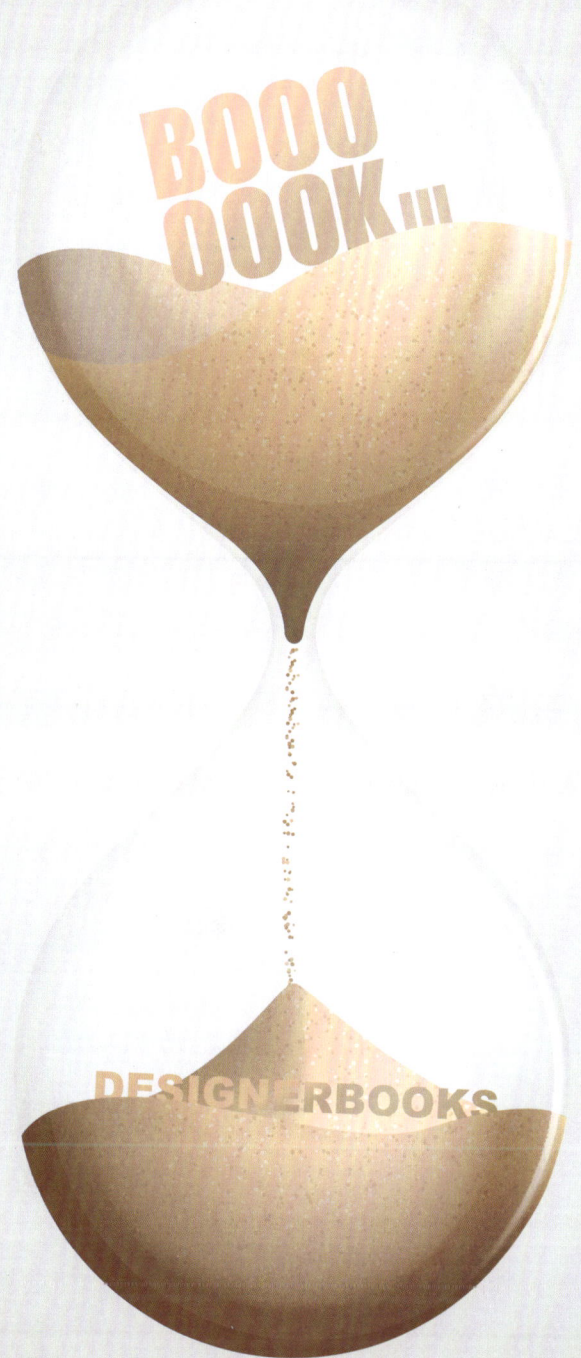

Editor-in-chief: Y&Y (Yang Liu & Jianing Yuan)
Editor: Qinghong Sun
Proofreader: Qinghong Sun
Art Director: Yannick (Jianing Yuan)
Design Director: Yang Liu
Printing Specialist: Yang Liu
Design and Layout: Qinghong Sun, Yang Liu

Publisher: DESIGNERBOOKS
2/F, Yau Tak Building, 167 Lockhart Road,
Wanchai, Hong Kong
Tel: +852-2575-5186
Fax: +852-2891-1996
E-mail: edit@designerbooks.com.cn

Distributor: DESIGNERBOOKS
Rm. 504-505, Bld. C, International Negotiate Garden,
NO. 3, Jinguanbei'er Str., Shunyi Dist., Beijing, China
Tel: 0086-10-6400-3080 (Beijing)
     0086-21-5596-7639 (Shanghai)
     0086-755-8825-0425 (Shenzhen)
     0086-20-8756-5010 (Guangzhou)
Fax: 0086-10-64018430-822
E-mail: import01@designerbooks.com.cn
http: //www.designerbooks.com.cn

Printed in China

ISBN: 978-988-79081-0-4

BOOO OOOK III

DESIGNERBOOKS

By the way - typography and material behavior

Designer: Thomas Wirtz
Design Agency: Thomas Wirtz Kommunikationsdesign
Country: Germany
Photographer: Thomas Wirtz

Client: Düsseldorf University of Applied Sciences
Others: Supervision: Prof. Philipp Teufel, Prof. Gabi Schillig

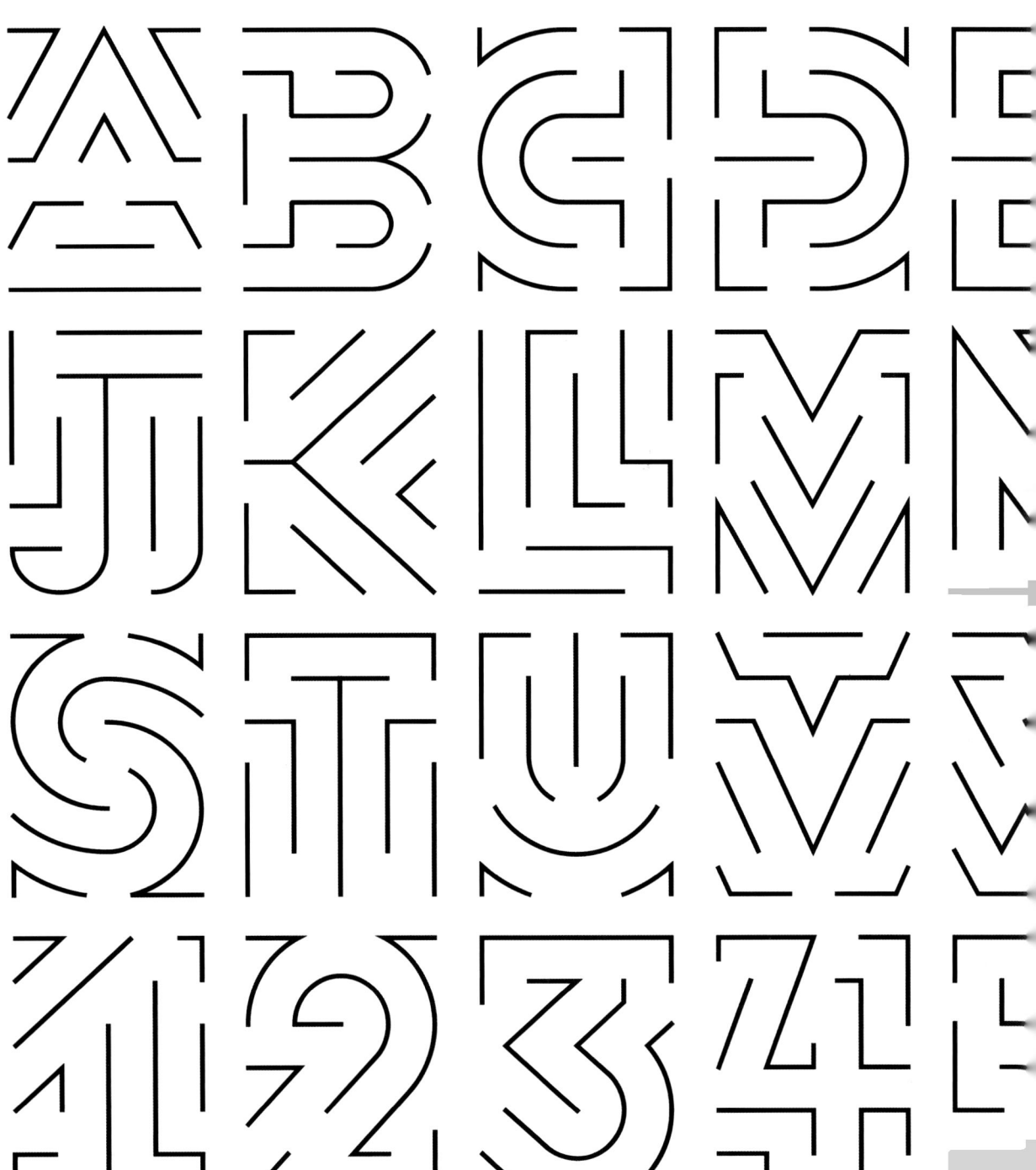

By the use of various media, the master thesis describes a free design experiment that has evolved over time into a modular system consisting of two components: The self-made font, produced by 3D printing, which is thereby associated with a variety of physical processes.

With references to the associated website, the book documents, among other things, the search for constants for the experiment, the design of the font, studies of different physical phenomena, the origin of 3D printing models, and the development of the own laboratory.

The project deliberately uses traits of digital applications and translates them to analogue media. Not only the acronyms of the models are common abbreviations used in the internet jargon, the experimental kit furthermore allows an analogue simulation of the effect of time dilation (Slow Motion), which is otherwise realised digitally.

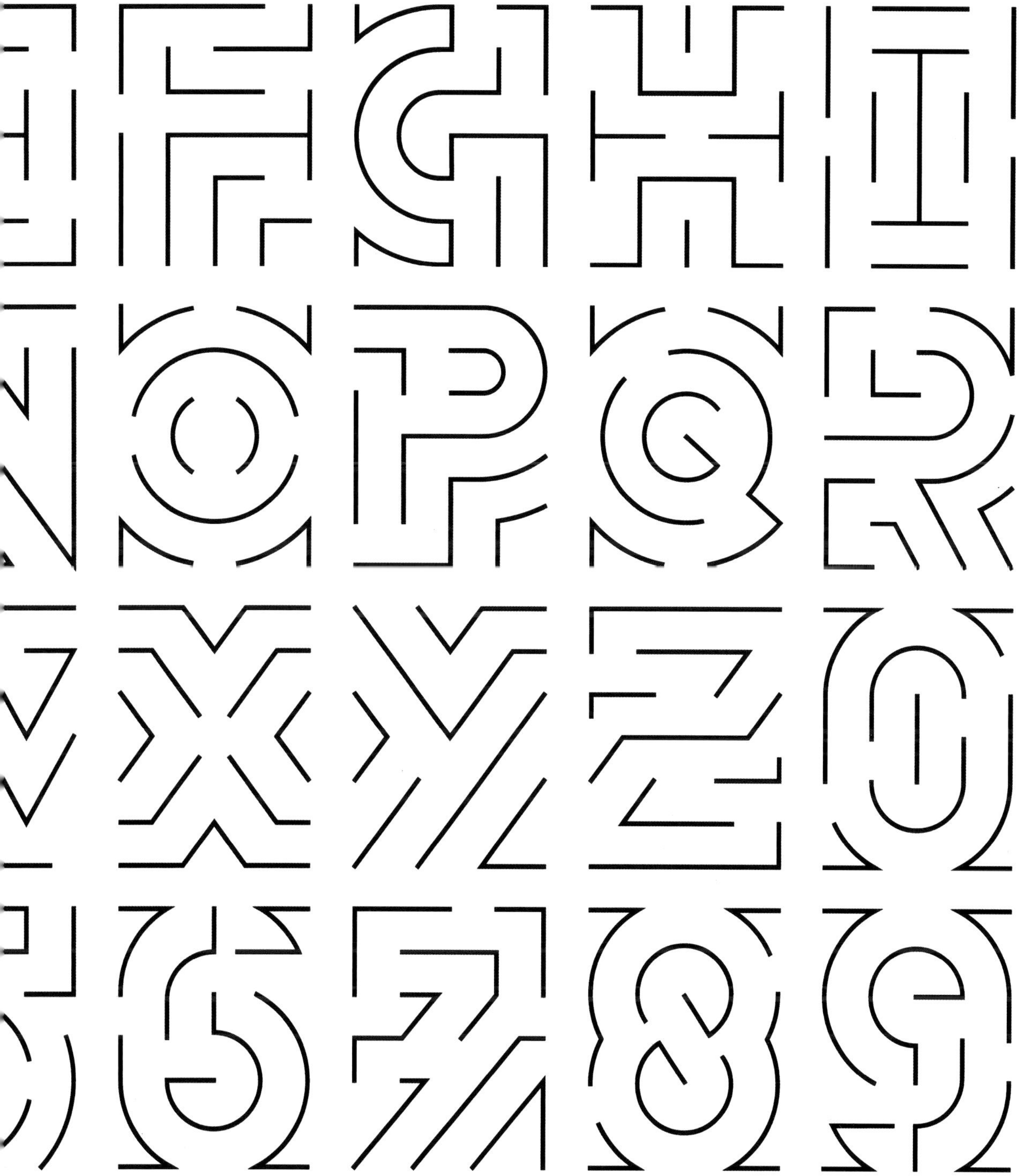

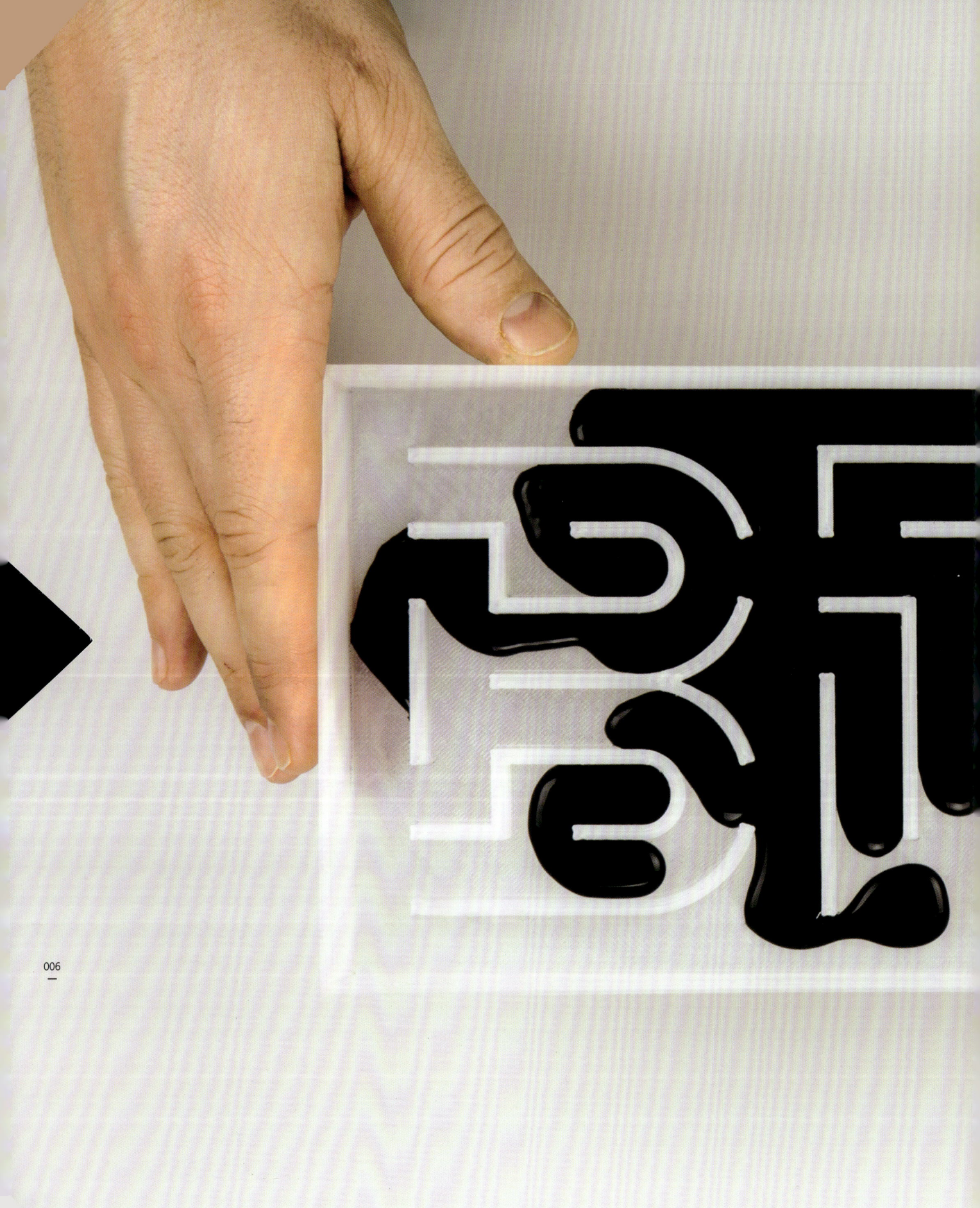

By the way - typography and material behavior

Designer: Thomas Wirtz
Design Agency: Thomas Wirtz Kommunikationsdesign
Country: Germany
Photographer: Thomas Wirtz

By the way - typography and material behavior

Designer: Thomas Wirtz
Design Agency: Thomas Wirtz Kommunikationsdesign
Country: Germany
Photographer: Thomas Wirtz

By the way - typography
and material behavior

Designer: Thomas Wirtz
Design Agency: Thomas Wirtz Kommunikationsdesign
Country: Germany
Photographer: Thomas Wirtz

By the way - typography and material behavior

Designer: Thomas Wirtz
Design Agency: Thomas Wirtz Kommunikationsdesign
Country: Germany
Photographer: Thomas Wirtz

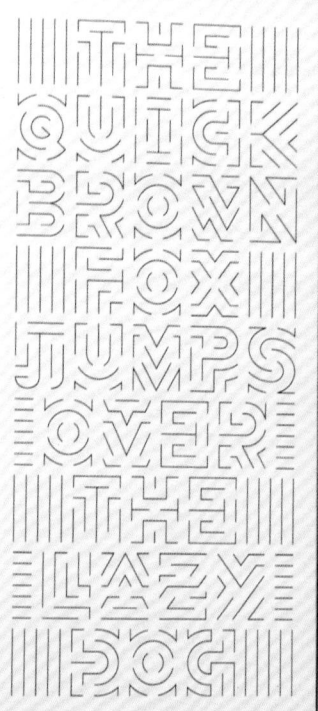

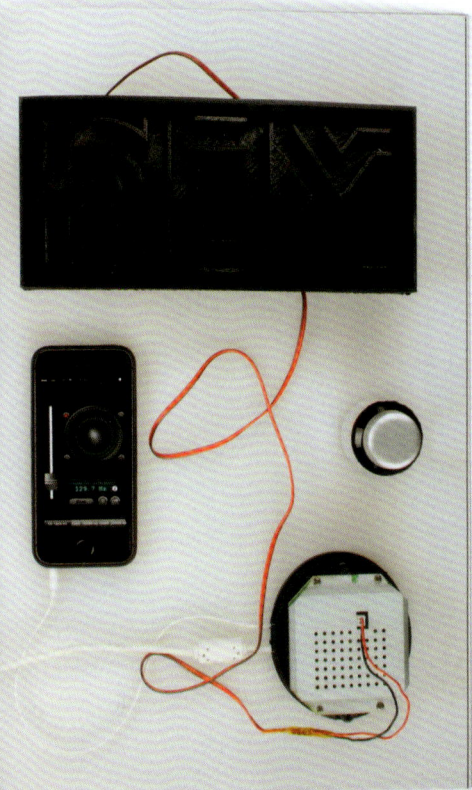

30/01
FILMSEQUENZEN
DER VERSUCHSREIHE
1 - SCHATTEN
2 - QUALM
3 - WASSEROBERFLÄCHE
▶ AFK 04
BTW:THOMASWIRTZ.NET

31/01
AUFEINANDERFOLGENDE
FRAMES DES DRITTEN
VERSUCHES

30/01

Die folgende Versuchsreihe hat eine „herkömmliche" Schrift im Bold-Schnitt als Grundlage und soll feststellen, inwieweit sich die Ergebnisse mit gleichem Versuchsaufbau aber flächigen und simplen Zeichen vom vorherigen Experiment (29/03) unterscheiden. Hierbei sind die Zahlen 1, 2 und 3 von unterschiedlichen Effekten verzerrt worden: Invertierter Schattenwurf durch eine Schablone (1). Zigarettenqualm durch eine Lichtprojektion (2). Lichtreflexion auf einer fließenden Wasseroberfläche, wie im vorangegangenen Experiment (3).

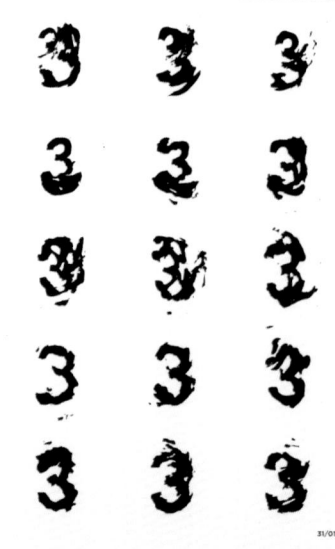

31/01

Die Analysen des dritten Versuchs zeigen, dass die Ergebnisse insbesondere für rein grafische Gestaltungsentwürfe interessant sind. Da aber die Experimente zuvor (Seite 27, 28) unter anderem mehr Möglichkeiten an Materialeinsatz versprechen, bleibt der Fokus auf den typografischen Grundrissen mit fließendem Inhalt.

DAS REGELWERK

Dieses besteht aus zwei Gruppen: Während die obligatorischen Regeln in jedem Fall angewendet werden müssen, besteht bei den fakultativen Regeln etwas mehr Freiraum. Sie sollten berücksichtigt werden, müssen aber nicht zwingend zum Einsatz kommen.

OBLIGATORISCHE REGELN

Monospace:
Alle Buchstaben besitzen die gleiche Grundfläche, die bespielt werden muss. Dies betrifft sowohl besonders breite Buchstaben wie das W, als auch schmale Buchstaben wie das I (38/1).

38/01

Keine geschlossenen Räume:
Die Buchstaben dürfen keine Punzen besitzen, da diese Bereiche für das darin befindliche Material nicht erreichbar wäre. Sollte eine Art Innenraum entstehen, so muss dieser mindestens eine Öffnung aufweisen (38/02).

38/02

Keine freien Flächen:
Normalerweise definiert sich ein einzelnes Zeichen auch durch seinen Weißraum und seine Lücken. Diese sollen hierbei jedoch möglichst vermieden werden. Das Grundraster der Schrift besteht aus acht mal neun Rechtecken. Jedes einzelne Rechteck muss wenigstens an den Kanten bespielt werden (38/03).

38/03

Keine gekreuzten Linien:
Zwar können Linienenden andere Linien berühren wie bei einem herkömmlichen T: es dürfen aber keine Linien gekreuzt werden wie bei einem gängigen X. Der optische Fokus würde im Gesamtbild sonst zu stark darauf gelenkt werden (38/04).

38/04

Eindeutigkeit des Zeichens:
Das konstruierte Zeichen sollte in jedem Fall eindeutig als solches zu erkennen sein. Man darf es nicht mit einem anderen Zeichen verwechseln.

FAKULTATIVE REGELN

Breite der Gänge:
Damit sich das Material möglichst gleichmäßig durch die Schleusen und Gänge der Schrift bewegen kann, sollten alle Gänge nach Möglichkeit gleich breit sein (39/01).

Größe der Öffnungen:
Ähnlich der Breite der Gänge sollte auch die Breite ihrer Öffnungen möglichst gleich sein. Ab einer bestimmten Größe wären unterschiedlich breite Durchgänge unter anderem in Abhängigkeit der Viskosität des Materials leichter oder schwerer erreichbar. Dies sollte vermieden werden (39/01).

39/01

Offene Außenachsen:
Damit das Material gut von einem Zeichen zum nächsten wandern kann, sollten insbesondere die vertikalen Außenachsen nicht komplett geschlossen sein. Auch Durchgänge bei den horizontalen Außenachsen können im mehrzeiligen Schriftbild von Vorteil sein (39/01).

Vorbild Grotesk:
Die Konstruktion des jeweiligen Buchstabens richtet sich in erster Linie nach ihrem ursprünglichen Vorbild, der Grotesk-Schrift, sprich ihre grafischen Elemente (Winkel, Linienrichtung, etc.) werden weitestgehend übernommen. Reicht dies im Sinne der Eindeutigkeit oder als Füllelement nicht aus, darf auf weitere zeichentypische Elemente der Antiqua (z.B. Serifen) zurückgegriffen werden (39/02).

39/02

Abstraktion des Zeichens:
Im besten Fall liegt das Zeichen nicht als optische Einheit in Form von geschlossenen Linien vor. Das Zeichen sollte durch Öffnungen unterbrochen sein. Ferner ist der Eindruck eines „Outline-Buchstabens" zu vermeiden. Das Zeichen bewahrt so einen gewissen Abstraktionsgrad (39/03).

39/03

DER BODENNEBULATOR

Mehr als zwei Wochen nach den letzten Experimenten mit Aerosolen findet auch die Bodennebelkonstruktion nach Abb. 71/02 ihre Umsetzung (80/01). Der Nebel wird vom Ausgang der Nebelmaschine mittels eines 10 Meter langen Aluflexschlauches, der sich in einer Plastiktonne mehrfach windet, bis hin zu einem Karton geführt, welcher wiederum einen Ausgang am unteren Ende von der Größe eines Briefkastens besitzt. Die Plastiktonne ist mit 4 kg Eis gefüllt (81/02). Auf diese Weise wird der Nebel über die lange Entfernung bis zum Ausgang des Karton abgekühlt.

Beim Austreten flutet der Nebel den Boden relativ dicht, bleibt aber konstant auf sehr geringer Höhe (81/03). Damit wäre das vorgegebene Ziel erreicht und gleichzeitig zwei von drei Herausforderungen hinsichtlich dieser schwer kontrollierbaren Umstände gemeistert: Dank des 360°-Linienlasers entsteht eine klar definierte Fläche an Licht und durch den jüngst umgesetzten „Bodennebulator", kann das eigenwillige

Aerosol flach am Boden gehalten werden: Der durch beide Komponenten ausgelöste Effekt kann nun betrachtet werden, ohne dass der Nebel die Sicht auf das Geschehen verdeckt (80/01).

Im letzten Schritt muss nun ein typografisches Modell erstellt werden, welches den gegebenen Anforderungen entspricht und mit beiden „Maschinen" korrespondiert (80/02). ▶ S. 90

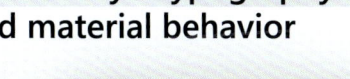

80

81

By the way - typography and material behavior

Designer: Thomas Wirtz
Design Agency: Thomas Wirtz Kommunikationsdesign
Country: Germany
Photographer: Thomas Wirtz

LABORINTH

EIN IRRGARTEN AUS SPONTANENTSCHEIDUNGEN

Das Vorexperiment startet mit knapp 300 ml Leitungswasser in einem 13 cm hohen Trinkglas. Die Entscheidung fällt bewusst auf ein alltägliches, fast schon langweilig wirkendes Objekt, das aber gleichzeitig viel Freiraum an Möglichkeiten zum Experimentieren lässt. Es soll als Ausgangspunkt dienen, um verschiedene Wege innerhalb des Experiments einschlagen zu können (22/01).

Die Fülle an Optionen wird nach eigenem Ermessen und Interesse auf genau vier Maßnahmen beschränkt, die auf das Wasserglas als nächstes angewendet werden dürfen. Eine dieser Richtungen ist die Erzeugung eines Wirbels an der Wasseroberfläche (23/01). Dieses Zwischenergebnis inspiriert zu weiteren kleinen Experimenten, die wiederum auf spontan am interessantesten erscheinenden Handlungen reduziert werden. Auf diese Weise wird durch eine Art Labyrinth aus kleinschrittigen Möglichkeiten navigiert, der der jeweilige Entwicklungsstand des Wasserglases anbietet bzw. dem,

was von dem Ausgangsobjekt übrig geblieben ist. Denn die Wahl des nächsten Schrittes steht jedes Mal völlig frei:

So wird der Wasserwirbel von oben betrachtet oder vor einem dunklen Hintergrund (23/02), das Wasser wird in die Luft geschüttet (23/04), es entstehen Reihenaufnahmen (23/05) und Assoziationen. An Stationen, welche die eigene Neugierde nicht weiter anregen, darf ein Schritt zurückgegangen werden, um eine andere der vier Möglichkeiten auszutesten. Auch der Schritt ganz zurück zum Ausgangsobjekt, dem Wasserglas, ist erlaubt. Es entstehen Lösungen mit Milch oder Tinte (23/07) auf je unterschiedlichem Hintergrund, mal um 180° gedreht, mal auf der vertikalen Mittelachse gespiegelt. Neben Bombenexplosion (23/08), Rorschachkleks, Typografie (23/06) und anderen Assoziationen wird das Wasser gegen ein anderes Material wie brennende Stahlwolle (23/03) ersetzt. Zudem werden die Dokumentationsmöglichkeiten um Filmaufnahmen erweitert.

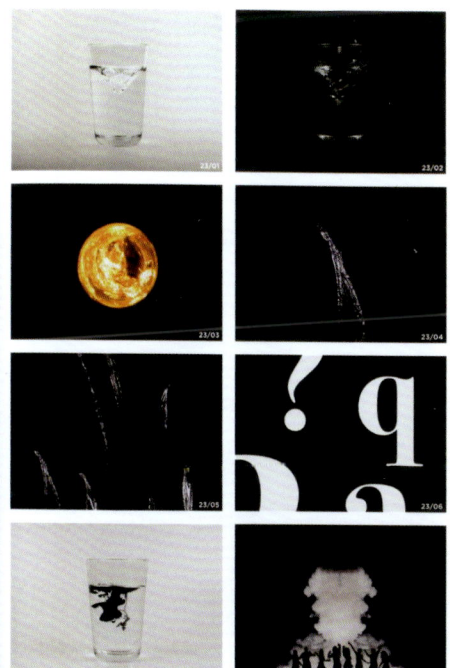

23/1
WIRBEL

23/2
WIRBEL VOR
DUNKLEM HINTERGRUND

23/3
GLÜHENDE STAHLWOLLE
BIRDVIEW

23/4
WASSER IN DER LUFT

23/5
WASSER IN DER LUFT
ALS SERIE

23/6
ASSOZIATION
TYPOGRAFIE

23/7
TINTE IN WASSER

23/8
ASSOZIATION MILCHBOMBE

22

23

015

The four seasons of country life

Designer: Masaomi Fujita
Design Agency: tegusu
Country: Japan

It is a collection of essays by the author on the subjects such as her relations with nature, harvesting of her produces and her cooking, in her reflections of her own country life in the changes of the seasons. It portrays the self-sustaining life in the country with ample illustrations.

The title of the book in Japanese literally means, "Life in the Country is Colored by the Seasons". I tried to express the implication of the title with abstract patterns of each season, applying them to the graphic motifs of the entire book, and to the typographies of the inside cover pages of 'Spring', 'Summer', 'Autumn' and 'Winter. The author also writes about the ideas of 'mottainai' (not wanting to waste things), and she uniquely called herself 'Mottainaissier'. I created an icon with this word in kanji and alphabets to make it a symbol of this book for the uniqueness.

The cover represents the image of the author enjoying changes of seasons in her life from her window, and designed to show the patterns of the four seasons from four windows. When the cover paper is removed, the inside of the cover shows free spread of the patterns of the four seasons that express the 'richness' and 'colors' of the country life.

I also had bookmarkers made from the excess of the cover paper, cutting the patterns randomly to express the idea of 'mottainai' in details.

mottainaissier

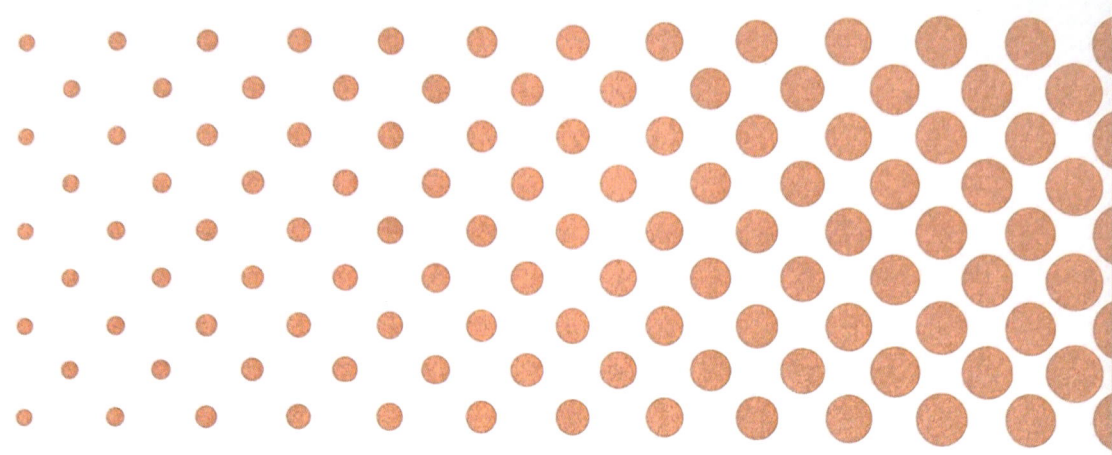

田舎
暮らしは
季節模様

The four seasons of
Country life
Mottainaissier
Kimiyo Nishiyama

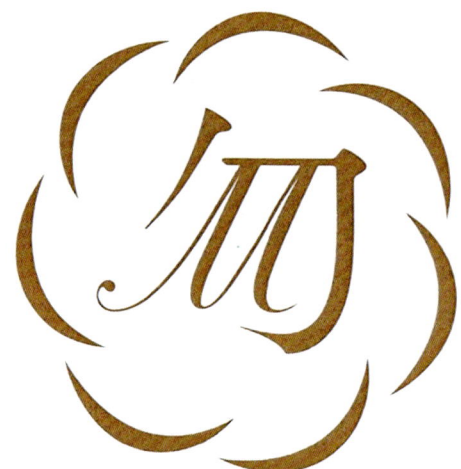

The four seasons of country life

Designer: Masaomi Fujita
Design Agency: tegusu
Country: Japan

The four seasons of country life

Designer: Masaomi Fujita
Design Agency: tegusu
Country: Japan

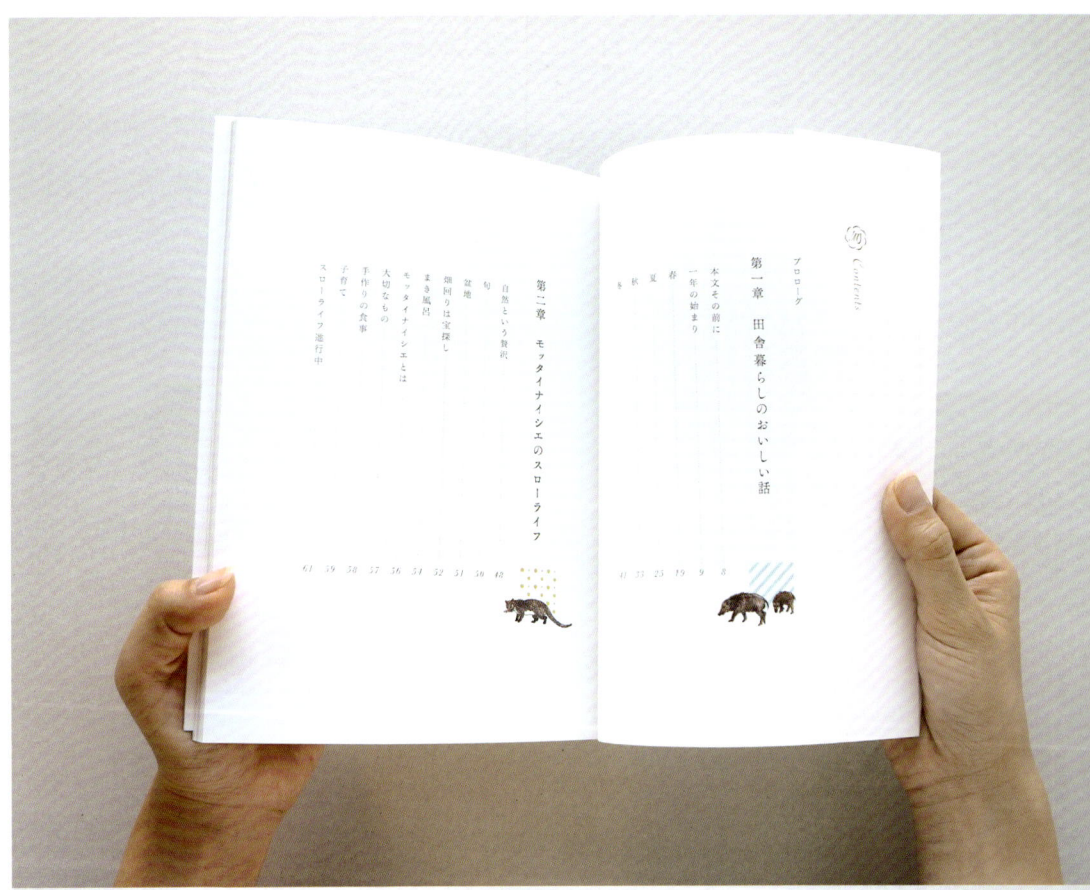

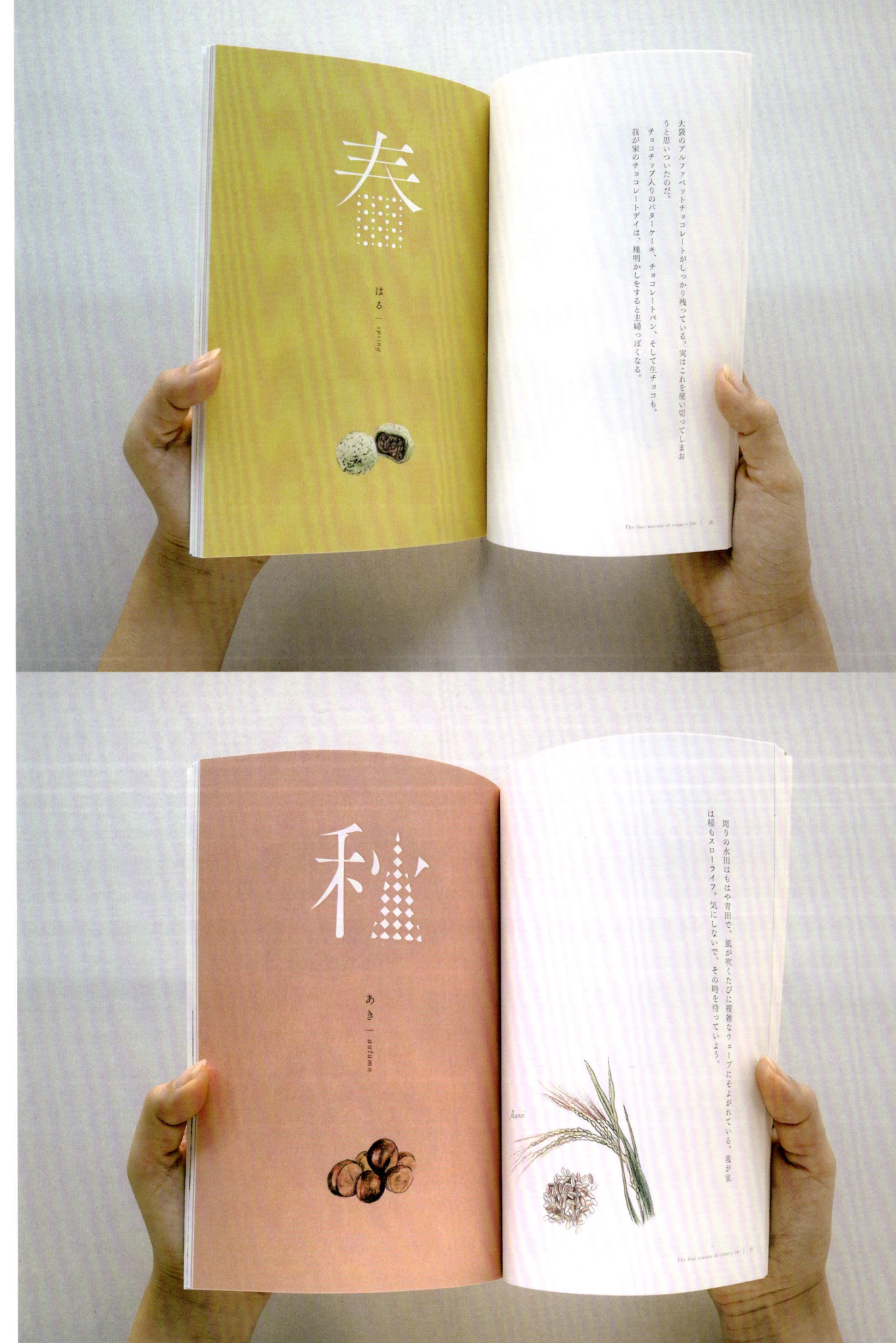

夏
なつ｜summer

春の山菜採りの終盤は、フキになるだろうか。フキは人気があるようで、山に入ってくる人をよく見かける。私も作り置き用にと、きゃらぶきを必ず作っている。この季節、初鰹とフキをゆっくり煮たお惣菜も我が家では度々登場する。

Katsuo to fuki no Souzai

冬
ふゆ｜winter

天然酵母の材料は柿の他、季節の果物でよく、熟しすぎてちょっと食べるにはという状態が酵母時なのである。柿酢もこのやわらかくなった柿が材料だ。初めて作るには、発酵を助けるために米こうじなどを使うといいかもしれない。後は、時間の仕事人に任せておけばいい。やがてアルコールから徐々に酢に変化する。十月ほどでフルーティーな柿酢が出来上がる。

Konnyaku no suihen

Konagakoimo

The four seasons of country life

Designer: Masaomi Fujita
Design Agency: tegusu
Country: Japan

The four seasons of country life

The four seasons of country life

Designer: Masaomi Fujita
Design Agency: tegusu
Country: Japan

春 夏

秋 冬

田舎暮らしは季節模様

The four seasons of country life

Designer: Masaomi Fujita
Design Agency: tegusu
Country: Japan

Collector's edition "Death and the Maiden" by Elfriede Jelinek

Designer: Alfidiya Kuchukbaeva
Country: Russia

Tutor: Natalia Agapova

This book contains plays "Death and the Maiden" by Austrian Nobel prize-winning author Elfriede Jelinek. Extraordinary form of the book inside the plastic sphere is a metaphor for unraveling complex meanings and truth. This concept became a reflection of provocative and sophisticated content of the play "Death and the Maiden".

The text of the book is printed on long paper type and then raveled. The process
of comprehension of truth and understanding the meaning of the

play has an analogy with reading this book by means of unraveling. The form factor of book inside the sphere influenced on typography and covers of these books. The book in the sphere can be used for a long time by means of removable construction of plastic sphere and re-entanglement of a paper type.

Standard book and book inside the sphere complement each other and represent one gift edition (it can be used for the theatrical premiere of play). This book concept can be a new form of theatrical souvenir instead of brochures or posters.

Collector's edition "Death and the Maiden" by Elfriede Jelinek

Designer: Alfidiya Kuchukbaeva
Country: Russia

Tutor: Natalia Agapova

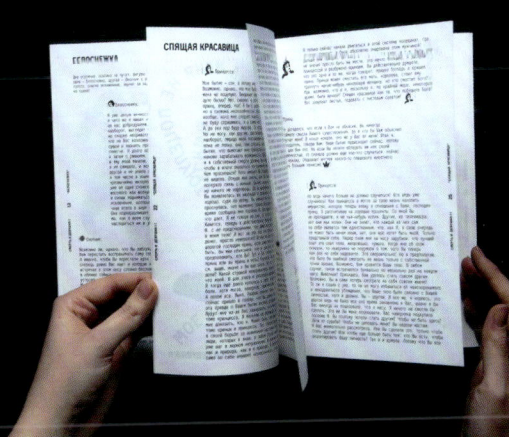

Linoleum packing for a book

Designer: Makekaky Mlouha
Country: Poland

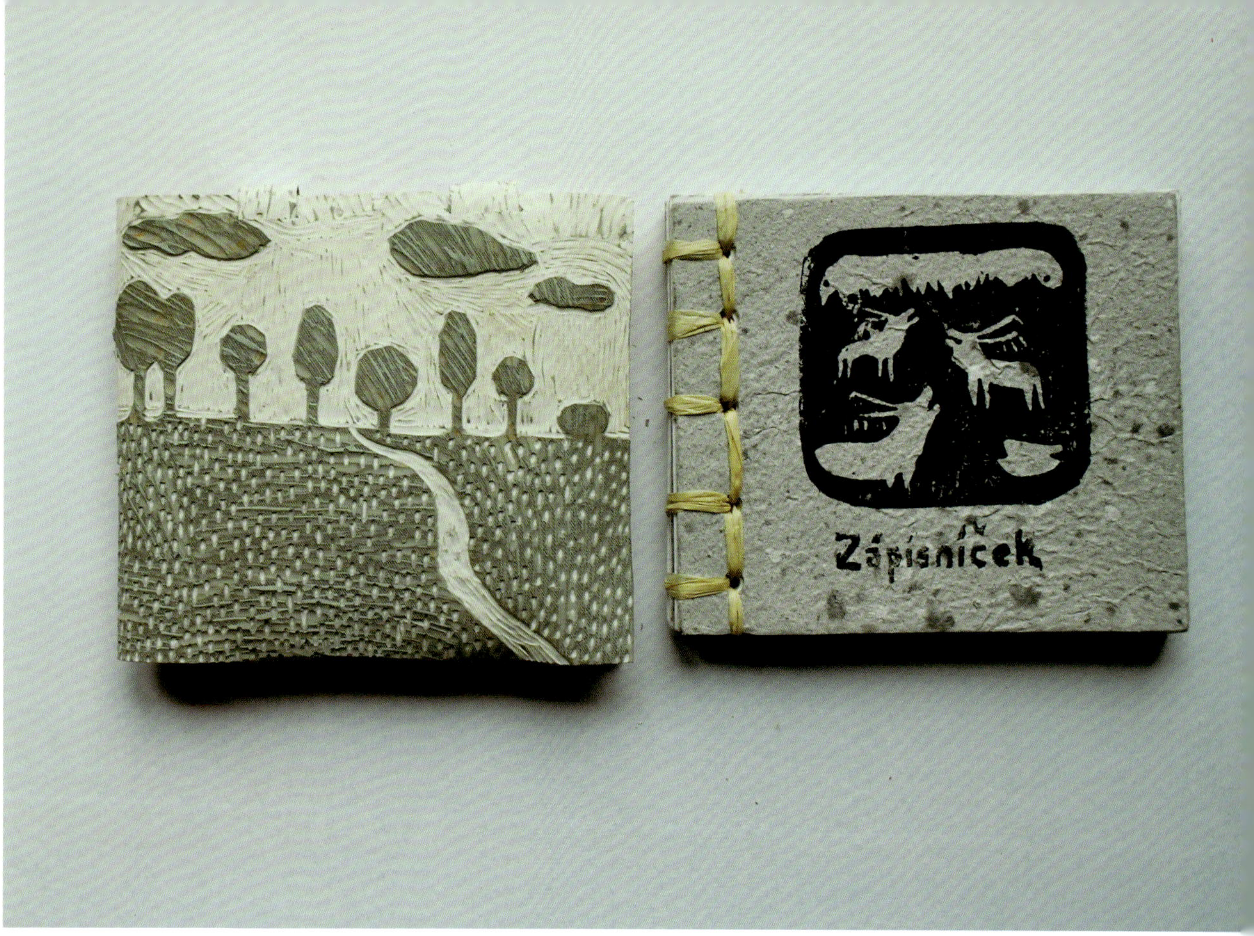
Zápisníček

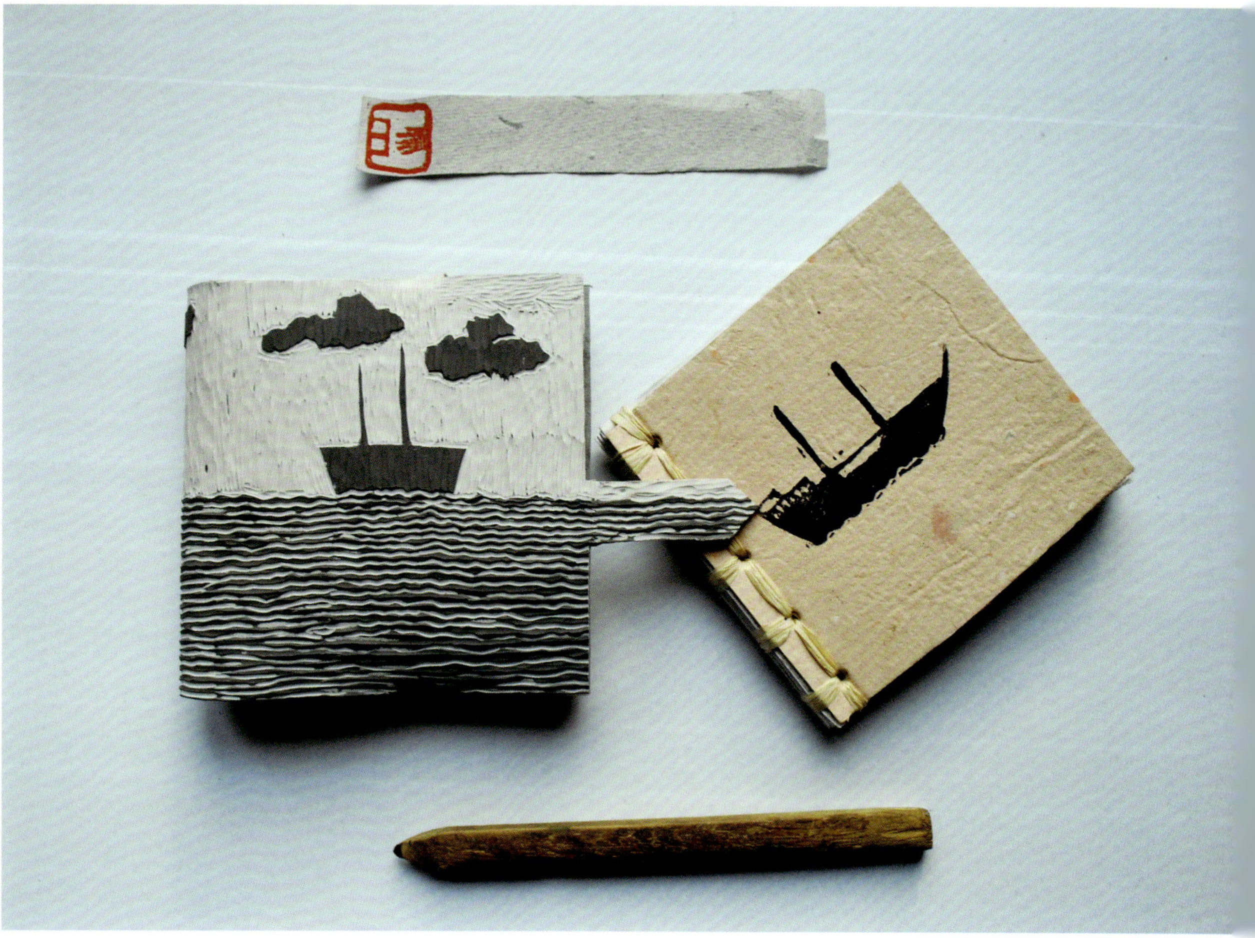

Linoleum packing for a book

Designer: Makekaky Mlouha
Country: Poland

First three handmade books

Designer: Makekaky Mlouha
Country: Poland

PŮLNOČNÍM LESEM
teskný hlas
táhle míjí

Jeleni
v říji.

Big recycled notebooks

Designer: Makekaky Mlouha
Country: Poland

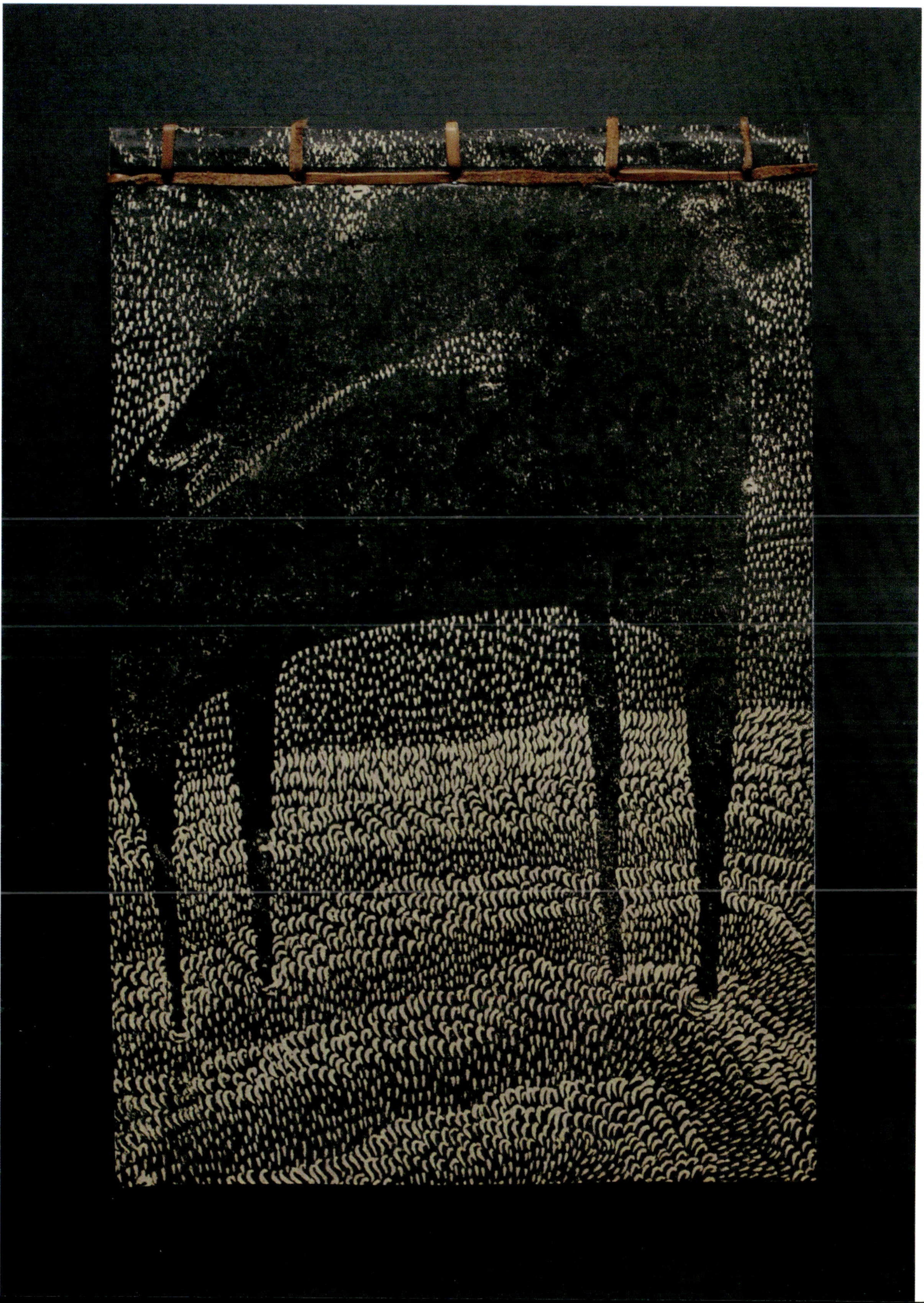

Big recycled notebooks

Designer: Makekaky Mlouha
Country: Poland

Book Design of Prose Collection "Qinghuan"

Designer: Chujing Long
Country: China
Photographer: Chujing Long

It's a conceptual book design of ''QingHuan'',a prose collection written by Lin-Qingxuan. The Binding form of the work is Fanjiazhuang from ancient India. The cover and back cover are made of yellow bamboo pieces. The spirit of bamboo in China is similar to that of Mr.Lin. The text on the cover uses laser engraving technology. Dark paper rope through the inside pages,readers can disassemble and assemble according to their preferences,or for bookmarks. Hoping readers feel fresh and elegant temperament of the bamboo while reading prose.

Book Design of Prose Collection "Qinghuan"

Designer: Chujing Long
Country: China
Photographer: Chujing Long

chat_Journal - MA Yearbook

Designer: Lucas Blat
Country: Brazil

The objective of my MA's last project was to design a journal as an year-book. I decided to make something different, so I collected all the history of messages between the Master students on Facebook.

Gathering links, images, songs, videos and files, I made this journal as an Index of everything that happened during the year. Using QR Codes and Hexadecimal language, it also shows statistics of the most used words, number of messages, characters and even how many laughters were typed.

To keep it safe for everybody, all the students' and teachers' names were cryptographed with glyphs chosen for each one, and images showing faces were pixelated or converted into ASCII.

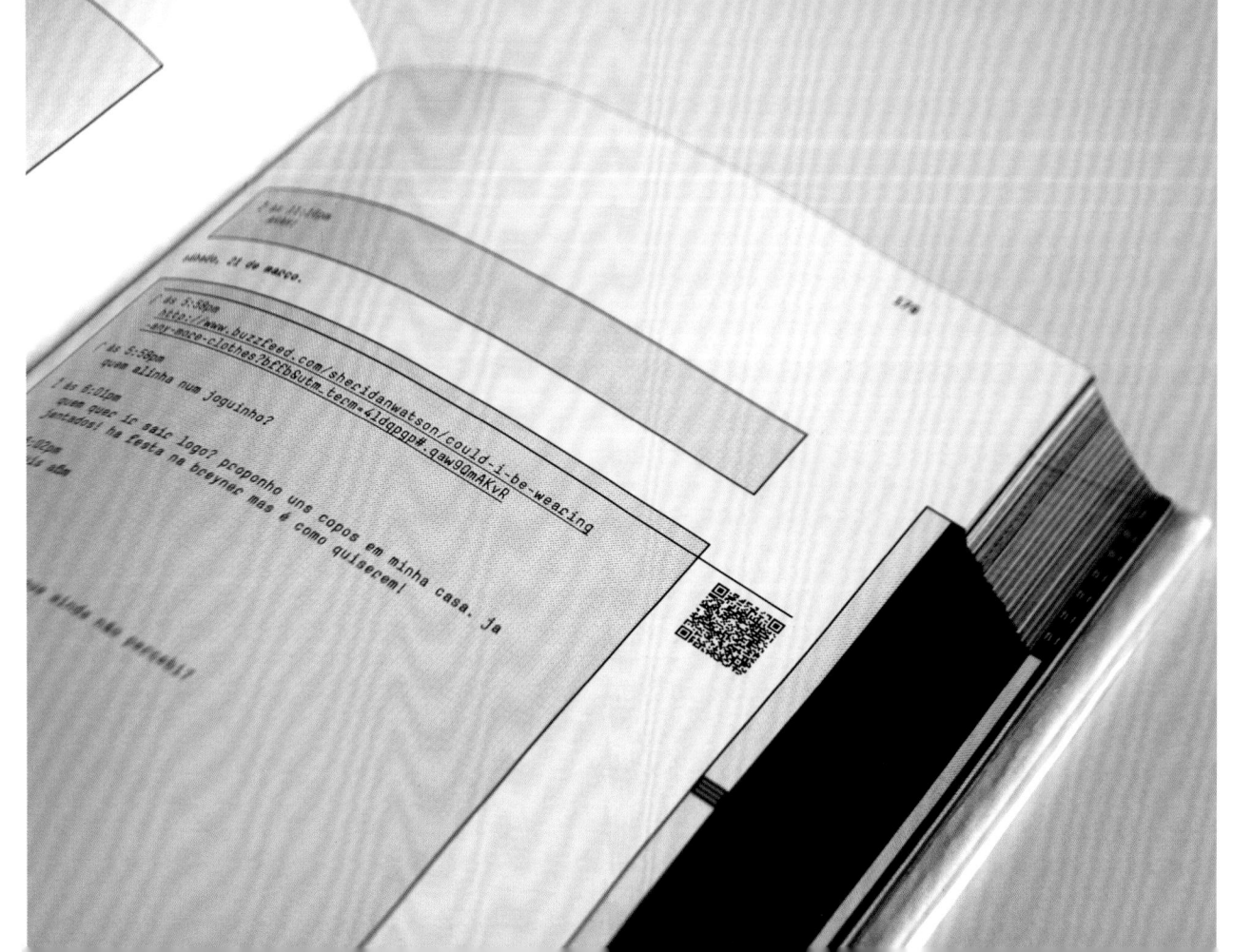

chat_Journal - MA Yearbook

Designer: Lucas Blat
Country: Brazil

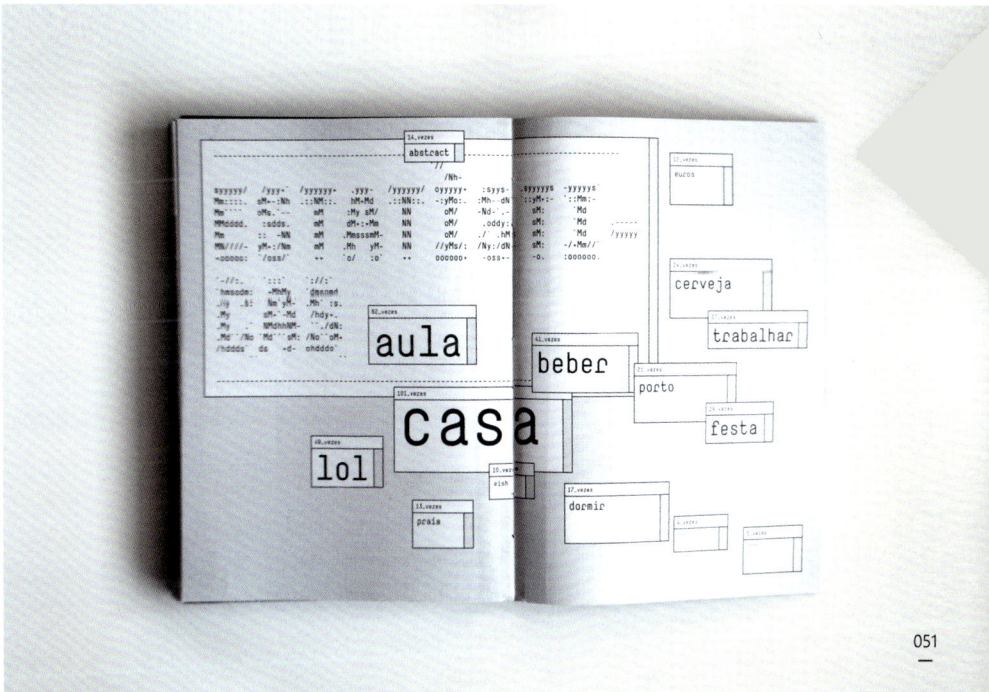

chat_Journal - MA Yearbook

Designer: Lucas Blat
Country: Brazil

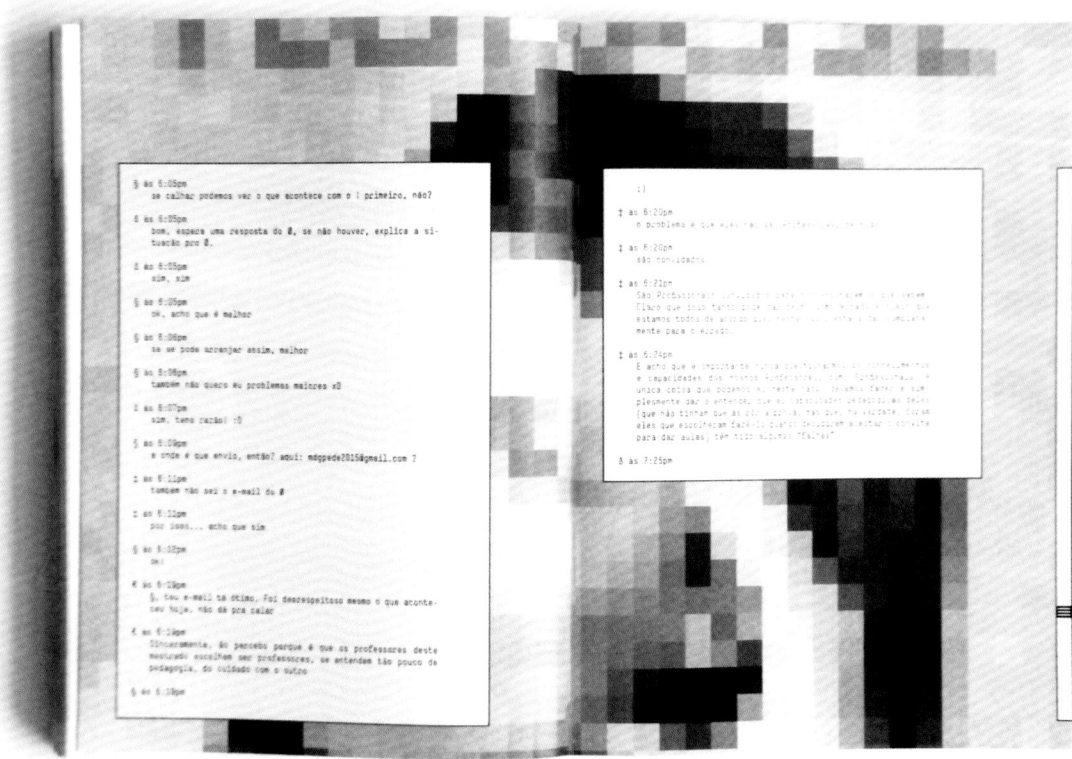

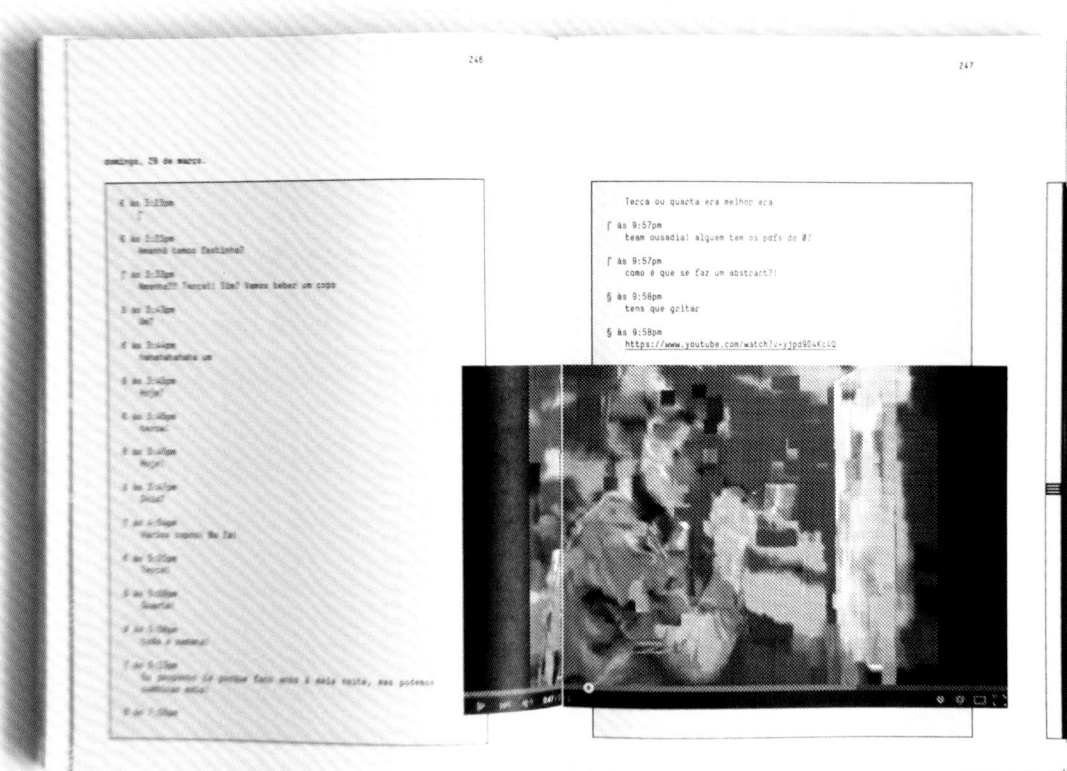

chat_Journal - MA Yearbook

Designer: Lucas Blat
Country: Brazil

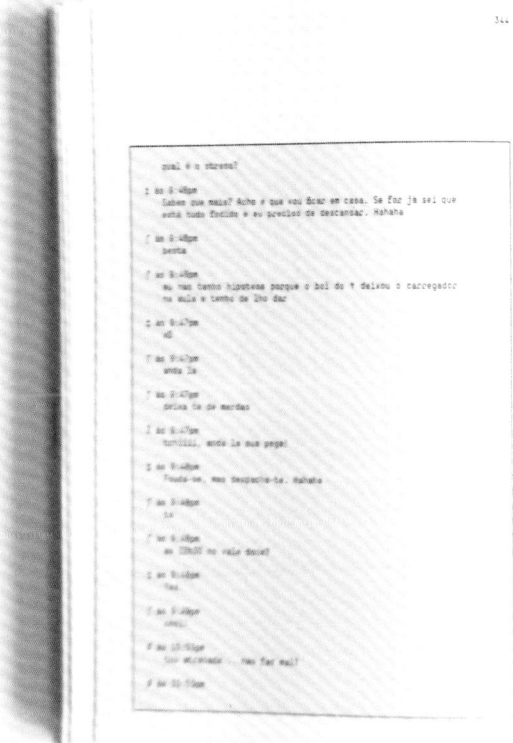

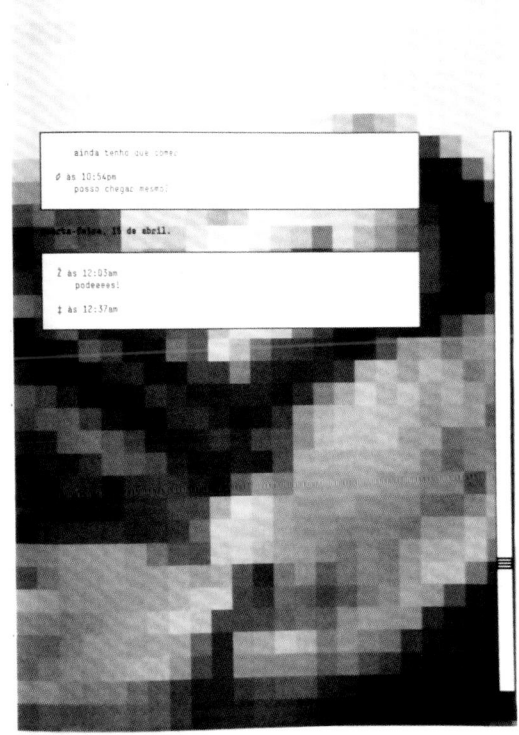

Cisma - Especial Haroldo de Campos

Designer: Lucas Blat
Country: Brazil

Client: Revista Cisma

Cisma is an independent academic journal from São Paulo, Brazil, run by a staff of volunteer undergraduate students of Literature at the University of São Paulo. The journal publishes only translations and essays on literature written by undergraduates from universities throughout the country, in biannual issues available both online and in print.

"Haroldo de Campos" is a special issue re-edited by the staff of Cisma of an original publication commissioned by the Pontifícia Universidade Católica de São Paulo in 1994. The issue is centered on the Brazilian poet and translator Haroldo de Campos, and comprises original texts on him by Jacques Derrida, Octávio Paz, Guillermo Cabrera Infante and João Cabral de Melo Neto. This new edition also brings a preface by Renan Nuernberger and an introduction by Diana Junkes Bueno, along with pastel illustrations by Victor Maia.

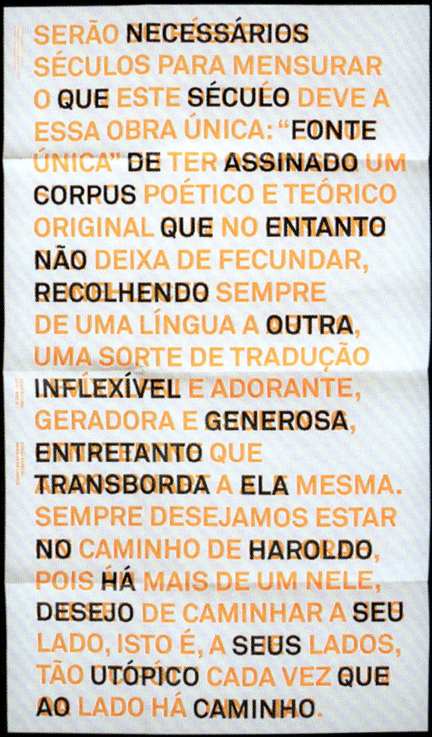

SERÃO NECESSÁRIOS
SÉCULOS PARA MENSURAR
O QUE ESTE SÉCULO DEVE A
ESSA OBRA ÚNICA: "FONTE
ÚNICA" DE TER ASSINADO UM
CORPUS POÉTICO E TEÓRICO
ORIGINAL QUE NO ENTANTO
NÃO DEIXA DE FECUNDAR,
RECOLHENDO SEMPRE
DE UMA LÍNGUA A OUTRA,
UMA SORTE DE TRADUÇÃO
INFLEXÍVEL E ADORANTE,
GERADORA E GENEROSA,
ENTRETANTO QUE
TRANSBORDA A ELA MESMA.
SEMPRE DESEJAMOS ESTAR
NO CAMINHO DE HAROLDO,
POIS HÁ MAIS DE UM NELE,
DESEJO DE CAMINHAR A SEU
LADO, ISTO É, A SEUS LADOS,
TÃO UTÓPICO CADA VEZ QUE
AO LADO HÁ CAMINHO.

Cisma - Especial Haroldo de Campos

Designer: Lucas Blat
Country: Brazil

17

CHAQUE FOIS, C'EST-À-DIRE, ET POURTANT, HAROLDO...
JACQUES DERRIDA

Chaque fois, c'est-à-dire souvent, chaque fois que je pense à la brièveté de la vie (« comme la vie aura été courte », ce sont hélas les mots de mon soupir préféré), c'est-à-dire chaque fois que je pense à toutes les figures de la finitude, c'est-à-dire à toutes les figures de ce qui m'aura manqué dans le temps, c'est-à-dire dans l'espace, alors chaque fois je compte ceux et celles que j'appelle pompeusement mais humblement mes grands-amis-admirables, mes grandes-amies-admirables, c'est-à-dire que je pleure alors chaque fois sur la rareté de nos rencontres, passées ou à venir, c'est-à-dire qu'incalculablement, au delà de toute arithmétique, car ces grandes personnes de tout âge sont si singulières, c'est-à-dire si uniques en elles mêmes et pour moi, je compte sans compter le temps qui reste, chaque fois je compte les fois qui restent, c'est-à-dire que je compte sans compter sur mes doigts, « hors d'anciens

calculs, où la manœuvre avec l'âge oubliée... ».

Une pensée du doigt, non de « la main crispée », jamais je n'ai su la dissocier d'un coup de dés.

Quand reverrai-je Haroldo de Campos ? Nous nous sommes si rarement rencontrés, une première fois à Paris il y a des décennies, et ce fut pour moi la révélation (« cet homme est un immense poète-penseur qui sait tout, me disai-je aussitôt, *quel est le secret qu'il détient ?* »), une autre fois il y a quelques mois à São Paulo, au cours d'une soirée bénie, chez Leyla Perrone-Moisés. Depuis décembre, je suis plongé dans les nouveaux chefs-d'œuvre que j'ai rapportés avec moi, en particulier *Bere'Shith, a cena da origem*— où entre tant d'autres trésors, je retrouve les mots qui décriraient le mieux, peut-être, la forme du génie haroldodecamposien dans sa fulgurance poético-pensante : *O palimpsesto proliferante, Hibridização generalizada, Intertextualidade, Um multicanto paralelo* et pour citer deux autres grands amis : *saber sem sabor.*

Deux fois seulement, c'est-à-dire que je crois m'avoir parlé que deux fois avec lui, littéralement, et *pourtant,* tout aussi littéralement, l'entretien est sans fin, et pourtant Haroldo est un intime, dès lors que j'apprends à le lire, et pourtant j'ai encore tant à apprendre de lui, en tant de langues, à commencer par la sienne, l'hébreu et quelques autres, et pourtant je sais déjà d'un savoir absolu, intemporel, définitif, inaltérable, indubitable, que je peux penser à lui,

CET HOMME EST UN IMMENSE POÈTE-PENSEUR QUI SAIT TOUT, ME DISAI-JE AUSSITÔT, QUEL EST LE SÉCRET QU'IL DÉTIENT ?

en permanence, comme à un de ces rares grands-amis-admirables que je n'aurai jamais rencontrés assez souvent, dont j'ai tant reçu mais dont je n'ai pas su assez recevoir, à qui je n'ai pas assez dit, manifesté, laissé savoir mon admiration et ma reconnaissance. Et pourtant, tout ce qui a pu signifier la loi, le désir aussi, l'urgence,

---

Cisma - Especial Haroldo de Campos

Designer: Lucas Blat
Country: Brazil

---

mais l'urgence la plus aventureuse et la plus audacieuse pour moi, dans l'ordre de la pensée, de l'écriture, de la poésie - « unique source » - dans l'horizon de la littérature, et avant tout dans l'intimité de la langue des langues, chaque fois tant de langues dans toute langue, je sais que Haroldo y aura eu accès comme moi avant moi, mieux que moi. C'est-à-dire qu'il m'attendait pourtant, déjà, de l'autre côté, arrivé avant moi, le premier, sur l'autre rive.

Je rêve donc à notre prochaine rencontre, j'attends la prochaine fois, j'attends de le lire encore, en ce temps, ici bas, mais en sachant déjà qu'il y faudra pourtant une autre vie. C'est-à-dire qu'il faudra des siècles pour mesurer ce que ce siècle doit à cette œuvre unique : « unique source » d'avoir signé un corpus poétique et théorique original tout en fécondant pourtant, volant chaque fois d'une langue à l'autre, une sorte de traduction inflexible et adorante, génératrice et généreuse, c'est-à-dire qui se déborde pourtant elle-même, penchant simultanément, avant de se poser sur la piste d'écriture, sur le sol du poème, pour ne renoncer à rien (ne renoncer à rien, c'est le génie de l'inconscient et l'inconscient du génie, l'unique source libidinale de toute pensée poétique), à la fois du côté de la mondialité et pourtant du côté de la plus irréductible singularité de l'idiome. On a toujours envie d'être du côté de chez Haroldo, parce qu'il y en a plus d'un, envie de rester chez lui, c'est-à-dire à ses côtés, si utopique chaque fois que cela demeure.

Entre ces deux vies, d'entre ces deux côtés à la fois, pourtant, je le salue, aujourd'hui, à cette date.

Je n'ai pas la force d'écrire longuement, je le fais entre deux voyages, entre deux continents, et je demande pardon à tous, à Haroldo pour commencer. Je ne voulais pas manquer aussi ce rendez-vous de l'amitié mais je prie pourtant tous les dieux à la fois pour qu'il y en ait beaucoup d'autres, c'est-à-dire beaucoup d'autres fois, d'un côté ou d'un autre, sur une côte ou sur une autre.

25 mai 1996

CADA VEZ, ISTO É, E NO ENTANTO, HAROLDO...
JACQUES DERRIDA

Cada vez, isto é, frequentemente, cada vez que penso na brevidade da vida ("como a vida terá sido curta", eis infelizmente as palavras de meu suspiro preferido), isto é, cada vez que penso em todas as figuras da finitude, isto é, em todas as figuras do que terá me faltado no tempo, isto é, no espaço, então cada vez eu conto aqueles e aquelas que denomino pomposamente mas humildemente meus grandes-amigos-admiráveis, minhas grandes-amigas-admiráveis, quer dizer que lamento então cada vez a raridade de nossos encontros, passados ou por vir, isto é, incalculavelmente, para além de toda aritmética, pois essas grandes pessoas de todas as idades são tão singulares, isto é, únicas nelas mesmas e para mim, eu conto sem contar o tempo que resta, cada vez conto as vezes que restam, quer dizer que conto sem contar nos dedos.

Quando verei novamente Haroldo de Campos? Nós nos encontramos tão raramente, uma primeira vez em Paris décadas atrás, e

HAROLDO DE CAMPOS É ESSA COISA EXTRAORDINÁRIA: UM POETA E TRADUTOR QUE VEIO PARA A LITERATURA ARMADO DE UM INVEJÁVEL CONHECIMENTO DO FENÔMENO LITERÁRIO.

EDITORIAL

Esta edição especial da *Cisma* reproduz quatro testemunhos sobre Haroldo de Campos: na ordem, um primeiro do filósofo franco-argelino Jacques Derrida; outro do pensador e poeta mexicano Octavio Paz; um terceiro do nosso João Cabral de Melo Neto; e, por último, um do escritor cubano, naturalizado britânico, Guillermo Cabrera Infante. Esse conjunto, pelo peso e variedade dos nomes, oferece uma amostra da extensão dos diálogos e relações de Haroldo, poeta, crítico, tradutor... e amigo – um grande amigo, admirável, no dizer de Derrida – cuja presença, textual e corpórea, é celebrada pelos quatro autores.

É por que re-*presentificar* Haroldo num número especial da *Cisma*, revista de crítica literária e tradução da graduação em Letras da USP, universidade que de resto costuma subestimá-lo? A resposta veio em *flashes*, numa sucessão de instantâneas (tal qual no poema de Octavio Paz), ao longo do processo de facção da revista, e nos obriga a rememorá-lo um pouco.

Ideia e possibilidade surgiram juntas, quando, ainda em 2014, obtivemos junto à editora da PUC os direitos de republicação dos textos constantes de um pequeno libreto impresso, em 1996, por ocasião de uma homenagem a Haroldo de Campos, professor emérito e um dos fundadores do programa de Pós-Graduação em Comunicação e Semiótica dessa universidade. Os textos – os mesmos que ora reproduzimos – nos seduziram de imediato, e logo demos início ao processo, que passou por: novas traduções dos originais em língua estrangeira, abrindo um espaço para três tradutores ainda da graduação; duas apresentações inéditas do material, uma da Diana Junkes Bueno Martha, professora de literatura brasileira da UFSCAR e estudiosa da obra de Haroldo de Campos, outra do Renan Nuernberger, poeta e mestre em teoria literária e literatura comparada pela USP; ilustrações feitas especialmente para a revista pelo Victor Maia; e, por fim, projeto gráfico idealizado pelo Lucas Blat.

Neste ano, graças ao financiamento obtido mediante edital da Secretaria de Cultura do Estado de São Paulo, conseguimos finalizar o projeto. E assim o devolvemos ao público, renovado, para que realize, cada vez mais, seu enorme potencial artístico, crítico, tradutológico... haroldiano.

EDITORIAL PRIMEIRO PUC

Poeta, tradutor, ensaísta e crítico, Haroldo de Cam[pos] uma das presenças mais marcantes no cenário literá[rio] brasileiro das últimas quatro décadas. Professor eme[rito da PUC] SP, foi um dos fundadores do programa de Pós-Gradu[ação em Co]municação e Semiótica, onde lecionou até aposentar-s[e.]

Em 1996, ano em que a PUC comemorou seu 50° a[niversário,] tivemos a grata satisfação de prestar essa homenagem. Na noite de 25 de setembro, em cerimónia especial no [Teatro da] Universidade (TUCA), foram lidos os textos aqui reunidos. [O pro]fessor foi presenteado com uma gravura de Tomie Ohtake. [Na] a semana seguinte, foi realizada uma exposição dos livros [de Ha]roldo de Campos na Biblioteca Central da PUC/SP, ocasião [em que] foram exibidos também dois vídeos sobre a sua obra, dirigi[dos por] Cristina Fonseca, e fotografias de Bob Wolfenson. Outra grav[ura de] Tomie Ohtake foi posteriormente reunida com os textos num[a edi]ção especial, com apenas trinta exemplares. A presente ediçã[o vem] somar-se, agora, à série "Autores Brasileiros", sob a coordena[ção] da Presidência da Comissão Geral de Pós-Graduação. Composta [de] dois mil exemplares, fora de comércio, destina-se a professor[es,] alunos, funcionários e amigos da PUC/SP.

A ligação duradoura do professor Haroldo de Campos com [a] universidade é para nós um motivo de orgulho. A convivência com [ele] ele permanece, hoje como sempre, uma educação, no modelo mais [elevado a que pode aspirar uma universidade.

Wild Man

Designer: Mose（叶昊）
Country: China

Wild Man is a series of book cover designs. It contains no fixed modal in form, no utilitarian color in content and no invariably standard answer in comprehension. Every design of Wild Man is the sentiment, is the understanding and interpretation of life, is the enthusiastically praise of frankness and unruliness.

If you ask me: "Where do you get your ideas?" The answer is very simple. I naturally focus on my inner world and am inspired by imagination. Wild Man doesn't have ornate character, only for most true feelings. Every detail of Wild Man is telling a story and maybe you can see yourself from it.

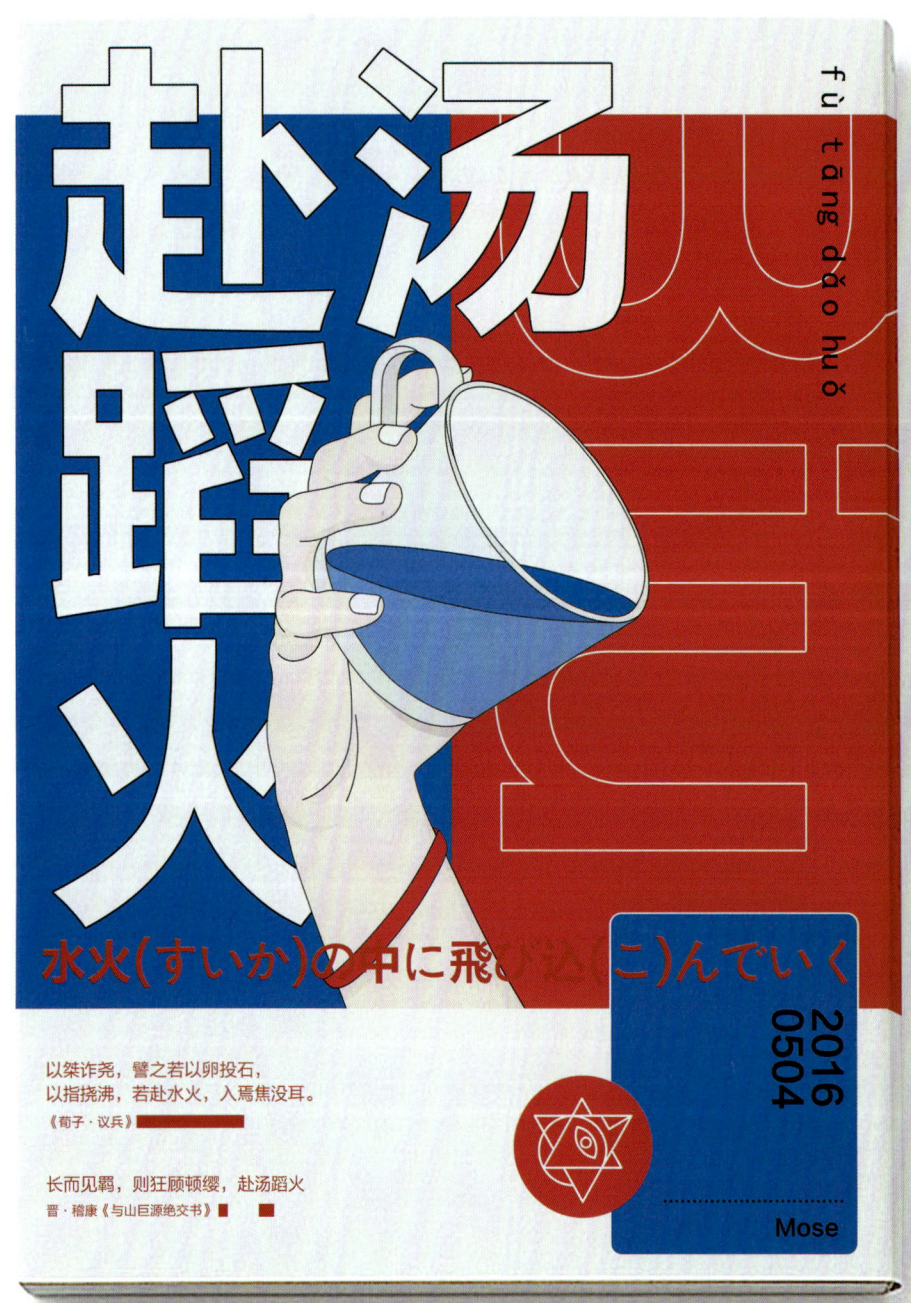

extraordinary
refined

mog

总觉得自己有超能力
会变很多很多的人民币······

2016
0503

超凡
脱俗

わかつ

Mose

Wild Man

Designer: Mose（叶昊）
Country: China

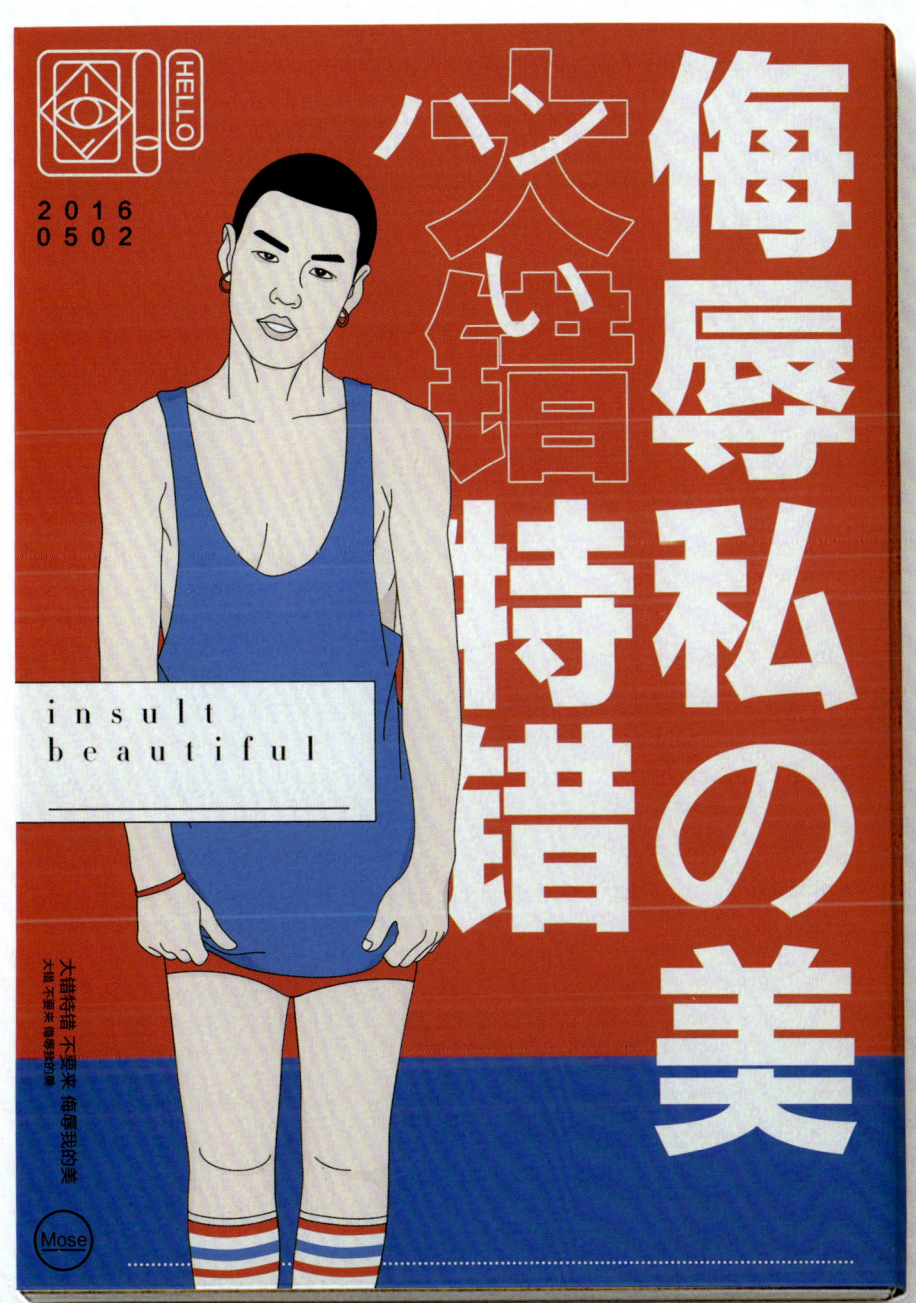

Wild Man

Designer: Mose（叶昊）
Country: China

Wild Man

Designer: Mose（叶昊）
Country: China

元气未成年子供少年

2016
0512

VITALITY YOUNG

Mose

指十岁左右至十五六岁这一时期的孩子

Wild Man

Designer: Mose（叶昊）
Country: China

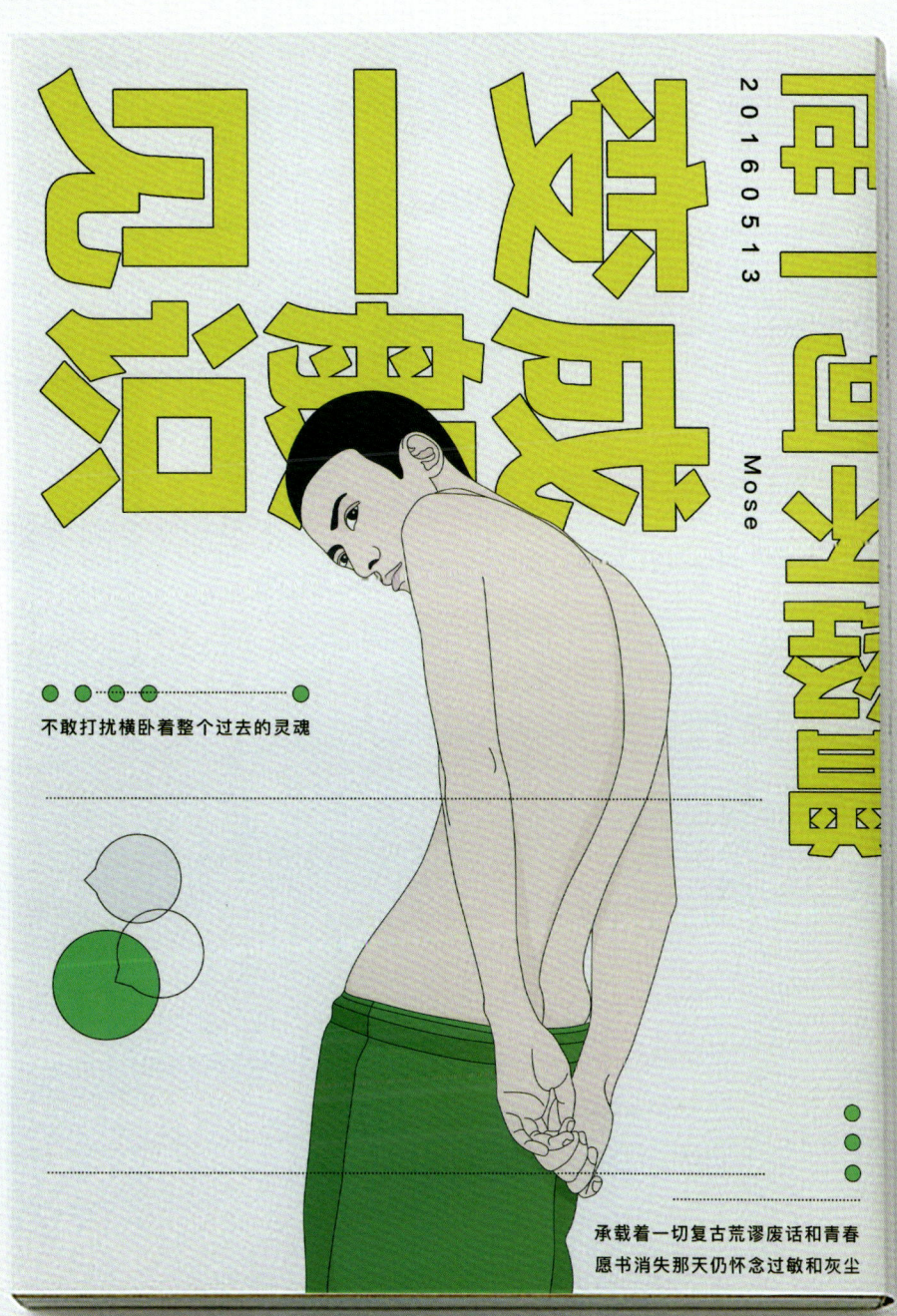

它只能够一直的
飞呀飞呀

这种鸟一辈子只能下地一次

那一次就是它死亡的时候

世界上有一种鸟
是没有脚的

2016
Mose

阿　飞　正　传　0514

追赶
CHASE

流放
EXILE

院落里往日喧与嚣在哪里　那么多的苍柏孤立
那张破碎的镜里　　　　　那张破旧的太师椅

20160513

Mose

Wild Man

Designer: Mose（叶昊）
Country: China

Wild Man

Designer: Mose（叶昊）
Country: China

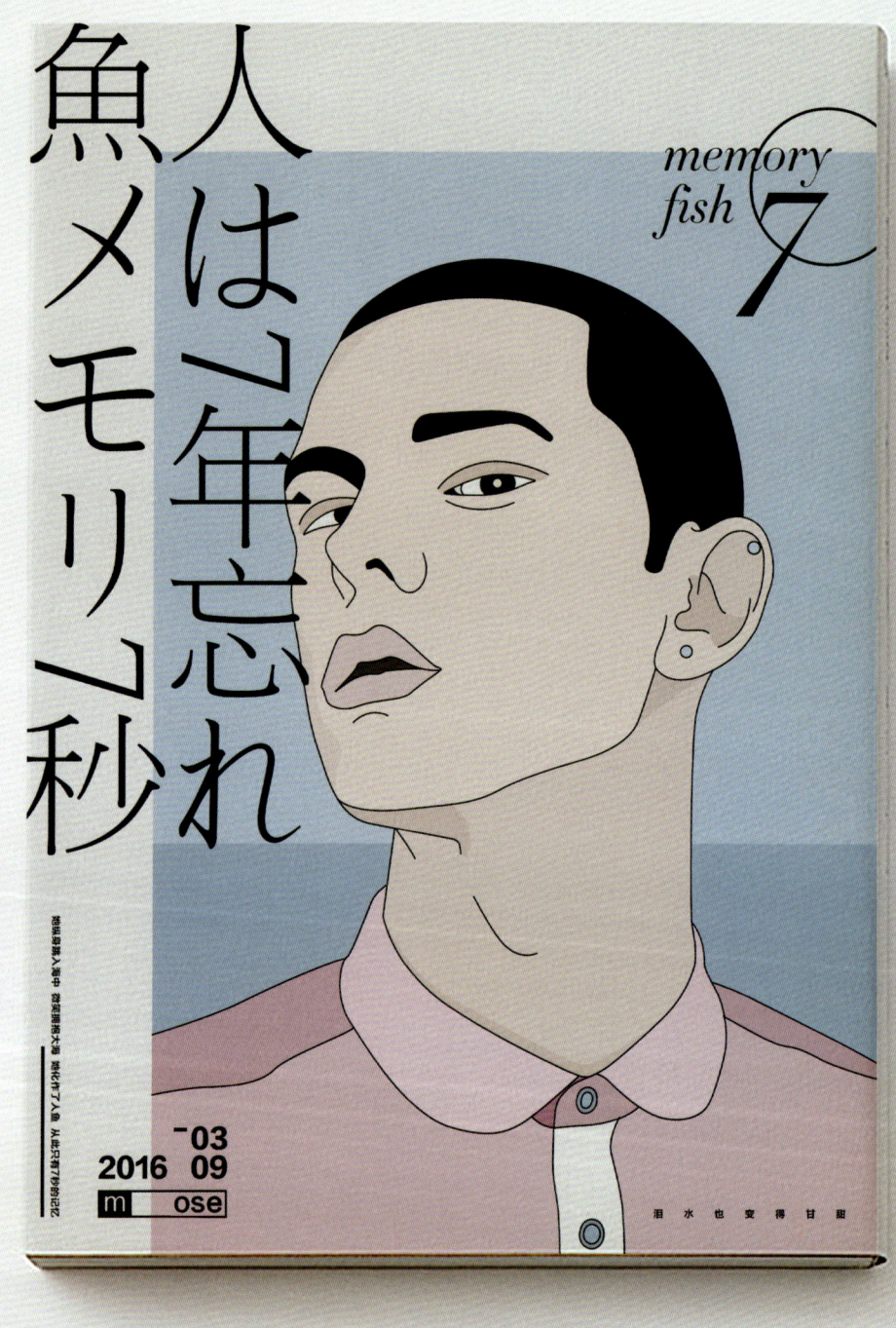

Wild Man

Designer: Mose（叶昊）
Country: China

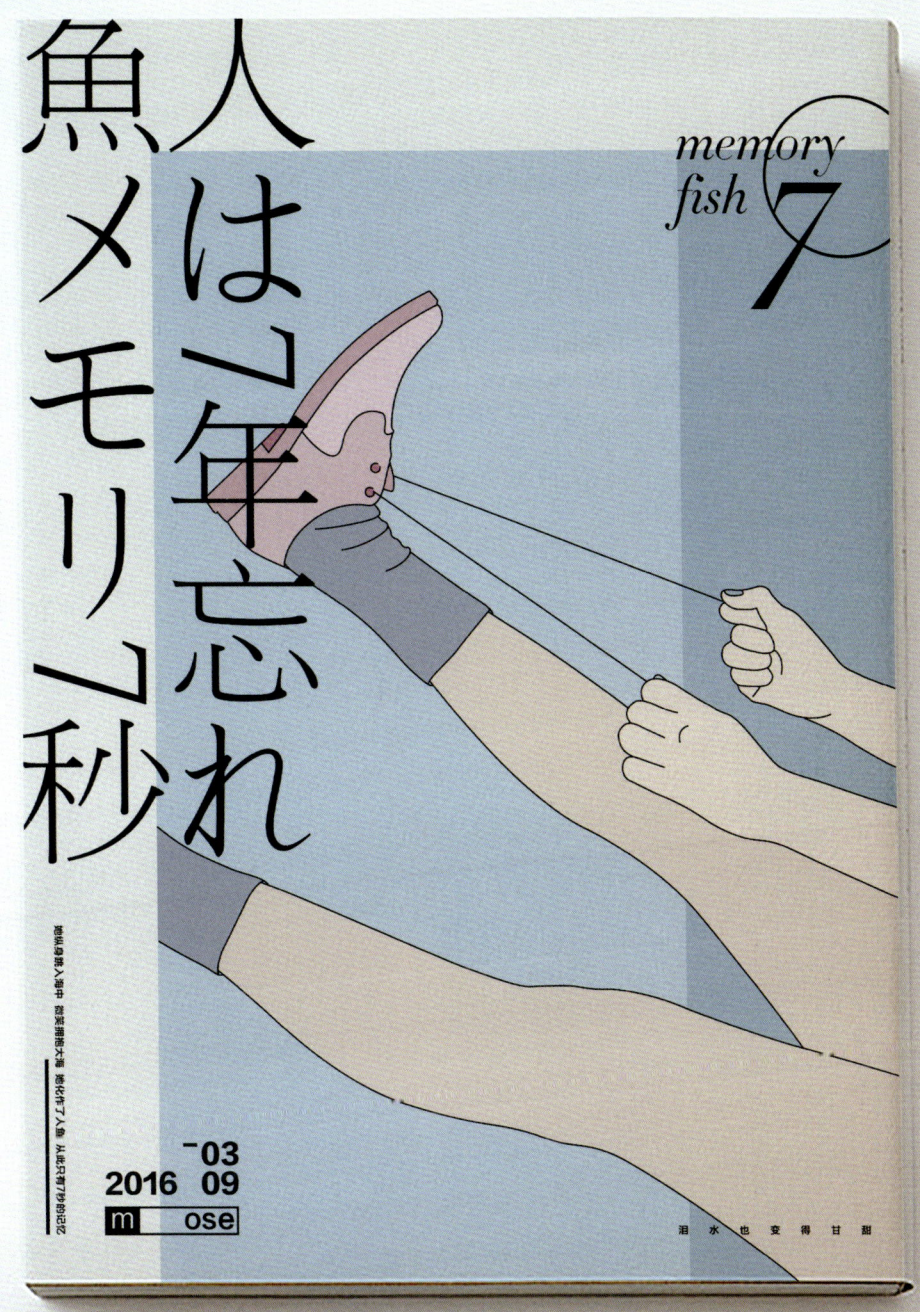

人は7年忘れ
魚メモリ7秒

魚メモリ7秒

memory
fish
7

—03
2016　09
m ose

泪 水 也 变 得 甘 甜

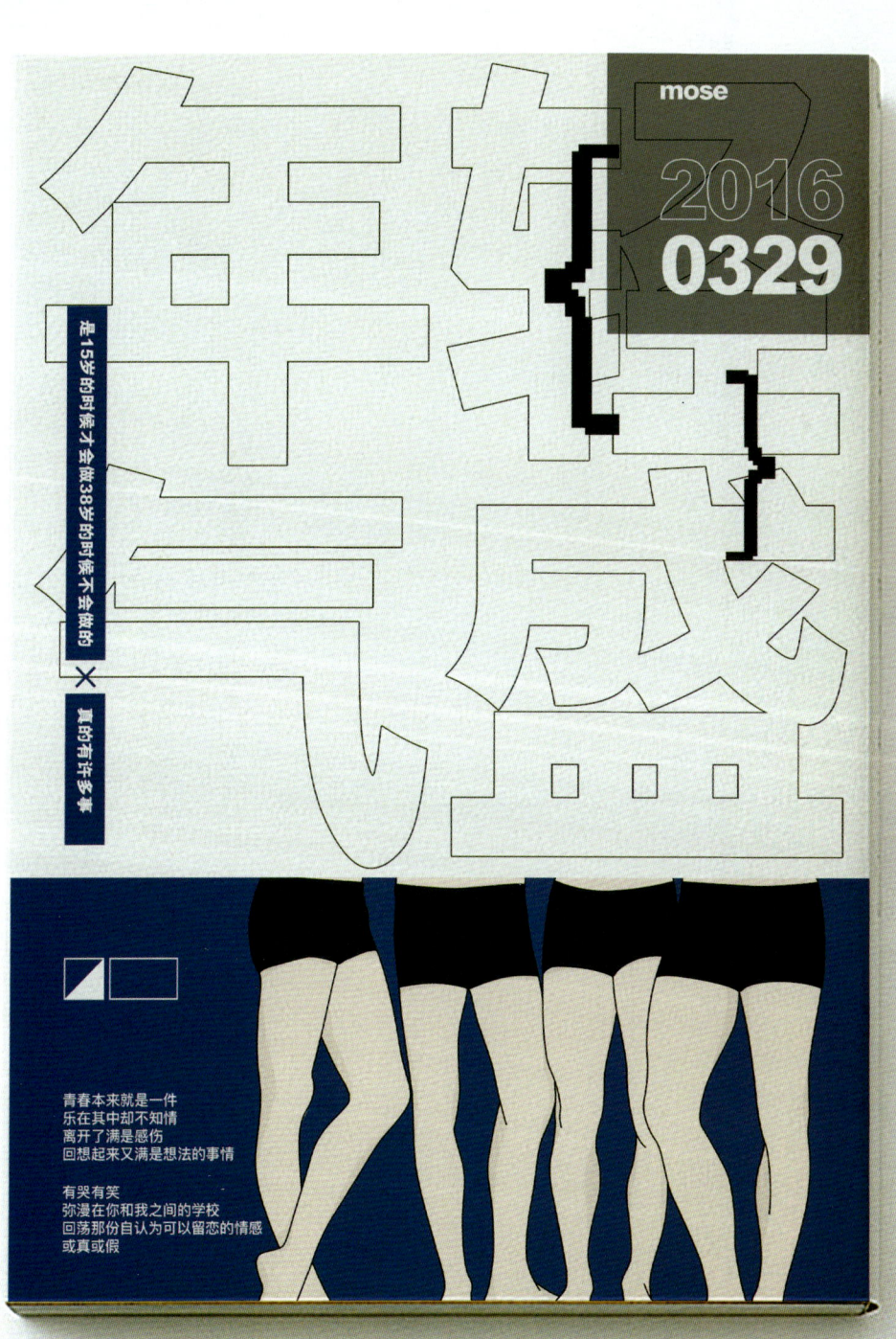

年轻气盛

年轻盛

mose
2016
0329

是15岁的时候才会做38岁的时候不会做的
真的有许多事

青春本来就是一件
乐在其中却不知情
离开了满是感伤
回想起来又满是想法的事情

有哭有笑
弥漫在你和我之间的学校
回荡那份自认为可以留恋的情感
或真或假

blue clothes

m ose

藍貓衣

我喜歡藍色 喜歡毛衣的男孩
世界裏都是大海 波瀾壯闊

Wild Man

Designer: Mose（叶昊）
Country: China

都
迷
茸
入
道

隐藏自己的疲倦 表达自己的狼狈
放纵自己的狂野 找寻自己的明天

03
26

In fact

mose

Wild Man

Designer: Mose（叶昊）
Country: China

社交
恐懼

不善言谈

-mose

やさげ

未滿拾捌請進

男女性號

野鶏文化

你迷恋完美身材是对的吗？
我从女人的背后追求女人。如果她转过头来，

一切便宣告结束。

pornographic poetry

PORNOGRAPHIC
ペナルティー・エリアの

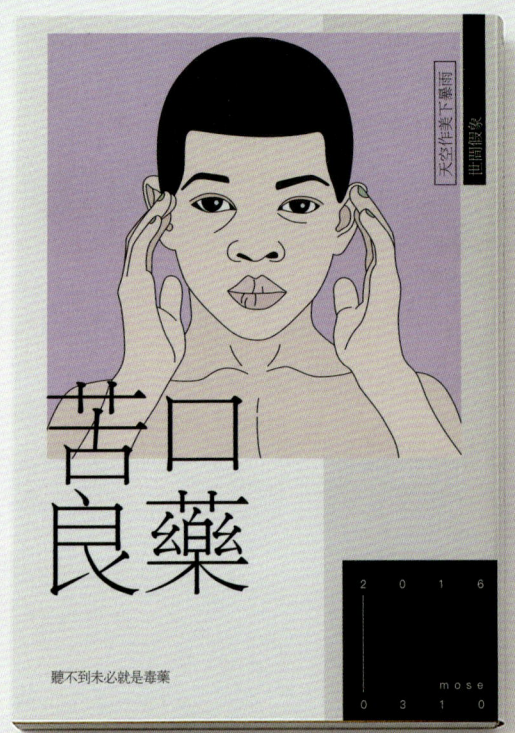

苦口
良藥

聽不到未必就是毒藥

蒙蔽
麻痺

不悅離我四十

Wild Man

Designer: Mose（叶昊）
Country: China

Wechat Book Design
-- Fabrication

Designer: Matto Lau
Design Agency: None
Country: China
Photographer: Matto Lau

The illusion of social network has created a stage for performing. The photos you choose, the lines you write, the music you share, the links you retweet, or even the sources, are all traces of your life.

Information like fact, time and location all interweave with each other, and manufacture a sense of reality. However, it is the cold electronic screen that displays all these pixels and data. The illusion of reality and undeniable distance has granted everyone a great chance to build a perfect self image.

The book recorded a good friend's life, sincere and emotional, with her WeChat chat history from 15:48, Oct. 2nd, 2014 to 19:01, Nov. 25th, 2015. Fabrication rearranged her chat history in random order, and put 12 pages in each day of October, 2015. That makes this calendar 372 pages in total.

Every page that you tear down on an odd-numbered day will become the daily record of the present day. While using this calendar, you will create daily records everyday. But you can never tell if these daily records are from the original day. There are 12 pages for every day. A new daily record of a new month will be created by those pages you tear down on any day randomly. By doing so, you can create a daily record for a year, and this is the illusion of reality.

01

❤️
🌼
💚
🌴

02

六郎七巷的誕生

03

菱葹的暖光

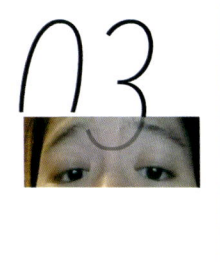

05

世界这么大，
最怕太在乎自己。

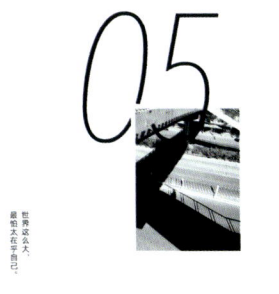

08

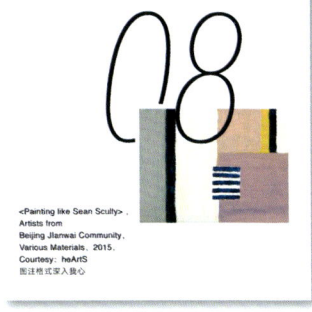

<Painting like Sean Scully>，
Artists from
Beijing Jianwai Community，
Various Materials，2015，
Courtesy: heArtS
图注格式寫入裝心

14

😋

15

他们不告诉我
海洋之心的下落
我就把他们
都杀了

17

善於沉睡的灵魂就该醒了

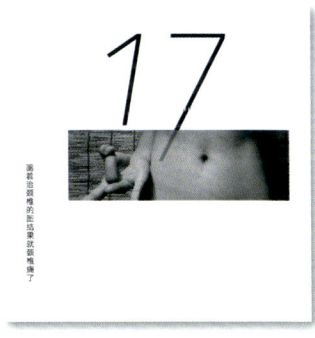

19

星星和残火
谁会先熄灭

20

他好像很愧

23

❤️
在23岁零一个月的时候
心里揣了一層皮

28

未來來，
让我来点走你的忧愁

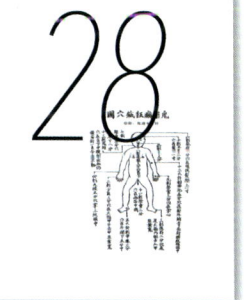

Wechat Book Design
-- Fabrication

Designer: Matto Lau
Design Agency: None
Country: China
Photographer: Matto Lau

Wechat Book Design
-- Fabrication

Designer: Matto Lau
Design Agency: None
Country: China
Photographer: Matto Lau

Time — Space — People

Continuity in Space & Object

A visual dialogue exploring traces of time within architectural spaces and objects of significance.

An attempt to connect time, space and people. An Experimental exploration into poetic expression of space within places, based upon spatial experience through photography, video, literature and various mediums. In hope that through the process, these places and objects can take on new meanings and that the collective memory of our nation could extend beyond our generation.

Time-Space-People

Designer: Cheryl Chong
Country: Singapore

A visual dialogue exploring traces of time within architectural spaces or objects of significance in Singapore. An attempt to connect time, space and people, an experimental exploration into poetic expression of space within places, based upon spatial experience through photography, video and various mediums. In hopes that through the process, these places and objects can take on new meanings; and that the collective memory of our nation could extend beyond our generation.

Time-Space-People

Designer: Cheryl Chong
Country: Singapore

02 — ARTICLES OF TIME

人・事 — People

Time — Space — People

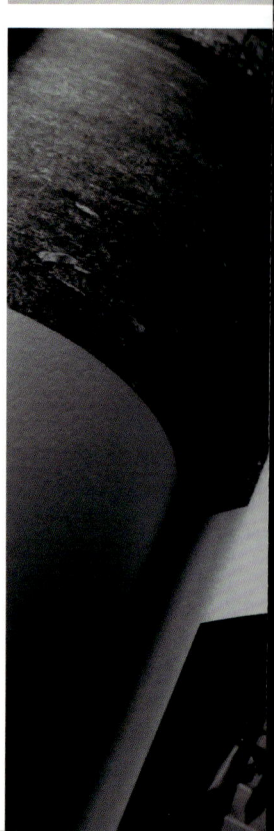

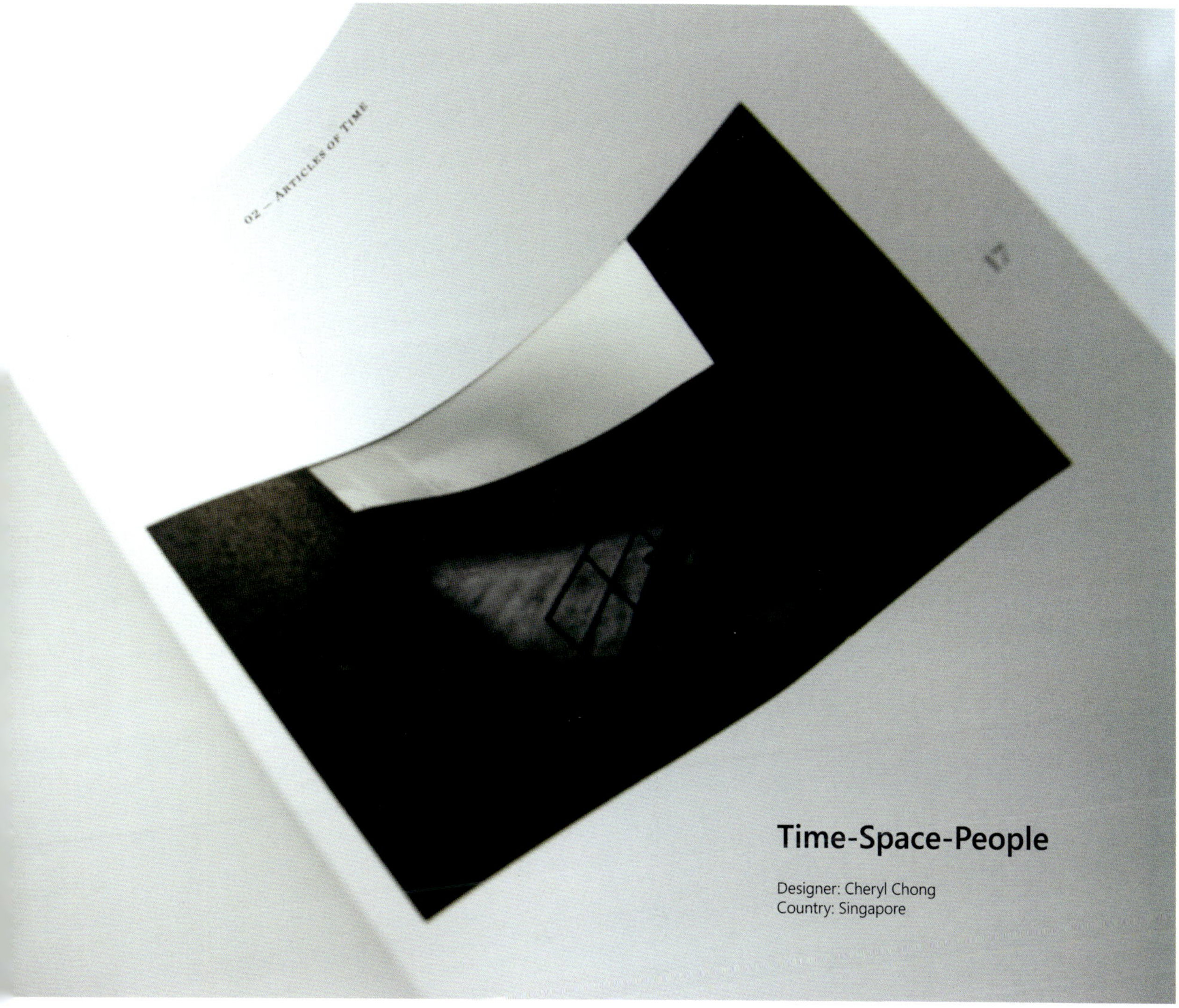

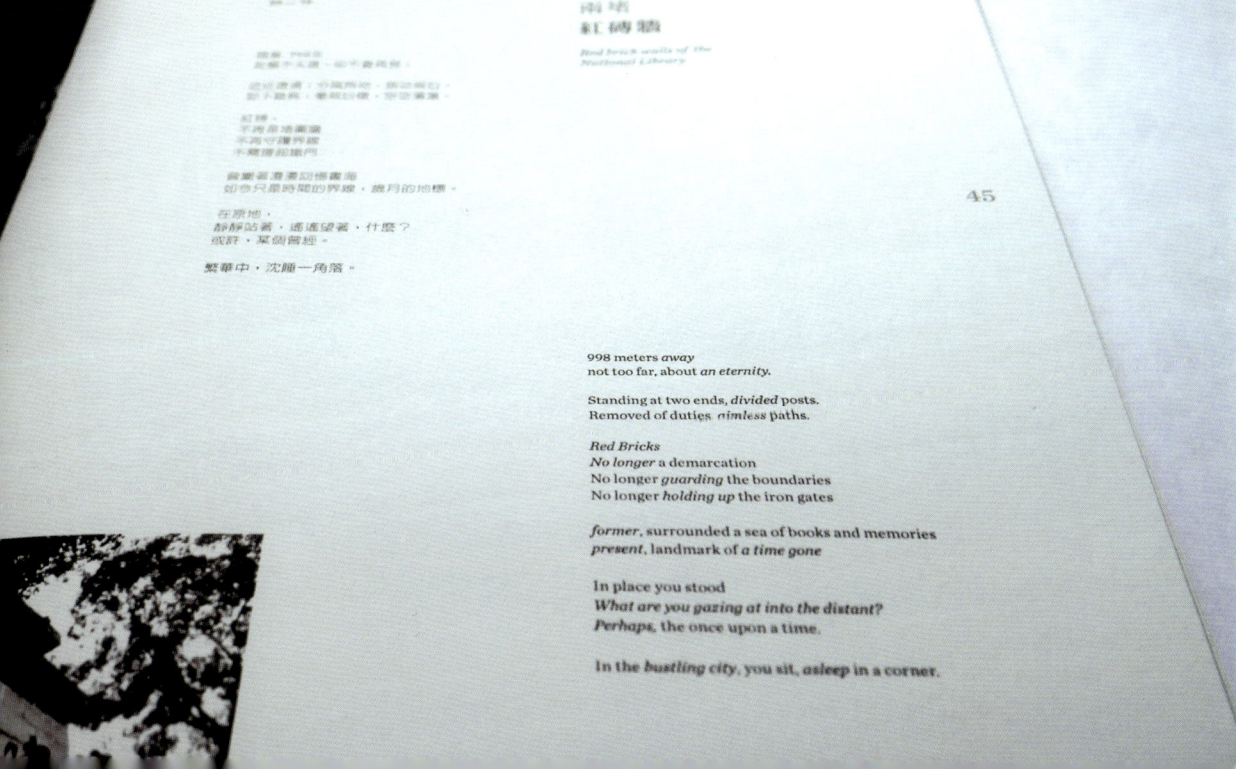

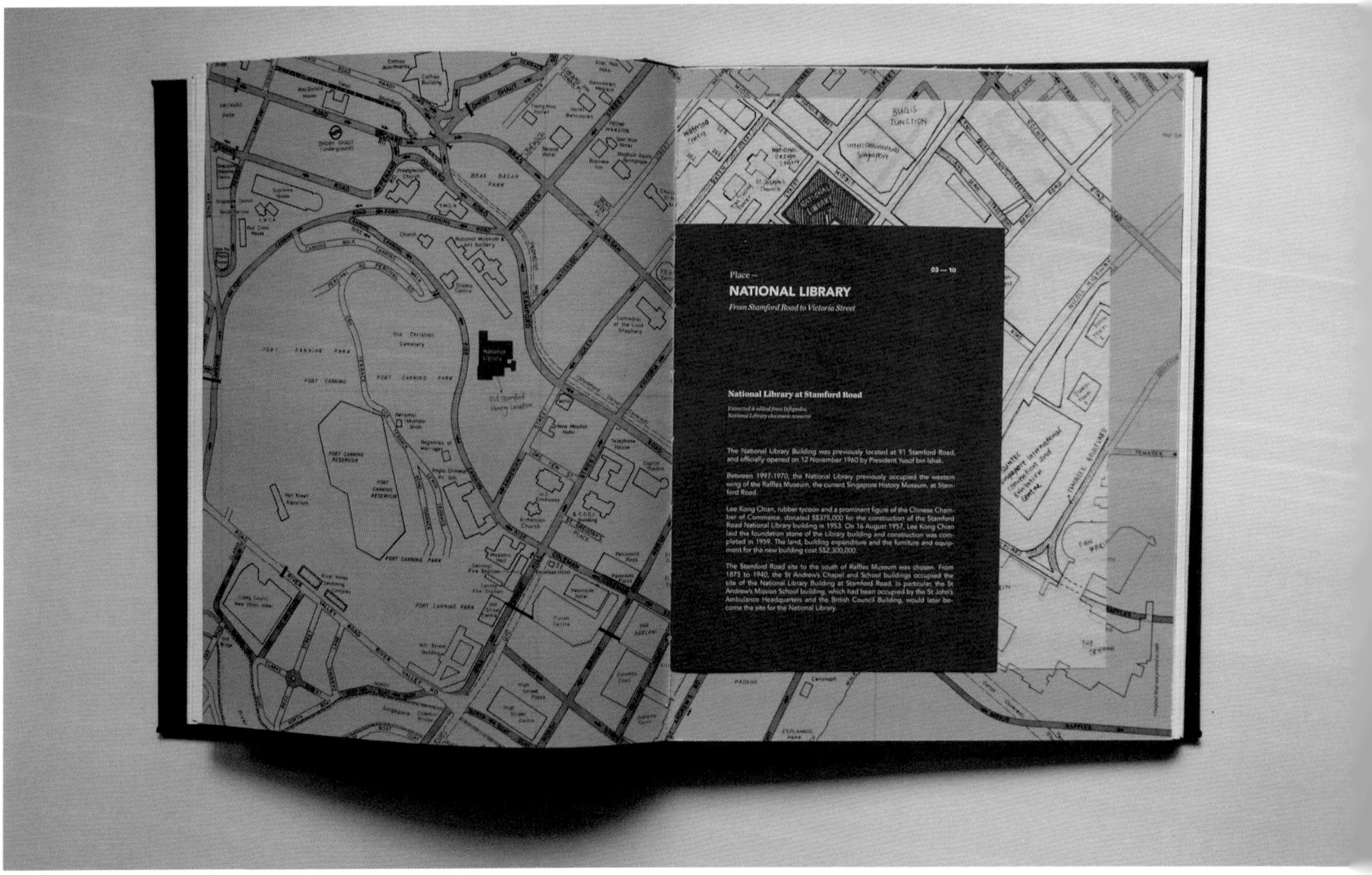

Time-Space-People

Designer: Cheryl Chong
Country: Singapore

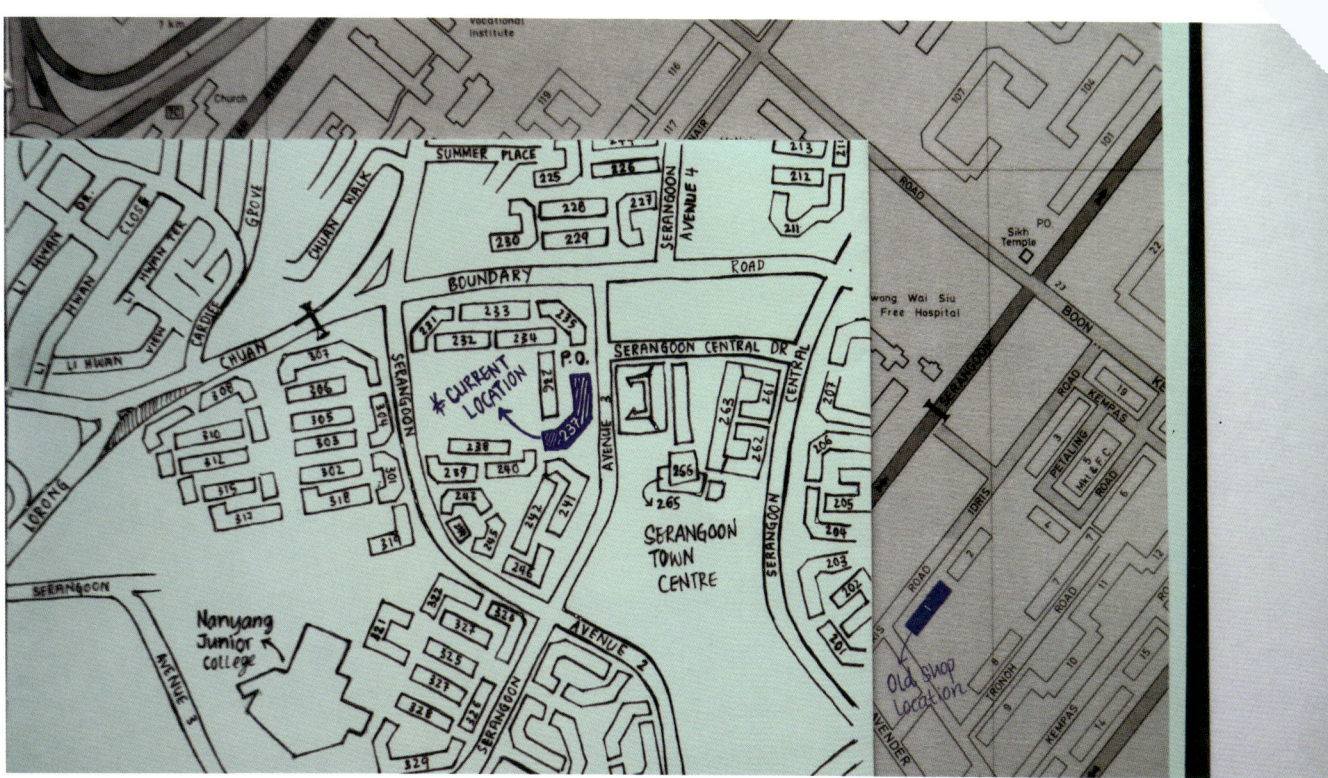

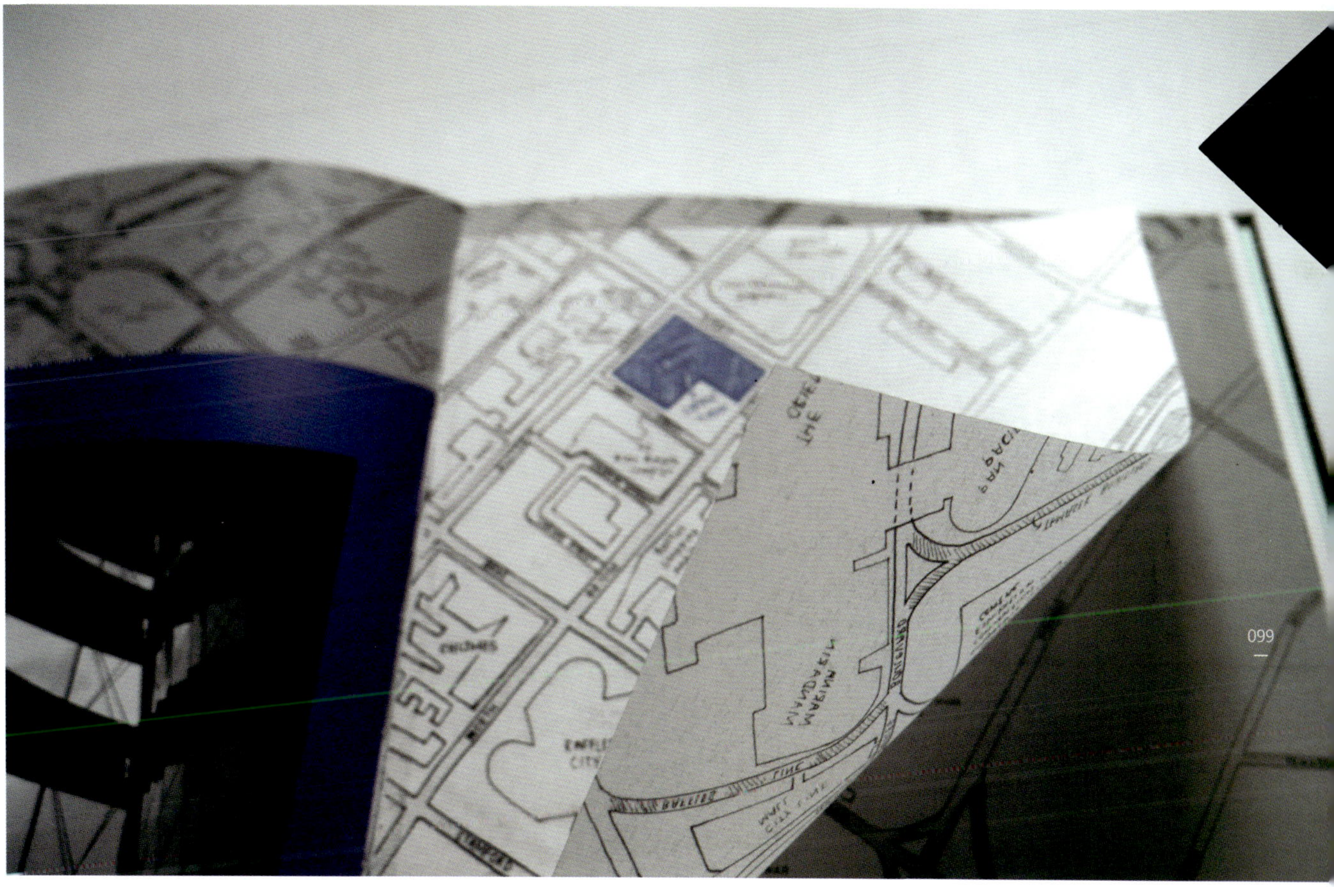

空・間 — Space

Time-Space-People

Designer: Cheryl Chong
Country: Singapore

Golden Mile Complex

Golden Mile Complex

Time — Space — People

Time-Space-People

Designer: Cheryl Chong
Country: Singapore

This project comprises of 3 publications, each publication focusing on an aspect — time, space and people:

Space focus on poetic expressions through poems and photography based upon spatial experience.
People consists of background history and location of place. Places featured are mostly famous architectural landmarks that are significant to Singapore's history, represents an era or a Golden period in Singapore.
Time features a collection of articles that record fragments of time. An attempt to "capture" traces of time in space and objects, metaphorically.

Portfolio

Designer: Alessandro Latela
Country: Italy

A single book which contains a selection of my works between 2013 and 2015, but also a few lines about my interests and my way of working. In the first and last page I attached my résumé and a CD-Rom with digital portfolio.
I love handmade productions, for this reason the cover simulates cardboard and the words are made with a marker. Lastly I used a labeller to make the title.

PORTFOLIO
2013/15

PORTFOLIO
2013/15

ESPERIENZE LAVORATIVE

· Villanova
2013
Graphic designer
CD musicale

· Oneglobal s.r.l
2014
Graphic designer
Depliant informativo

· Andar s.n.c
2013
Graphic designer
Brand identity

· L'altra Casalnuovo
2015
Graphic designer
Flyer per Stefano Iorio

· Gedi s.r.l
2013 > 2014
Graphic designer
Catalogo e Roll-Up

· Motortecno
2015
Graphic designer
immagini pubblicitarie

· Protezione Civile
2013
Graphic designer
Impaginazione opuscolo

· Crespine gel
2014
Graphic designer
Depliant medico

· Futuroremoto
2015
Graphic designer
Brand e manifesti

SOFTWARE

Id Ai Ps Lr Mu

105

LINGUE

· Italiano (lingua madre)
· Inglese (livello medio)

INTERESSI

· Fotografia
· Cinema
· Letteratura

MOSTRE

· Mostra personale
2012
First Floor
Pomigliano D'Arco (NA)

· Esposizione collettiva
2012
Cratere
Ercolano (NA)

· Esposizione collettiva
2014
A01 Fine Art Gallery
Napoli

· Mostra personale
2012
Feltrinelli Point
Pomigliano D'Arco (NA)

· Mostra personale
2013
Centro Polifunzionale "Pasolini"
Casalnuovo di Napoli (NA)

· Esposizione collettiva
2015
PAN "Palazzo delle Arti di Napoli"
Napoli

COMPETENZE & CAPACITÀ

Creatività

Gestione dei clienti   Progettazione

Rapporti interpersonali   Organizzazione

                                                    Cooperazione

Tempistiche   Affidabilità

Portfolio

Designer: Alessandro Latela
Country: Italy

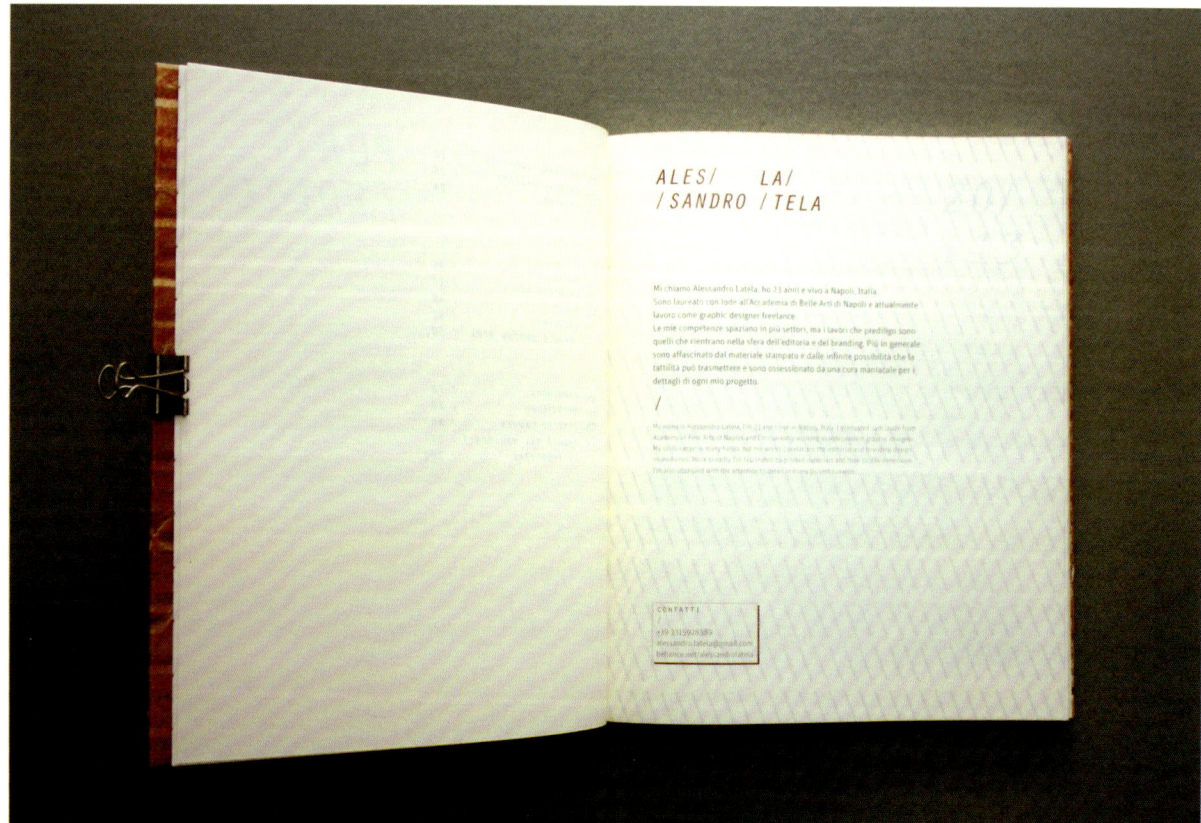

ALES/   LA/
/SANDRO /TELA

Mi chiamo Alessandro Lutela, ho 23 anni e vivo a Napoli, Italia.
Sono laureati con lode all'Accademia di Belle Arti di Napoli e attualmente
lavoro come graphic designer freelance.
Le mie competenze spaziano in più settori, ma i lavori che prediligo sono
quelli che rientrano nella sfera dell'editoria e del branding. Più in generale
sono affascinato dal materiale stampato e dalle infinite possibilità che la
tattilità può trasmettere e sono ossessionato da una cura maniacale per i
dettagli di ogni mio progetto.

/

CONTATTI
+39 3315970389
alessandro.lutela@gmail.com
behance.net/alessandrolutela

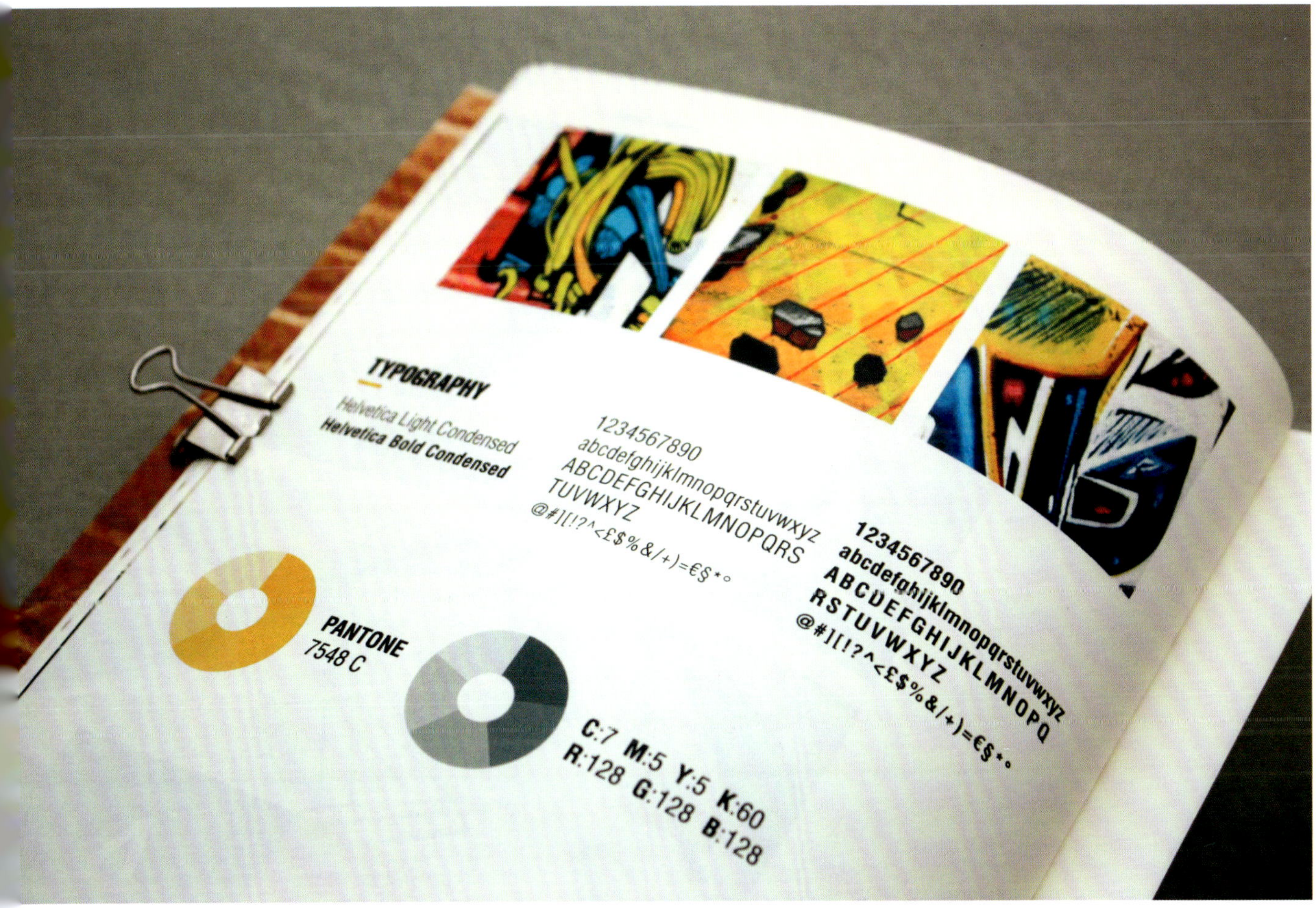

Graphic Design Book

Designer: Alessandro Latela
Country: Italy

Composition in seven/sixteenth, handmade bound
Paperback thread stitched
Matt lamination of the cover
Format 17 x 24 cm.

This project contains all the lessons, explanations, exercises, so all the knowledges learned during the three years of the Graphic Design course at the Academy of Fine Arts of Naples.
For the realization of the cover, the title was obtained by cutting bubble wrap, applied into the cover with photographic technique.

GRAPHIC
DESIGN

Graphic Design Book

Designer: Alessandro Latela
Country: Italy

The Creativity Beyond Essence

Designer: Chun-Ta Chu
Country: Taiwan, China

Client: National Taiwan Normal University Department of Design

The brand is developed via not only reflecting on the interaction between the designer, design work and portfolio, but expressing the designer's personality. The hanger is to the designer, and the shirt to his design work. These two elements lie at the intersection between time and continuous creation. Every piece is about the present self and also the encouragement for the future work.

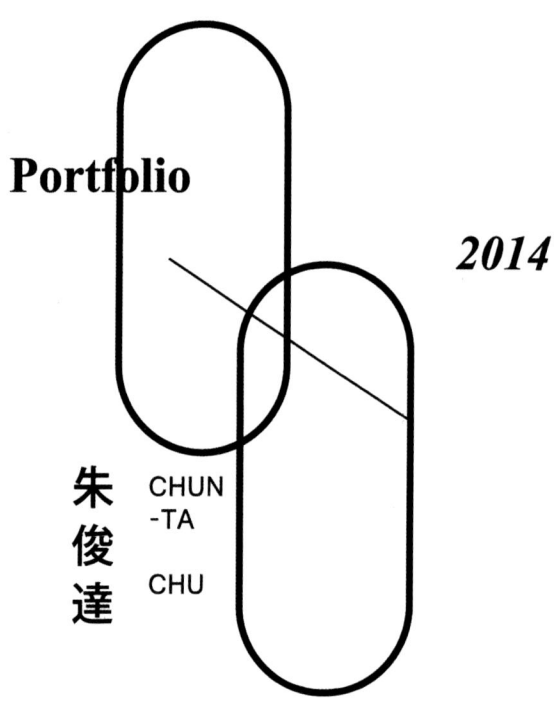

The Creativity Beyond Essence

Designer: Chun-Ta Chu
Country: Taiwan, China

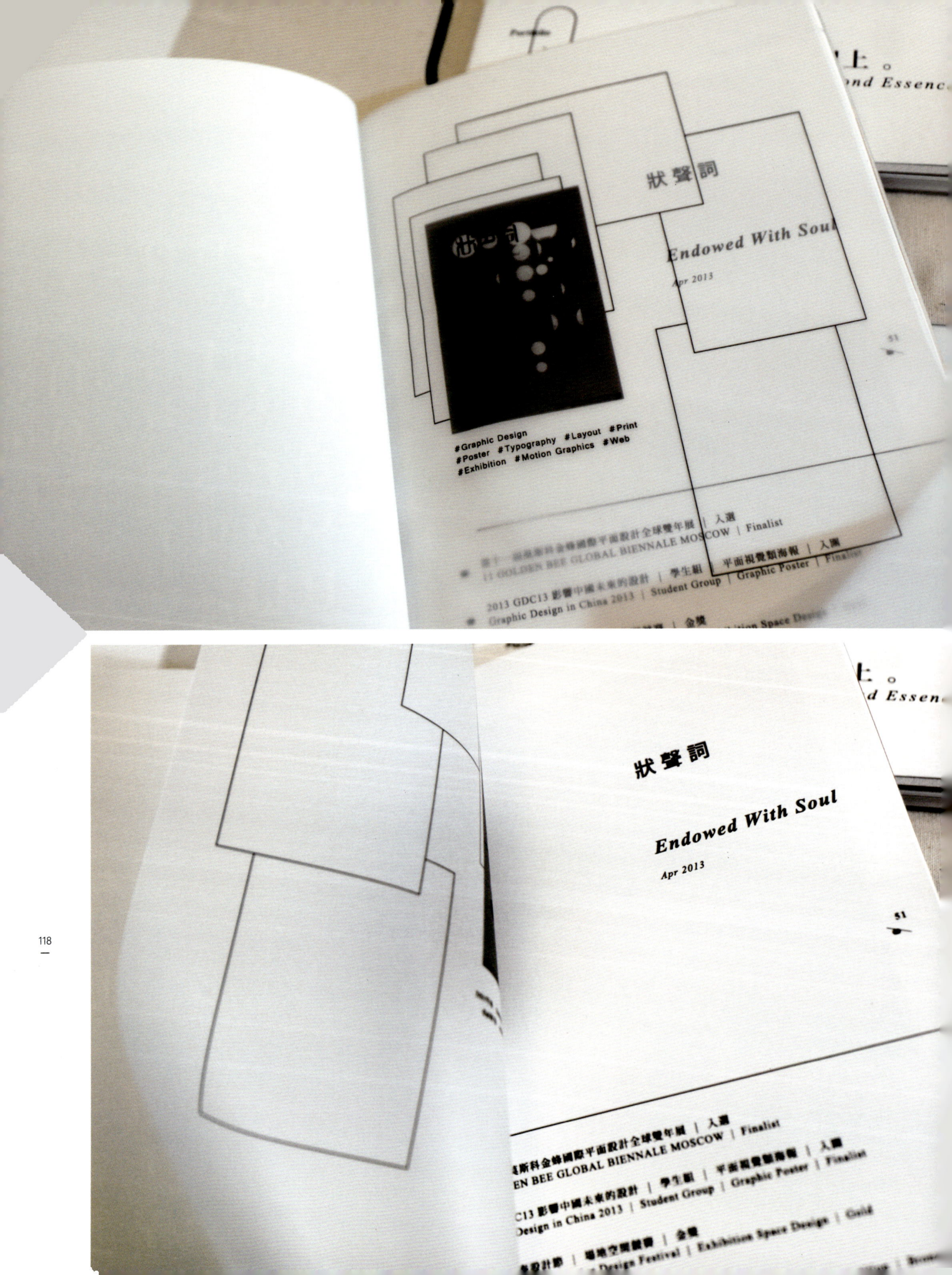

狀聲詞

Endowed With Soul

Apr 2013

#Graphic Design
#Poster #Typography #Layout #Print
#Exhibition #Motion Graphics #Web

第十一屆莫斯科金蜂國際平面設計全球雙年展 ｜ 入選
11 GOLDEN BEE GLOBAL BIENNALE MOSCOW ｜ Finalist   平面視覺類海報 ｜ 入選
                                                    Graphic Poster ｜ Finalist
2013 GDC13 影響中國未來的設計 ｜ 學生組
Graphic Design in China 2013 ｜ Student Group

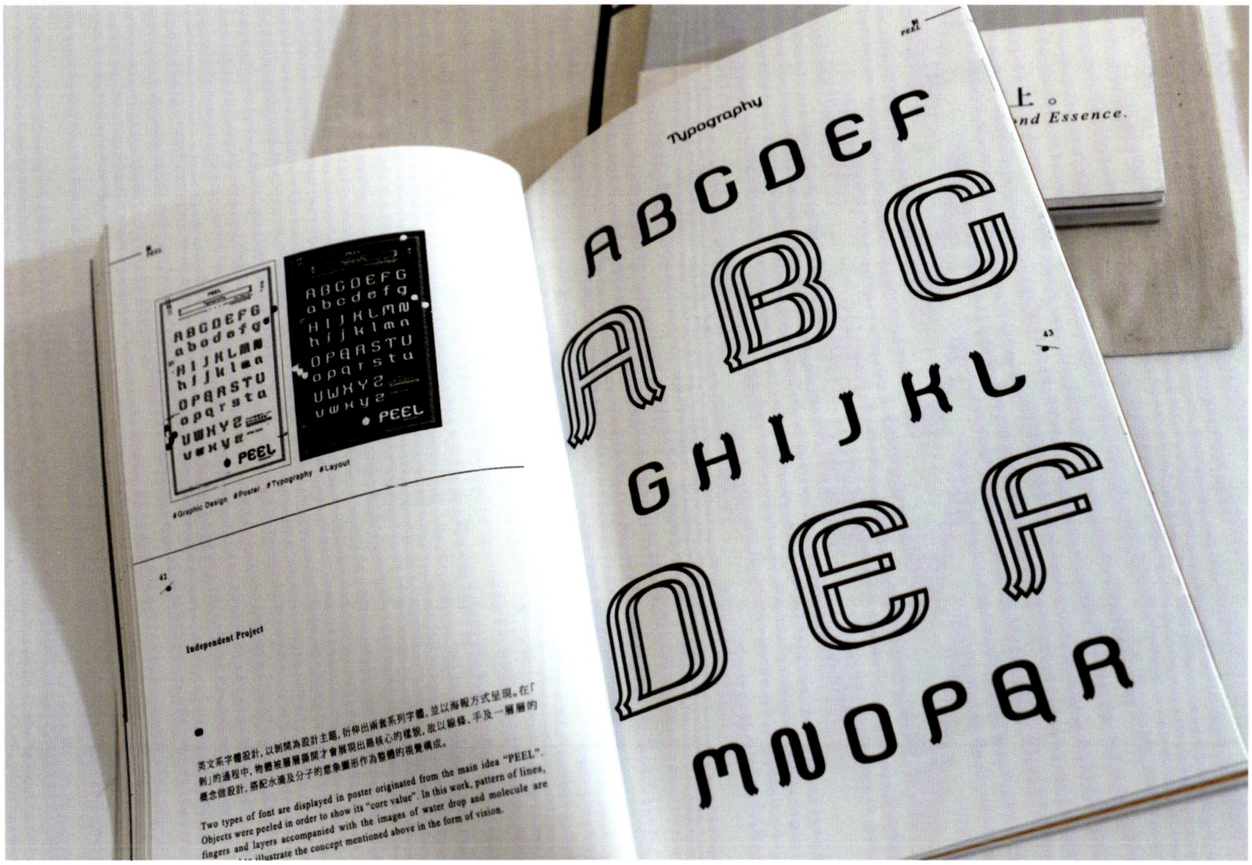

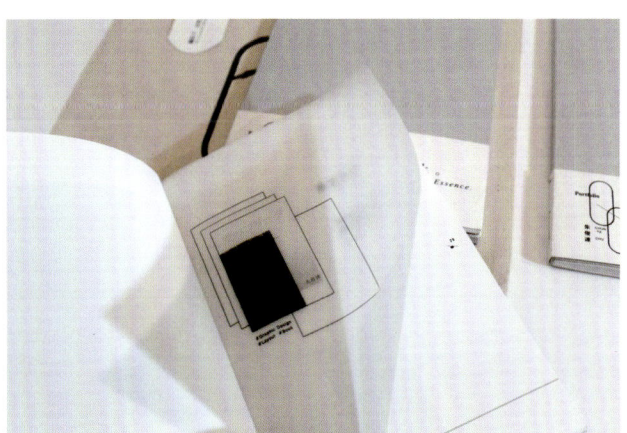

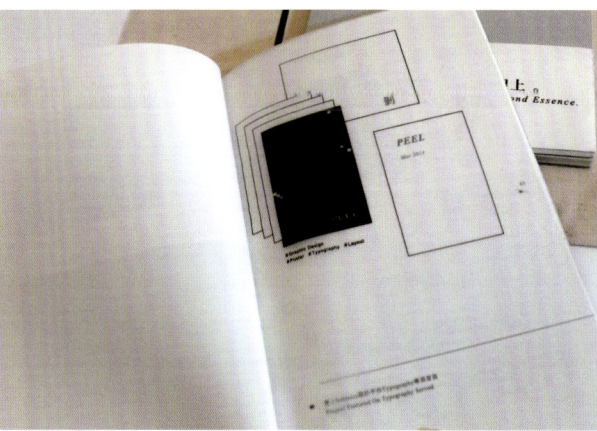

The Creativity Beyond Essence

Designer: Chun-Ta Chu
Country: Taiwan, China

The Creativity Beyond Essence

Designer: Chun-Ta Chu
Country: Taiwan, China

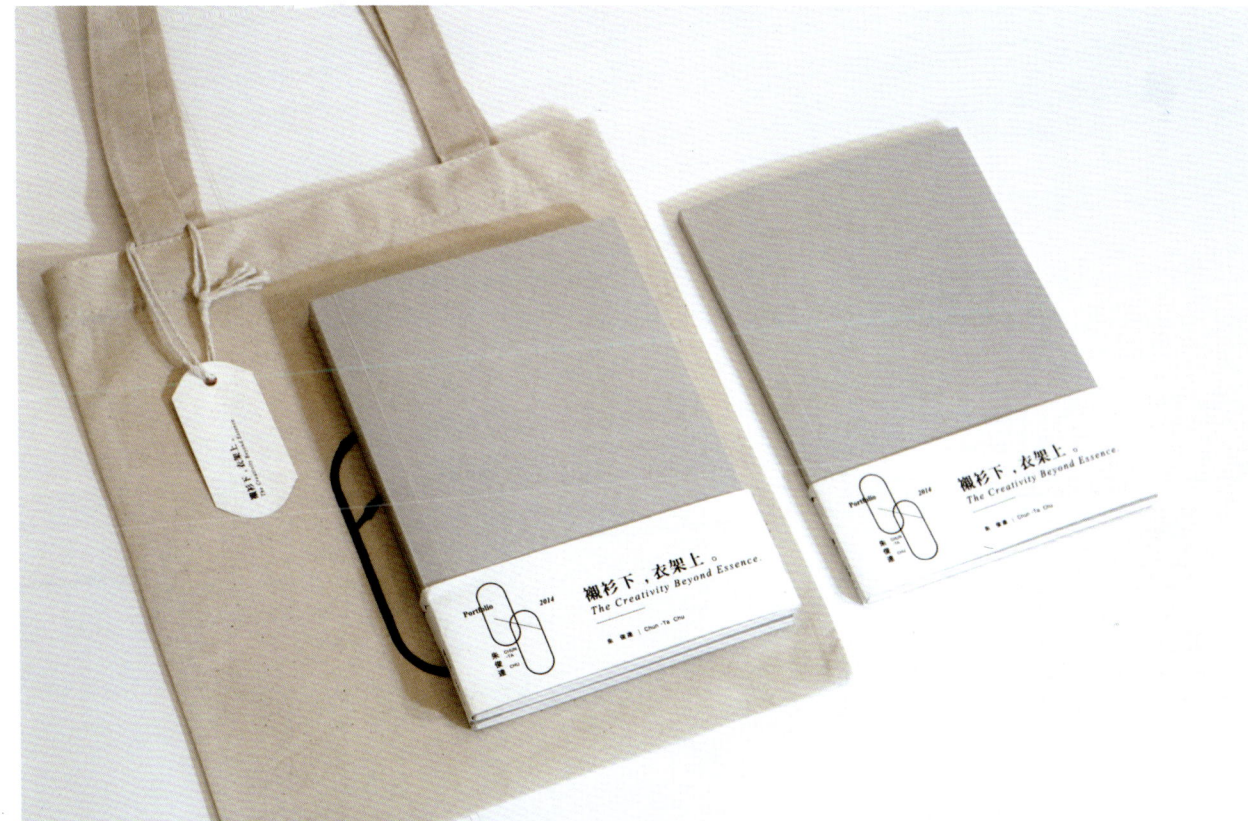

Chang Jung Christian University
Department of Computer...
長榮大學媒體設計...
102th academic...

C.V.

Hsinchu, Taiw...

Exhibition

畢業成果校內展 ｜ 長榮大學
宜蘭大賞 ｜ 高雄數位科技資訊館
青春設計節 ｜ 籃 · 藝術特區
新一代設計展 ｜ 台北世貿一館
GDC13 影響中國未來的設計 ｜ 深圳華美術館
第9屆創意達人設計大賽「歸錄」 ｜ 台北當代藝術館MOCA
第11屆莫斯科金蜂平面設計雙年展 ｜ Moscow, Central...

Publish

《GDC13》Graphic Design in China 2013 作品年鑑
《dpi》雜誌177期1月號
《設計印象》雜誌66期1月號
《2013青春設計節》青春影展》

Work Experience

助理設計師 ｜ 門陣俱樂部 ｜ Sep 2010 - Jun 2011 ｜ Jul 2012 - Jun 2013
專案助理 ｜ 教育部補助智慧生活影視計畫案 ｜ Mar 2012 - Jul 2012 ｜ Dec 2013 - Dec 2014
工讀生 ｜ 大台南西基電腦動畫公司建模培訓班
替代役役男 ｜ 教育部學生事務及特殊教育司全民國防教育科

Award

第十一屆莫斯科金蜂國際平面設計雙年展 ｜ 入選2件 ｜ 學生組平面視覺類海報 ｜ 入圍
GDC13 影響中國未來的設計 ｜ 平面視覺類 ｜ 評審團特別獎
第9屆創意達人設計大賽「歸錄」 ｜ 全勝 · 銅獎
2013青春設計節 場地空間競賽
2013新一代設計展 展場設校競賽 ｜ 平面類 ｜ 入圍
第二屆台南創意新人獎 ｜ 入圍
2013微視大賞（Vision Get Wild） ｜ 多媒體類 ｜ 入圍
2013微視大賞（Vision Get Wild） ｜ 跨領域類 ｜ 入圍
2013微視大賞（Vision Get Wild） ｜ 展場空間獎 ｜ 佳作

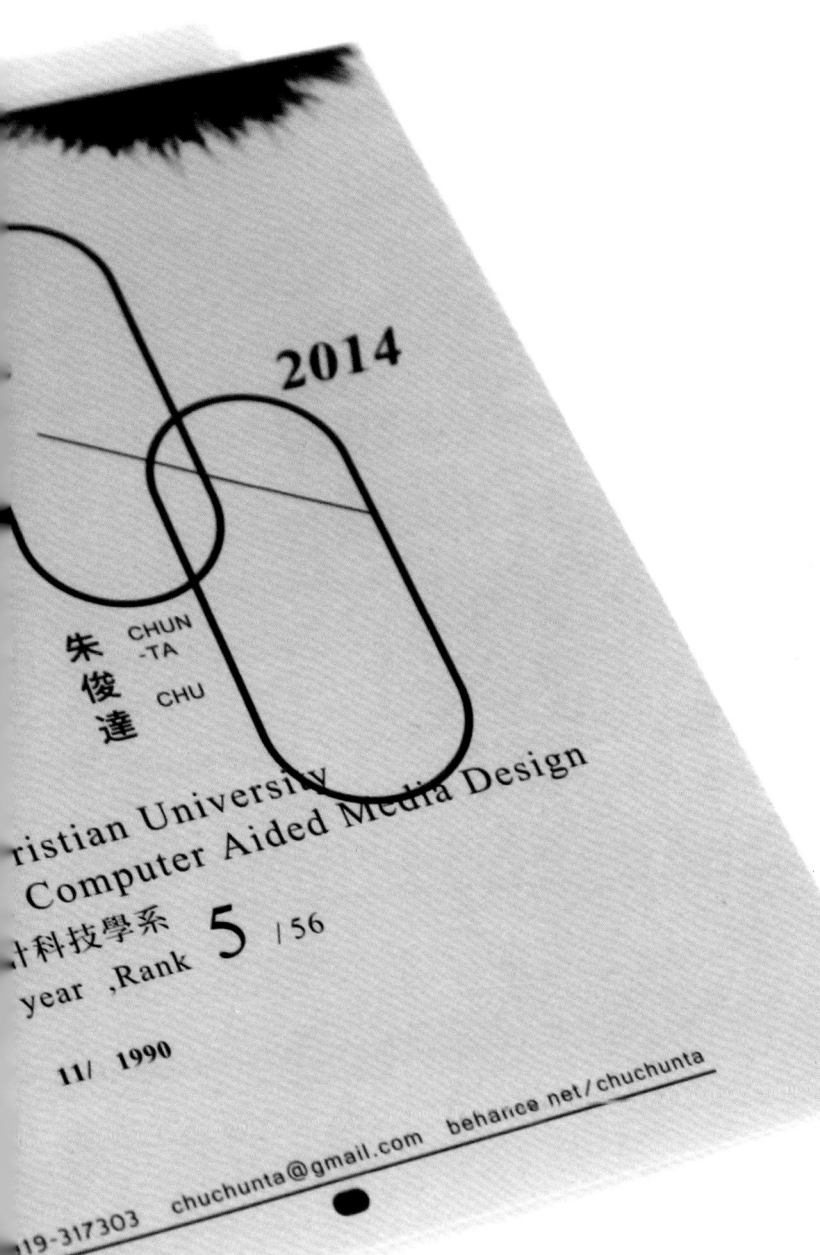

The Creativity Beyond Essence

Designer: Chun-Ta Chu
Country: Taiwan, China

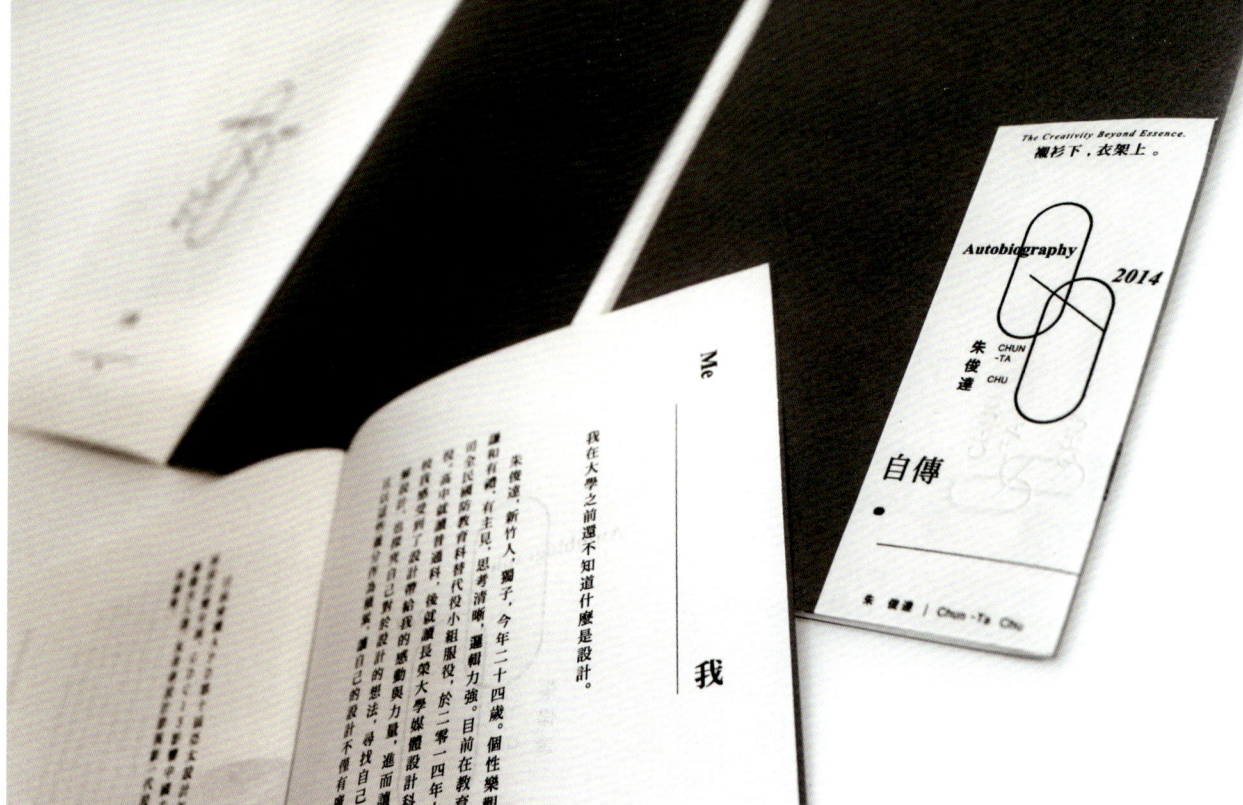

The Creativity Beyond Essence

Designer: Chun-Ta Chu
Country: Taiwan, China

澳門
藝術家推廣計劃
專輯

Livro de
Projecto de Promoção de
Artistas de Macau

ISBN 978-99937-119-9-5
MOP$ 180

5

中西共融

50

澳門藝術家

書法 ✕ 繪畫 ✕ 雕塑 ✕ 攝影

以自己的藝術為城市增
光添彩，記憶過去，描
繪現在，饋贈未來！

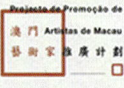

Projecto de Promoção de
澳門 Artistas de Macau
藝術家 推廣計劃

澳門基金會
FUNDAÇÃO MACAU

具象⋯印象⋯現代⋯抽象

「毋庸諱言，他們當中的佼佼者都經過艱苦的實踐，方在同代人中脫
穎而出，進入當代澳門藝壇」⋯⋯吳志良《澳門藝術家叢書・總序》

50: Works collection of Macao Artists promotion program

Designer: Chiwai Cheang
Design Agency: SomethingMoon Design
Country: Macau, China

Client: Macau Foundation

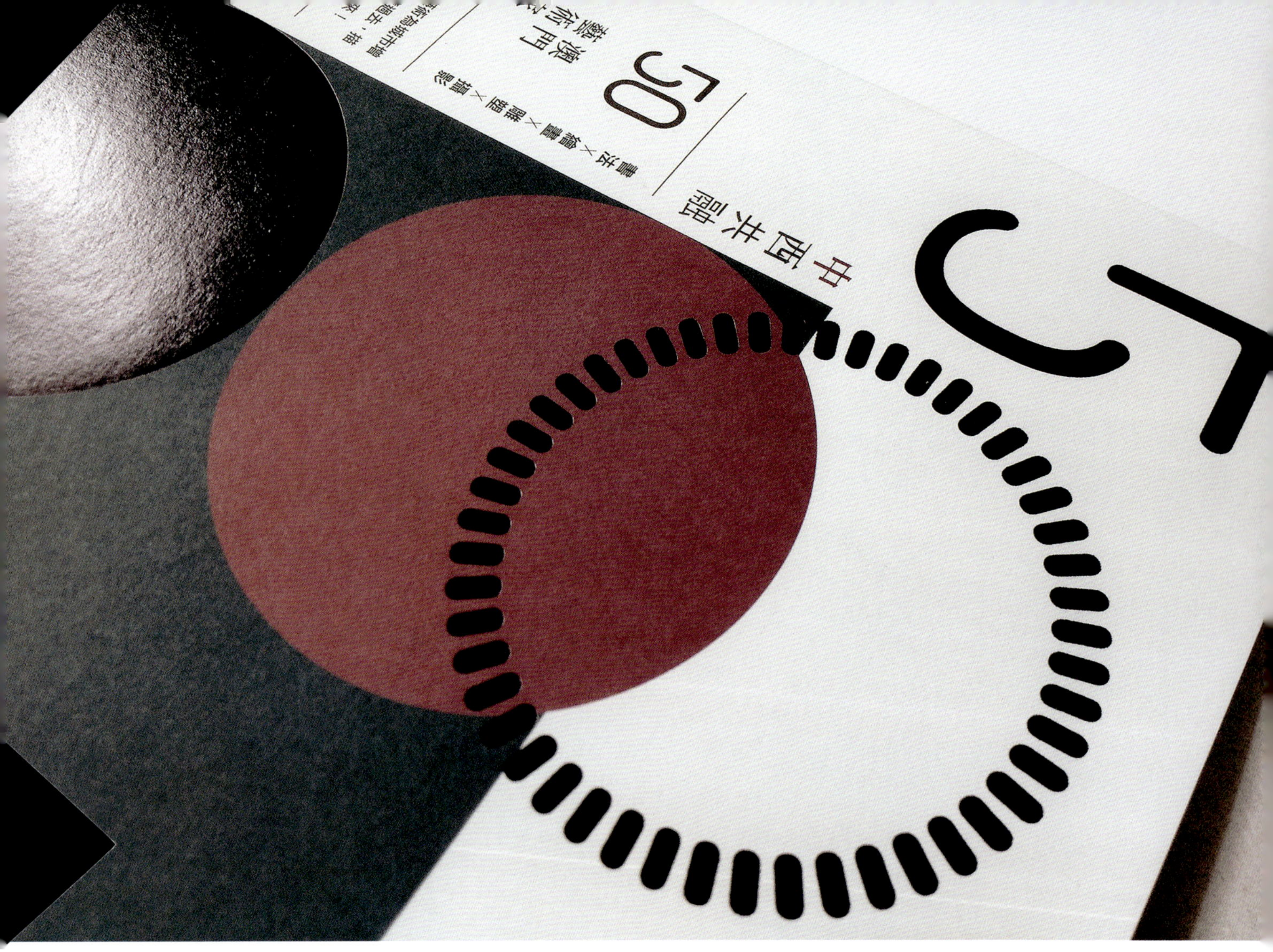
中西共融
50
書法×繪畫×雕塑×攝影

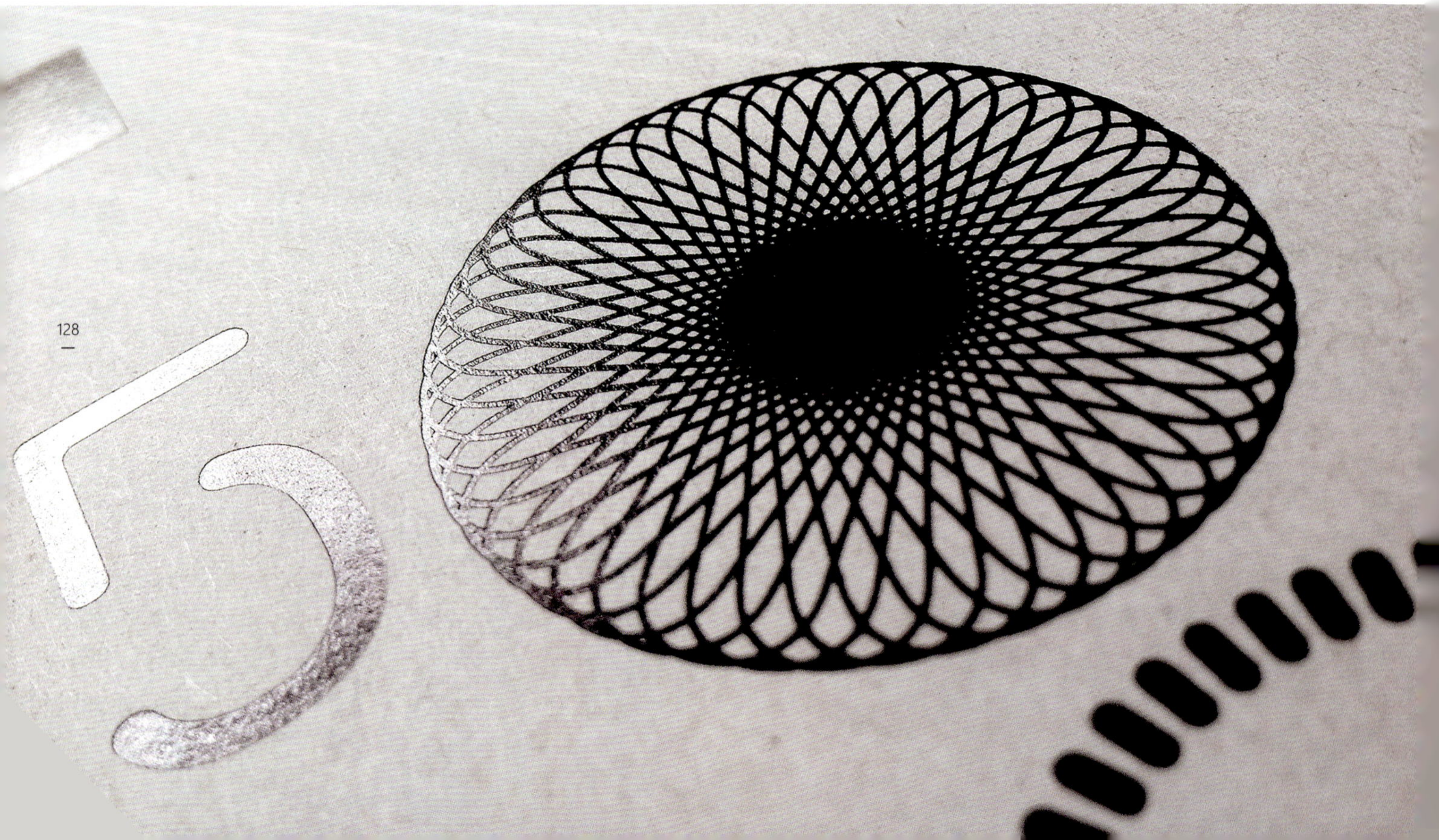

50: Works collection of Macao Artists promotion program

Designer: Chiwai Cheang
Design Agency: SomethingMoon Design
Country: Macau, China

50: Works collection of Macao
Artists promotion program

Designer: Chiwai Cheang
Design Agency: SomethingMoon Design
Country: Macau, China

鶴齡，「文晶」，廣東省番禺人，1930 年出生家廣東，中學與於
香港中文大學教育，曾於人。擅長水彩等工作當任校長，由此時起，
師範大學教育，而且注重從大自然汲取營養。師法自然，自成一格，其書畫作品
直醒洛虹，面注重從大自然汲取題材，師法自然，自成一格，其書畫作品
於京省紅，所到之處，二、現集書畫、目屬臻臻。高麗的
勝。廣州，港八方父又草書，自成，自成，自成，美加等地
的書法從人案入手，港澳，中國台灣以及其南亞，及珍藏
公祝鑑裱及藏家珍藏。

119

Actually We Are IV

Designer: Chiwai Cheang
Design Agency: SomethingMoon Design
Country: Macau, China

Client: Artistry of Wind Box Community Development Association

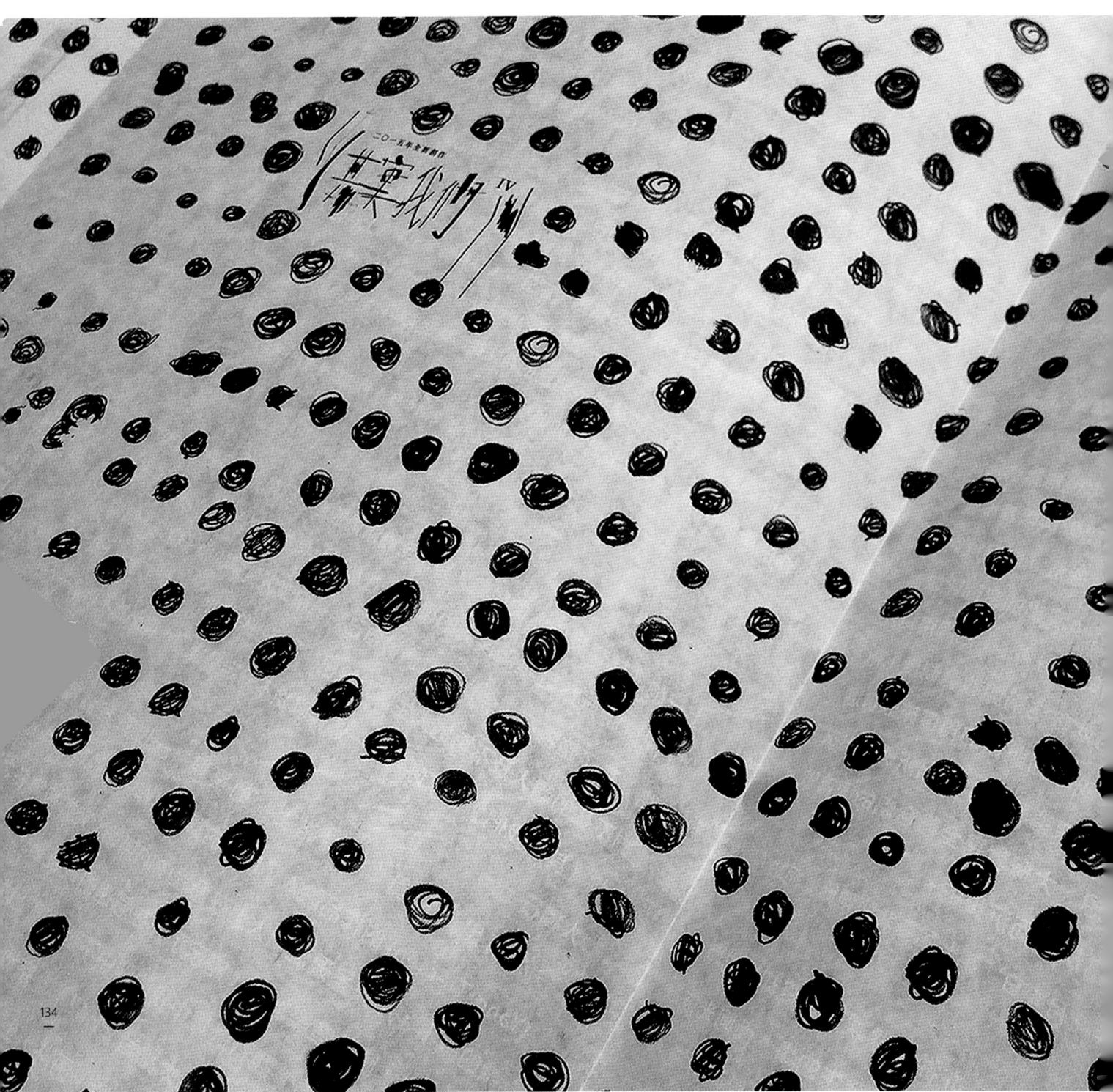

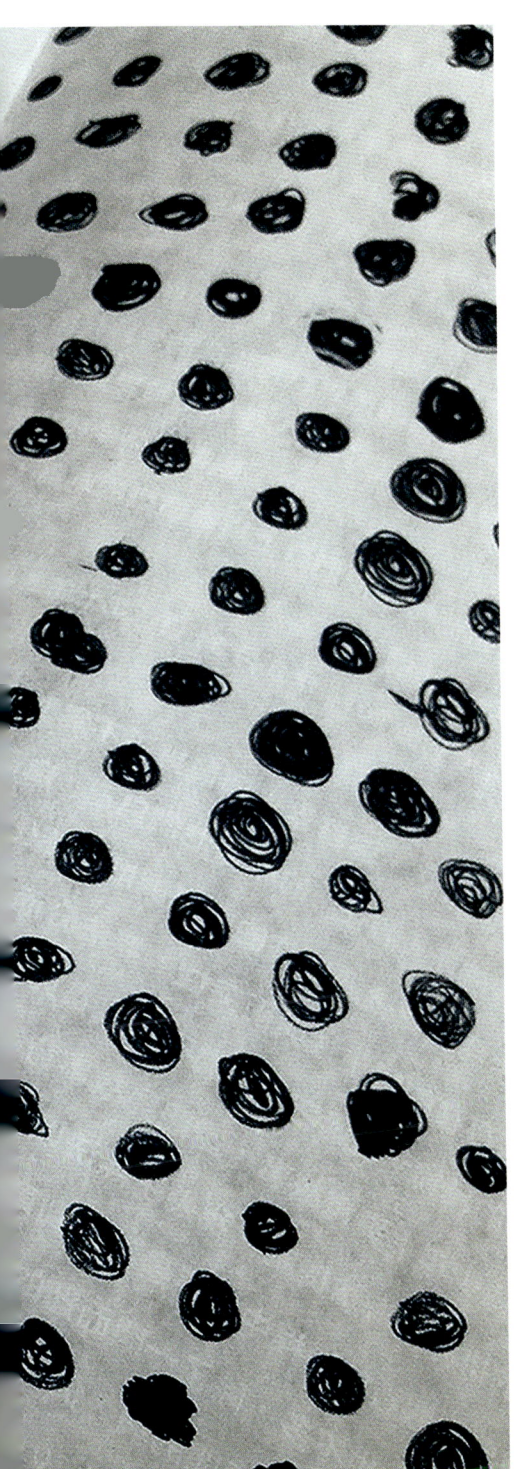

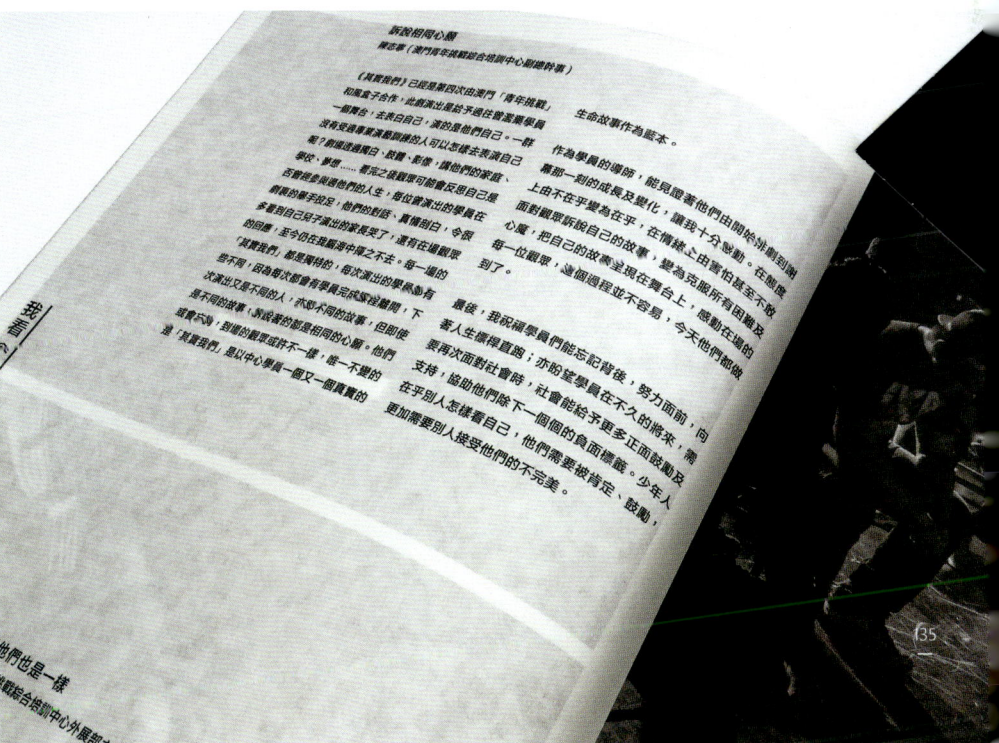

Actually We Are IV

Designer: Chiwai Cheang
Design Agency: SomethingMoon Design
Country: Macau, China

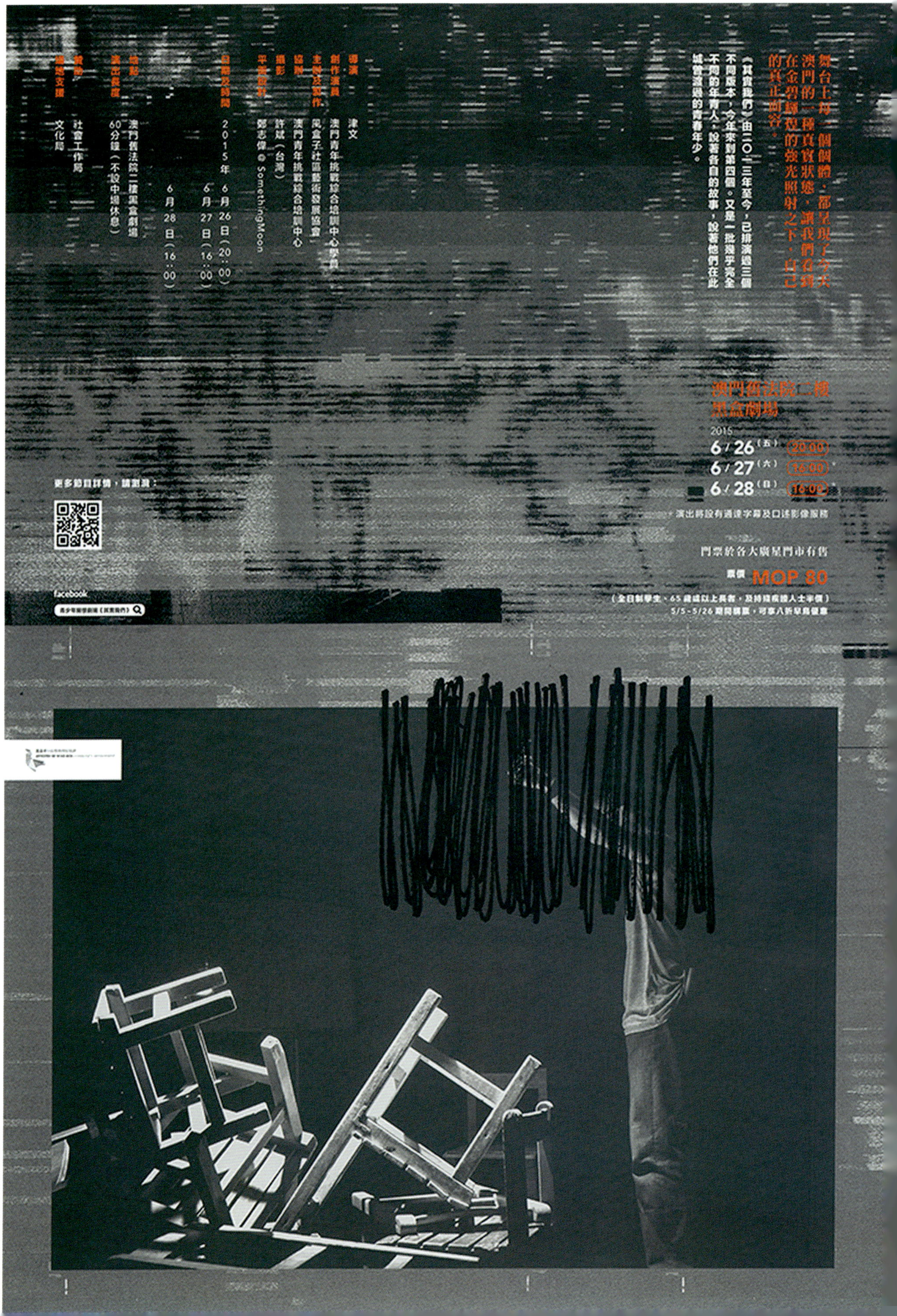

舞台上每一個個體，都呈現了字裏澳門的一種真實狀態，讓我們看到在金碧輝煌的強光照射之下，自己的真正面容。

《其實我們》由二〇一三年至今，已排演過三個不同版本，今年來到第四個。又是一批學完全不同的年青人，說著各自的故事，說著他們在此城裡渡過的青春年少。

導演　津文
創作演員　澳門青年挑戰綜合培訓中心學員
主辦及製作　飛皇子社區藝術發展協會
協辦　澳門青年挑戰綜合培訓中心
攝影　許斌（台灣）
平面設計　鄭志偉 © SomethingMoon
日期及時間　2015年 6月26日（五）20：00 / 6月27日（六）16：00 / 6月28日（日）16：00
演出長度　60分鐘（不設中場休息）
地點　澳門舊法院二樓黑盒劇場
贊助　社會工作局
場地支援　文化局

澳門舊法院二樓
黑盒劇場
2015
6/26（五）20:00
6/27（六）16:00
6/28（日）16:00

演出將設有通達字幕及口述影像服務

門票於各大廣星門市有售
票價　MOP 80

（全日制學生、65 歲或以上長者，及持殘疾powers人士半價）
5/5 - 5/26 期間購票，可享八折早鳥優惠

更多節目詳情，請瀏覽：
facebook.
青少年劇藝劇場《其實我們》

136
一

二〇一五年全新創作

《其實是我們 IV》

「這不是一個演出，更是一次真實的展示。
台上站著的不是演員，更是每一個真實的個體。」

Actually We Are IV

Designer: Chiwai Cheang
Design Agency: SomethingMoon Design
Country: Macau, China

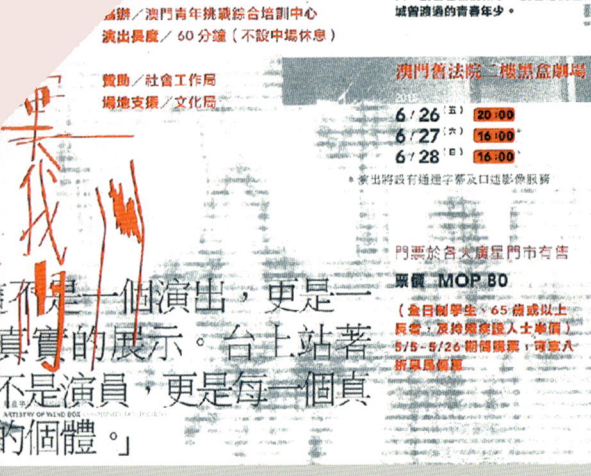

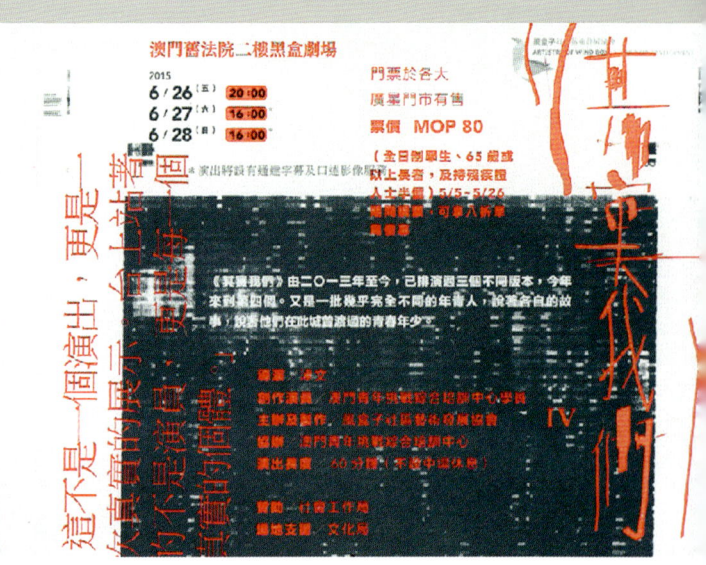

Actually We Are IV

Designer: Chiwai Cheang
Design Agency: SomethingMoon Design
Country: Macau, China

A Gambling World II

Designer: Chiwai Cheang
Design Agency: SomethingMoon Design
Country: Macau, China

Client: Step Out

A Gambling World II

Designer: Chiwai Cheang
Design Agency: SomethingMoon Design
Country: Macau, China

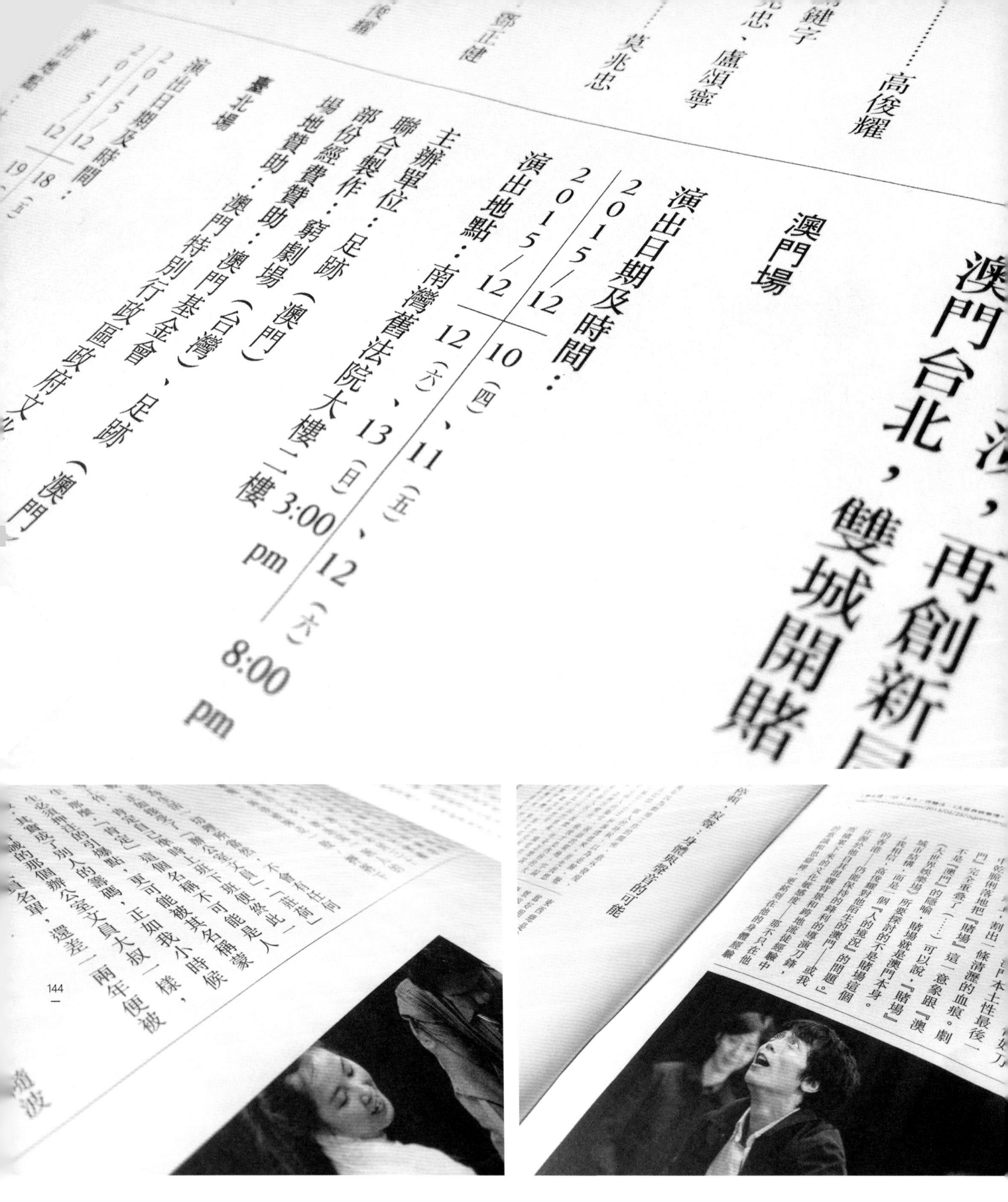

澳門合北，再創新局，雙城開賭

……高俊耀

……盧頌寧

……莫兆忠

……鄧正健

澳門場

演出日期及時間：
2015/12
10（四）

演出地點：南灣舊法院大樓二樓

12（六）、11（五）、13（日）、12（六）
3:00 pm
8:00 pm

主辦單位：足跡
聯合製作：足跡、窮劇場
部分經費贊助：窮劇場（澳門）
場地贊助：窮劇場（澳門）
澳門（台灣）、足跡（澳門）
澳門特別基金會、足跡（澳門）
澳門特別行政區政府文...

臺北場
演出日期及時間：
2015/12/18―19（五）...

A Gambling World II

Designer: Chiwai Cheang
Design Agency: SomethingMoon Design
Country: Macau, China

Macau 525

Designer: Chiwai Cheang
Design Agency: SomethingMoon Design
Country: Macau, China

Client: "Macau 525" Association

mo_st_ moholy_nagy_typophoto_studies

Designer: Dora Balla
Country: Hungary

Client: Moholy-Nagy University of Art and Design

Moholy-Nagy's philosophy and essay entitled Typophoto is more up-to-date now than ever before. How does the new generation of artists reinterpret the contemporary relation of classical photography and typography? How do young artists represent Moholy-Nagy's ideas today? How do they design typefaces in the new context of the spiritual heritage of Bauhaus? The book mo_st_ showcasing a selection from the works of the students of Moholy-Nagy University of Art and Design to answer the above questions. Professor: Dora Balla

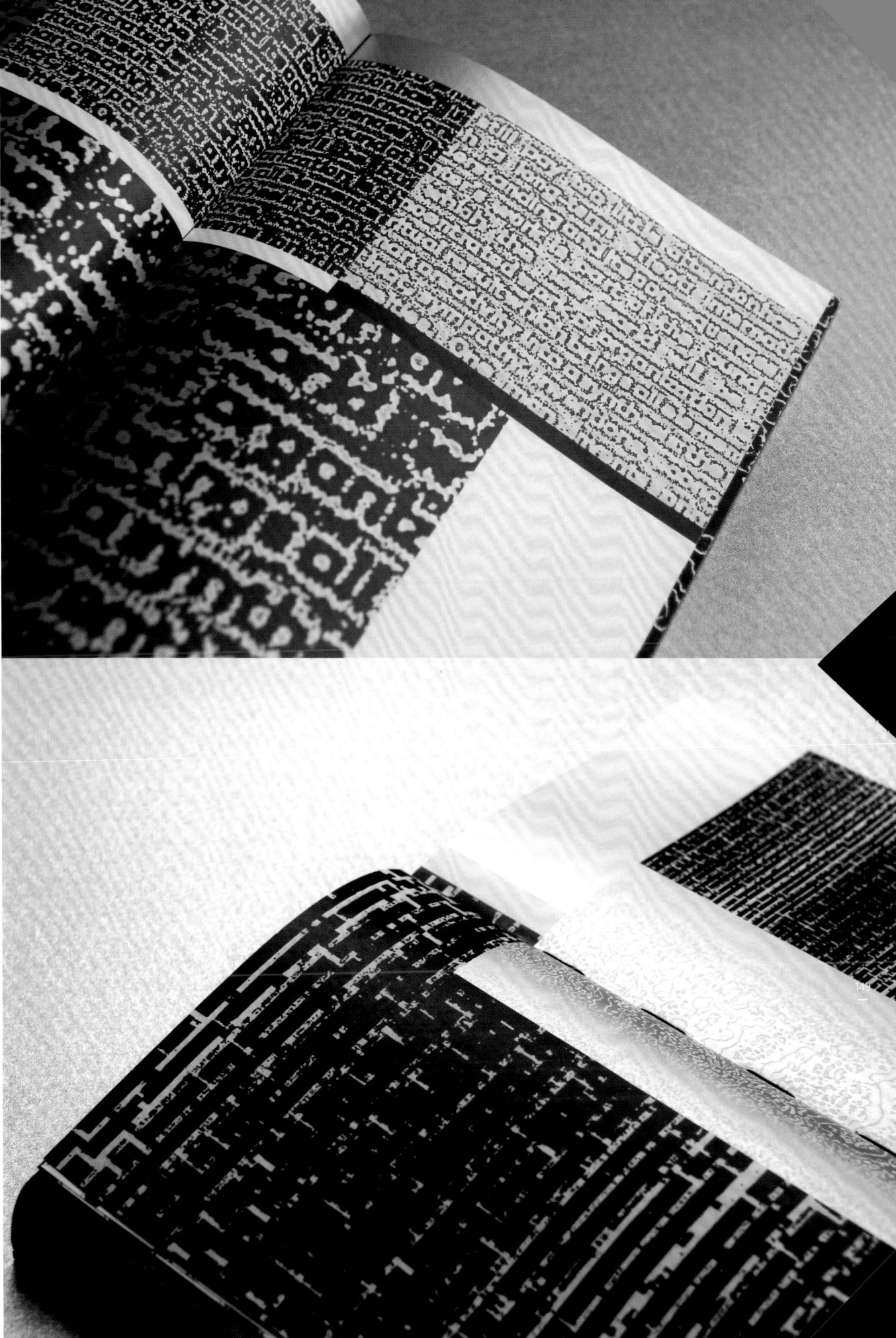

mo_st_ moholy_nagy_
typophoto_studies

Designer: Dora Balla
Country: Hungary

module; moby; text; experiment

module; moby; text; experiment

mo_st_ moho-
ly_nagy_typo-
photo_studies

Designer: Dora Balla
Country: Hungary

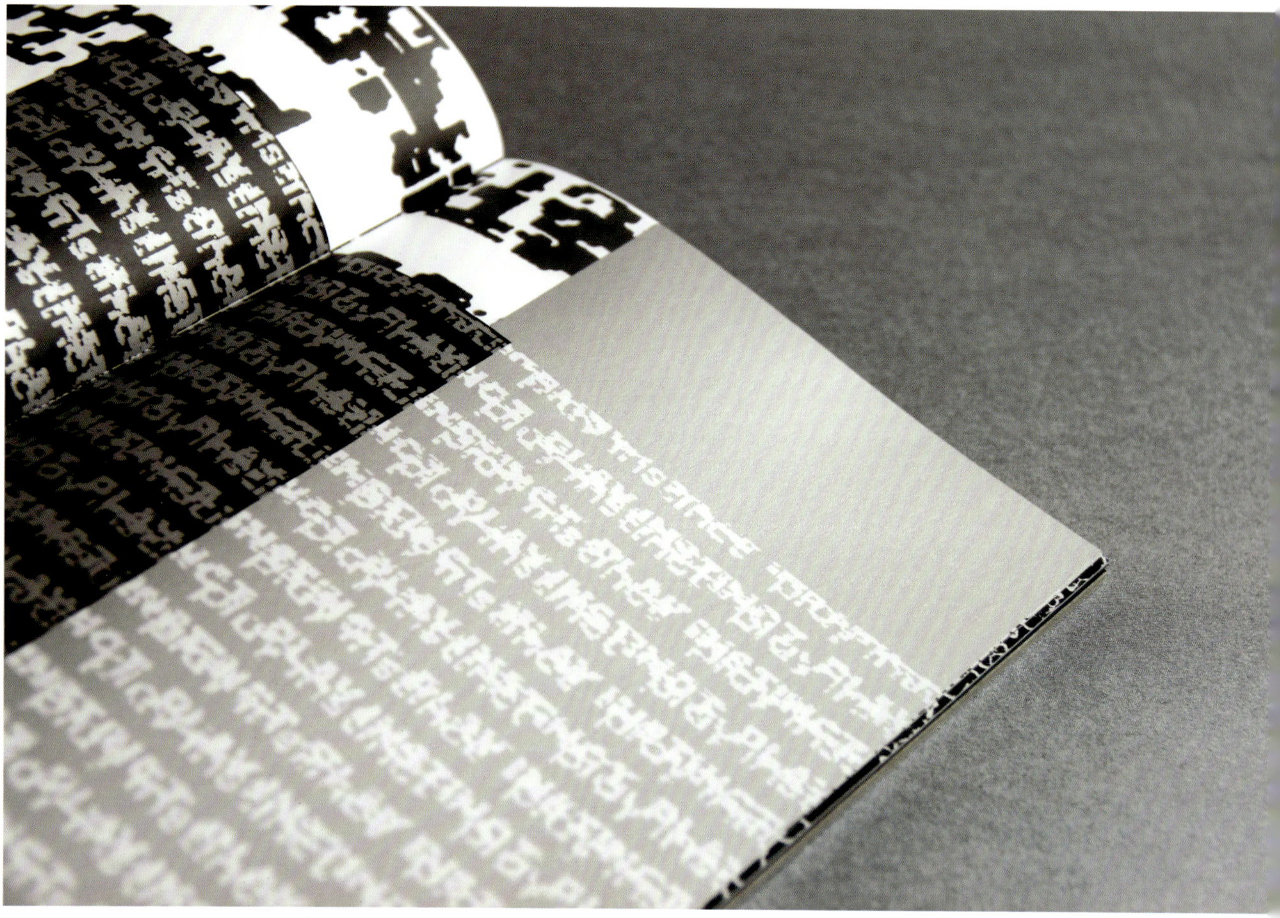

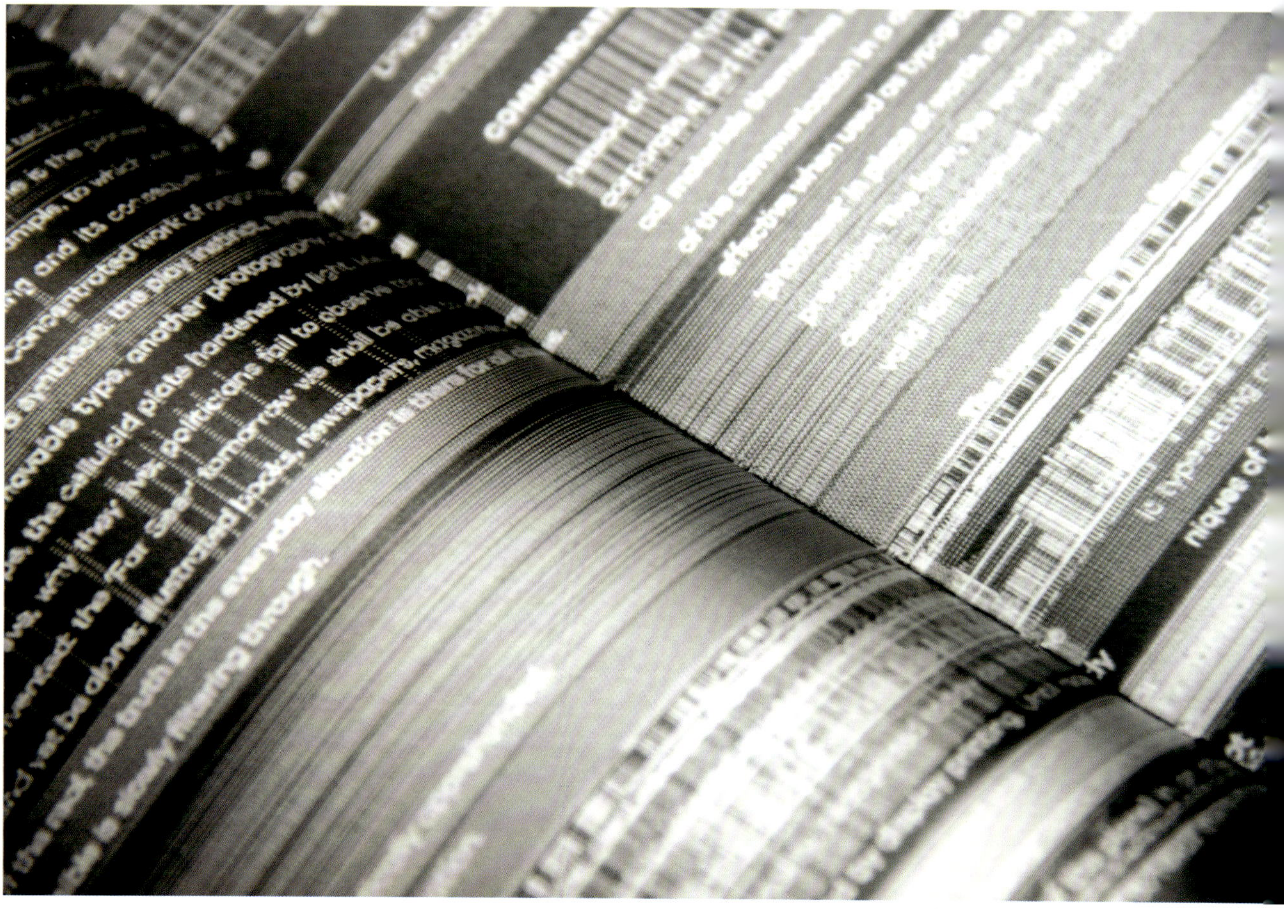

mo_st_ moho-
ly_nagy_typo-
photo_studies

Designer: Dora Balla
Country: Hungary

155

mo_st_ moho-
ly_nagy_typo-
photo_studies

Designer: Dora Balla
Country: Hungary

**mo_st_ moho-
ly_nagy_typo-
photo_studies**

Designer: Dora Balla
Country: Hungary

**mo_st_ moho-
ly_nagy_typo-
photo_studies**

Designer: Dora Balla
Country: Hungary

160

Dora Balla, Doctoral Dissertation Book - Henri Bergson, Creative Evolution

Designer: Dora Balla
Country: Hungary

Client: Moholy-Nagy University of Art and Design

Graphic Design for personal Doctoral Dissertation: Henri Bergson, Creative Evolution, Reinvention Project. The way of thinking from the Perception of the Creation. Experimental Book project.

Dora Balla, Doctoral Dissertation Book - Henri Bergson, Creative Evolution

Designer: Dora Balla
Country: Hungary

Dora Balla, Doctoral Dissertation Book
- Henri Bergson, Creative Evolution

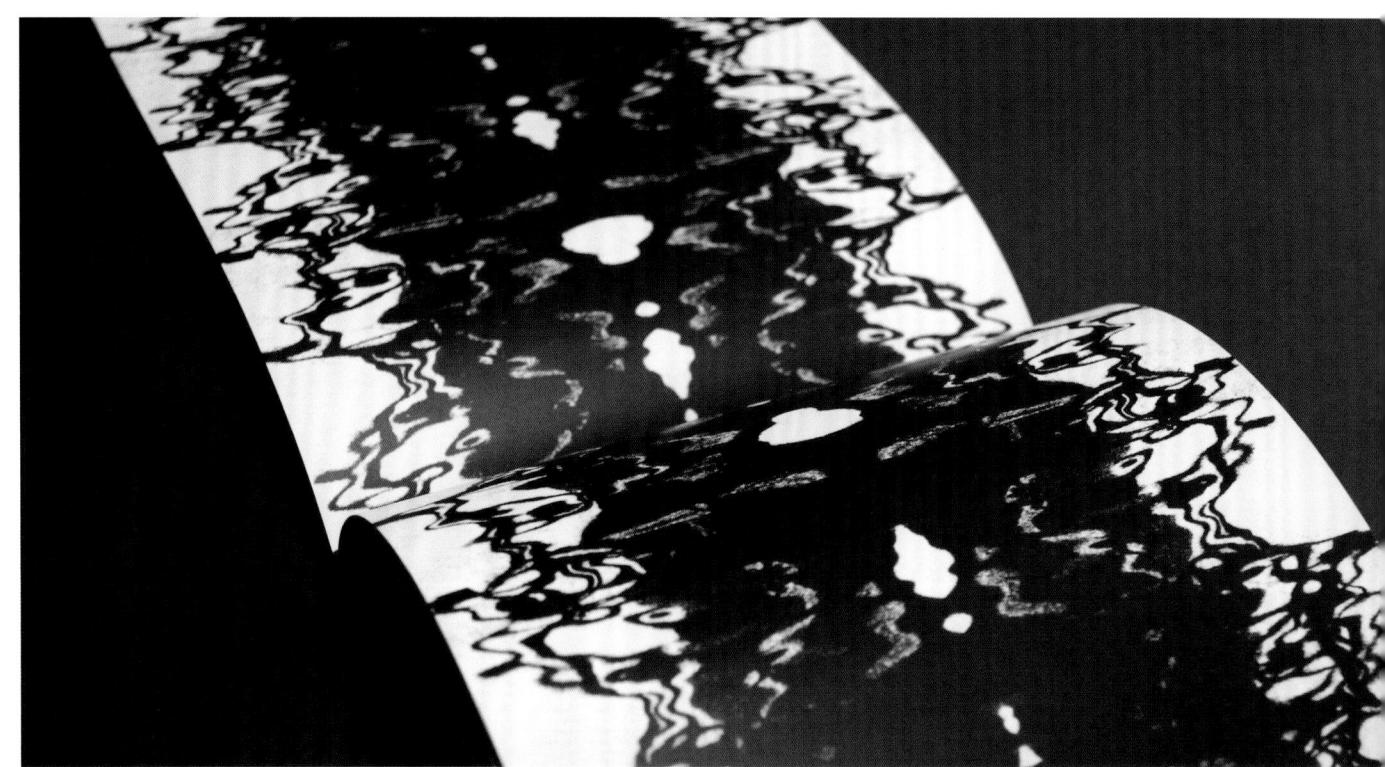

Designer: Dora Balla
Country: Hungary

Dora Balla, Doctoral Dissertation Book
- Henri Bergson, Creative Evolution

Designer: Dora Balla
Country: Hungary

rész elhagyta helyét

Dora Balla, Doctoral Dissertation Book - Henri Bergson, Creative Evolution

Designer: Dora Balla
Country: Hungary

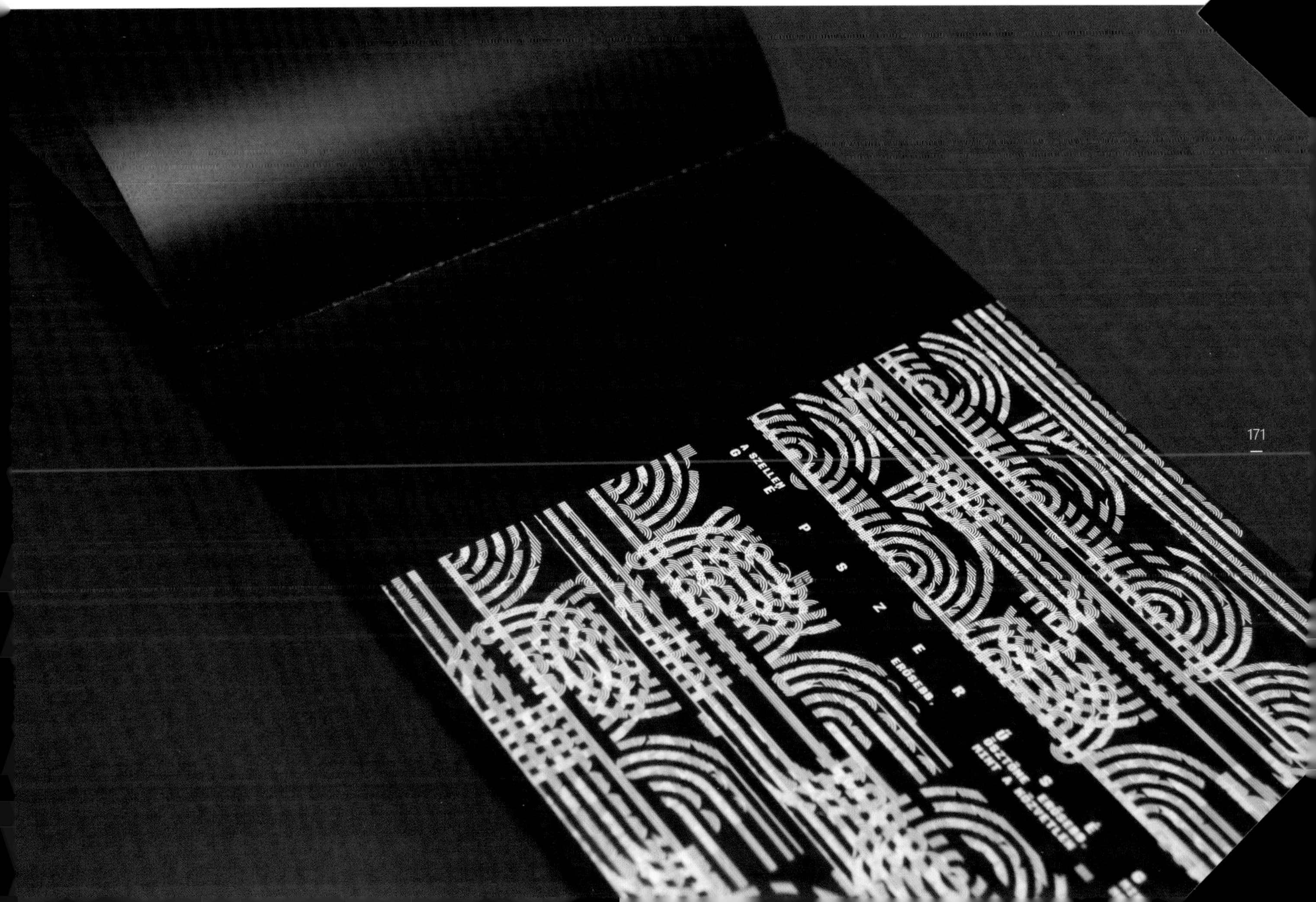

Cantigas de Amor & Maldizer

Designers: Daniel Bilac and Valquíria Rabelo
Design Agency: Estúdio Guayabo
Country: Brazil
Photographer: Daniel Bilac

Client: Jovino Machado
Woodcut [cover]: Rachel Leão; Printing: Alessandro Lima

Cantigas de Amor & Maldizer (or Songs of Love & Cursing) is a book by Jovino Machado – a Brazilian poet who has been publishing his work since the 1980's. The texts are about the excitement of love and the injuries of breaking up. In-tending to be a collector's edition, there were printed only fifty copies, each one signed and numbered by the author.

With just 4 x 5 inches, the book is delivered for the reader sealed. In the cover, there is a red woodcut of the artist Rachel Leão, reprinted by the engraver Alessandro Lima especially for this edition. However, in the inside, the reader can find a title page in emerald green apart some delicate botanic drawings and scientific illustrations of beetles. The contrasting pallet and the different kinds of images follow the main concept of the project: the duality, present both in the title and in the poems.

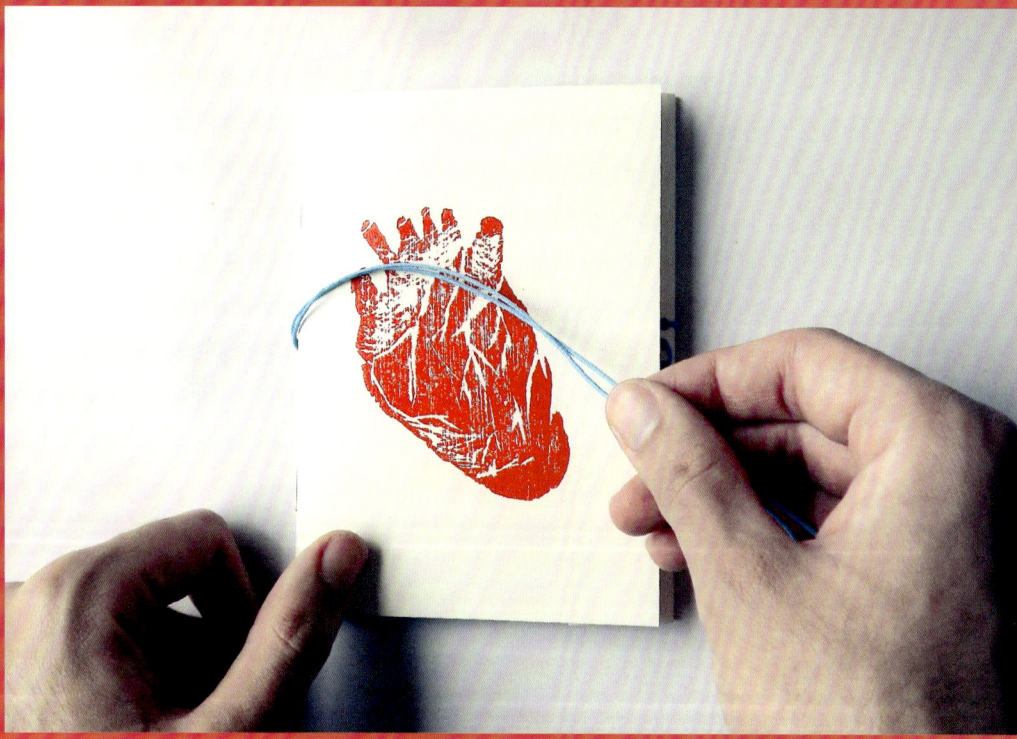

/50
CANTIGAS DE AMOR & MALDIZER
JOVINO MACHADO

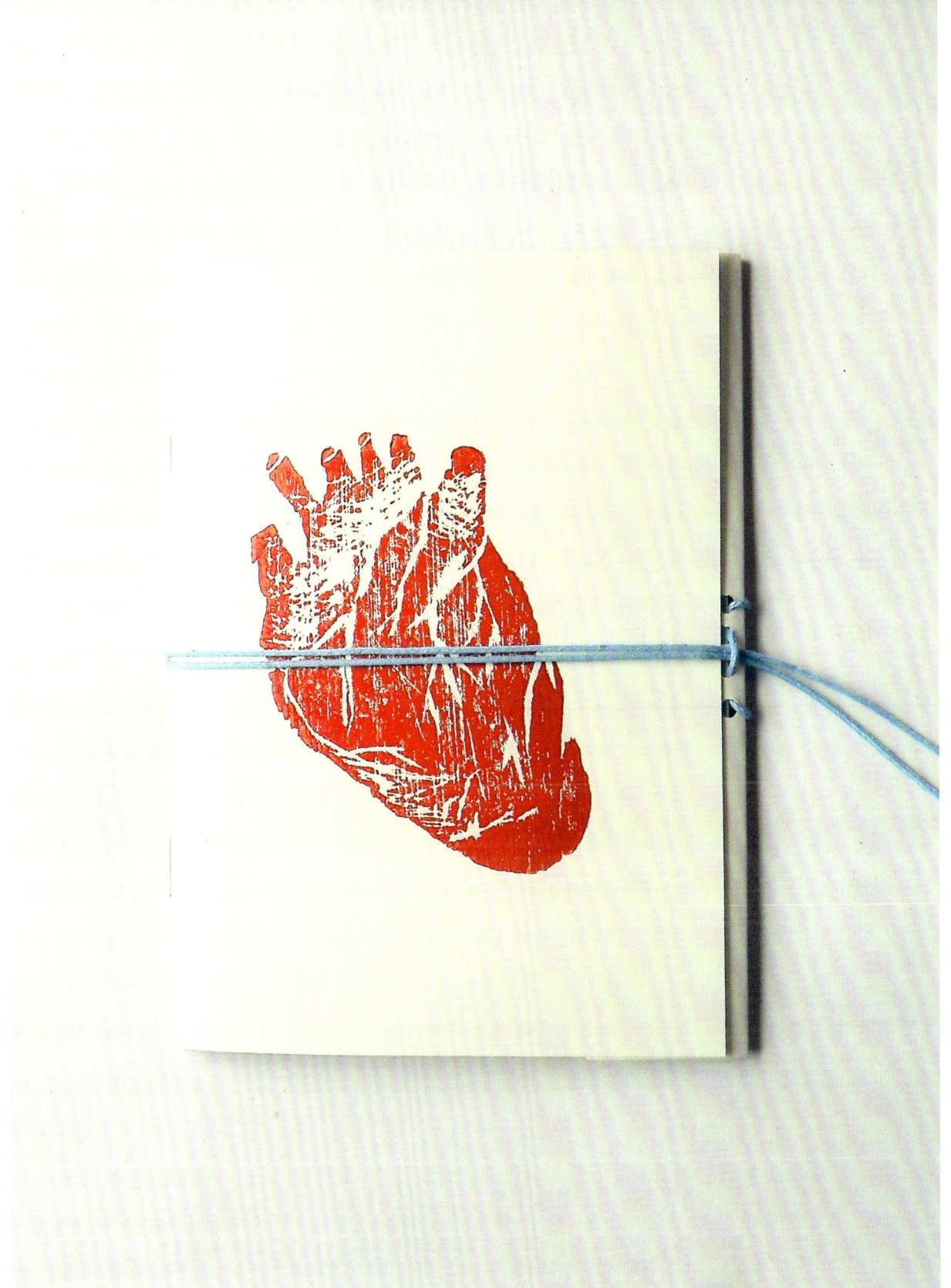

Cantigas de Amor & Maldizer

Designer: Daniel Bilac e Valquíria Rabelo
Design Agency: Estúdio Guayabo
Country: Brazil
Photographer: Daniel Bilac

CANTIGAS DE AMOR & MALDIZER

>> a sobrecapa desta plaquette traz uma xilogravura de **Rachel Leão** reimpressa por **Alessandro Lima** // grave produtos para gravura// especialmente para esta edição. foram utilizadas as tipografias veneer e leitura sans. o projeto gráfico é assinado por **Daniel Bilac** e **Valquíria Rabelo** //excelente projetos// . a tiragem de 50 exemplares foi lançada na primavera de 2013, aos cinquenta anos do poeta **Jovino Machado**, natural de Formiga, signo de Leão.

176

Cantigas de Amor & Maldizer

Designer: Daniel Bilac e Valquíria Rabelo
Design Agency: Estúdio Guayabo
Country: Brazil
Photographer: Daniel Bilac

Unpacking my library

Designer: Valquíria Rabelo
Design Agency: Estúdio Guayabo
Country: Brazil

Client: Estúdio Guayabo (experimental project)

Most of the academic texts are published in large editions, that gather essays, thesis and articles in very funtional volumes: books to be read, in an strict sense. For so, I wanted to develop an experimental project, where I could use attractive and unusual graphic resources, capable of creating a sensorial reading experience. Having this in my mind, I've selected a Walter Benjamin's small essay, named "Unpacking my library" (usually found in the book One-Way Street, published in 1900). In this text, Benjamin describes the book collectionism in a very personal manner. The caos of the memory, the boring order of the shelves, the fascination for the rare or the ancient – the author describes all this while unpacking his books in a dusty room.

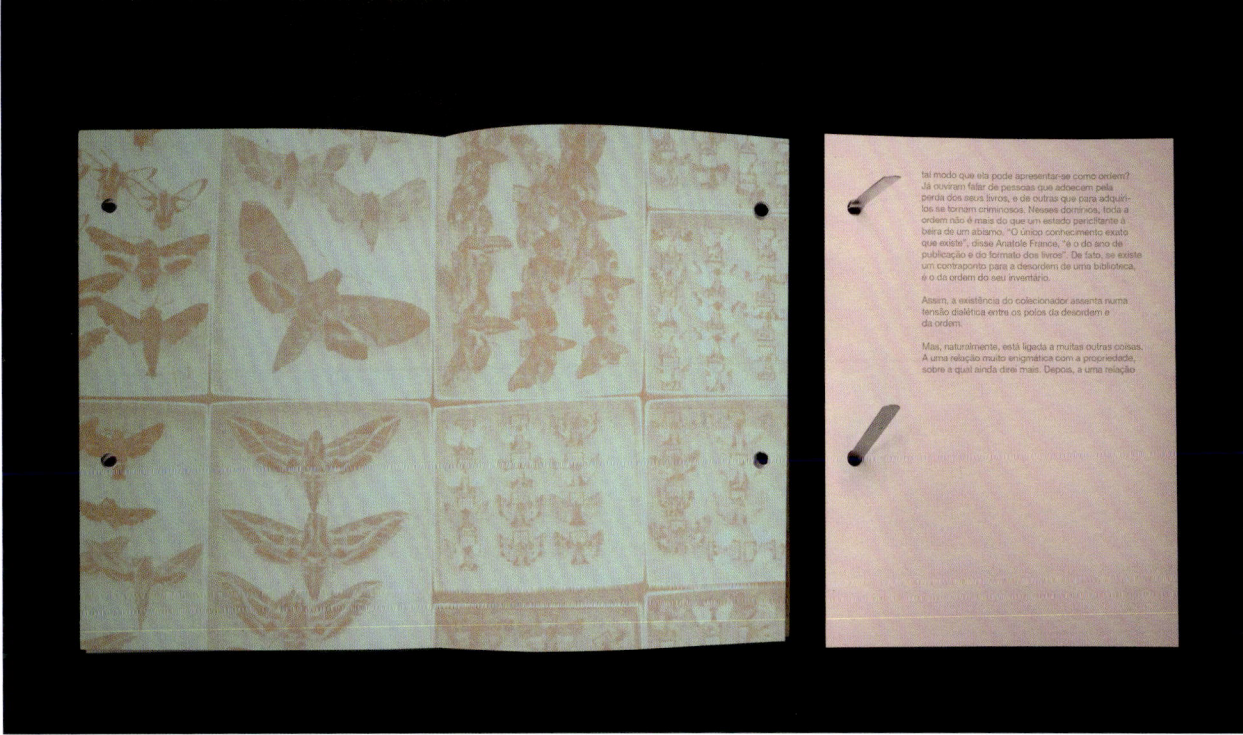

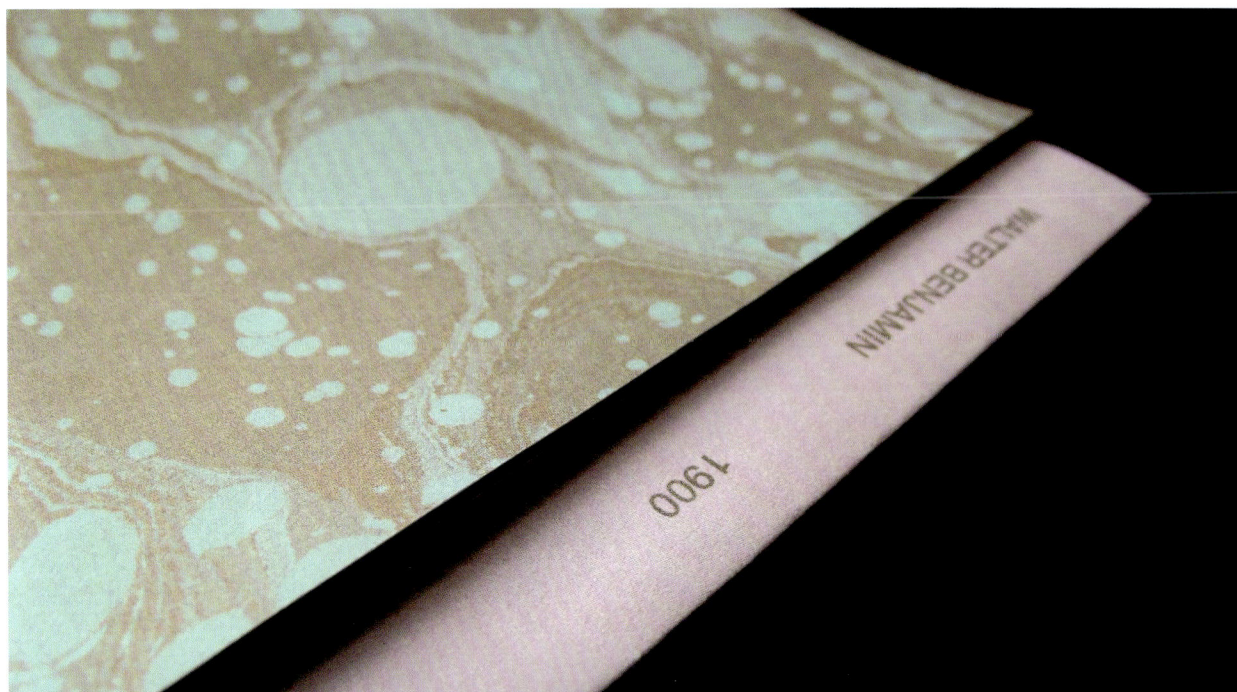

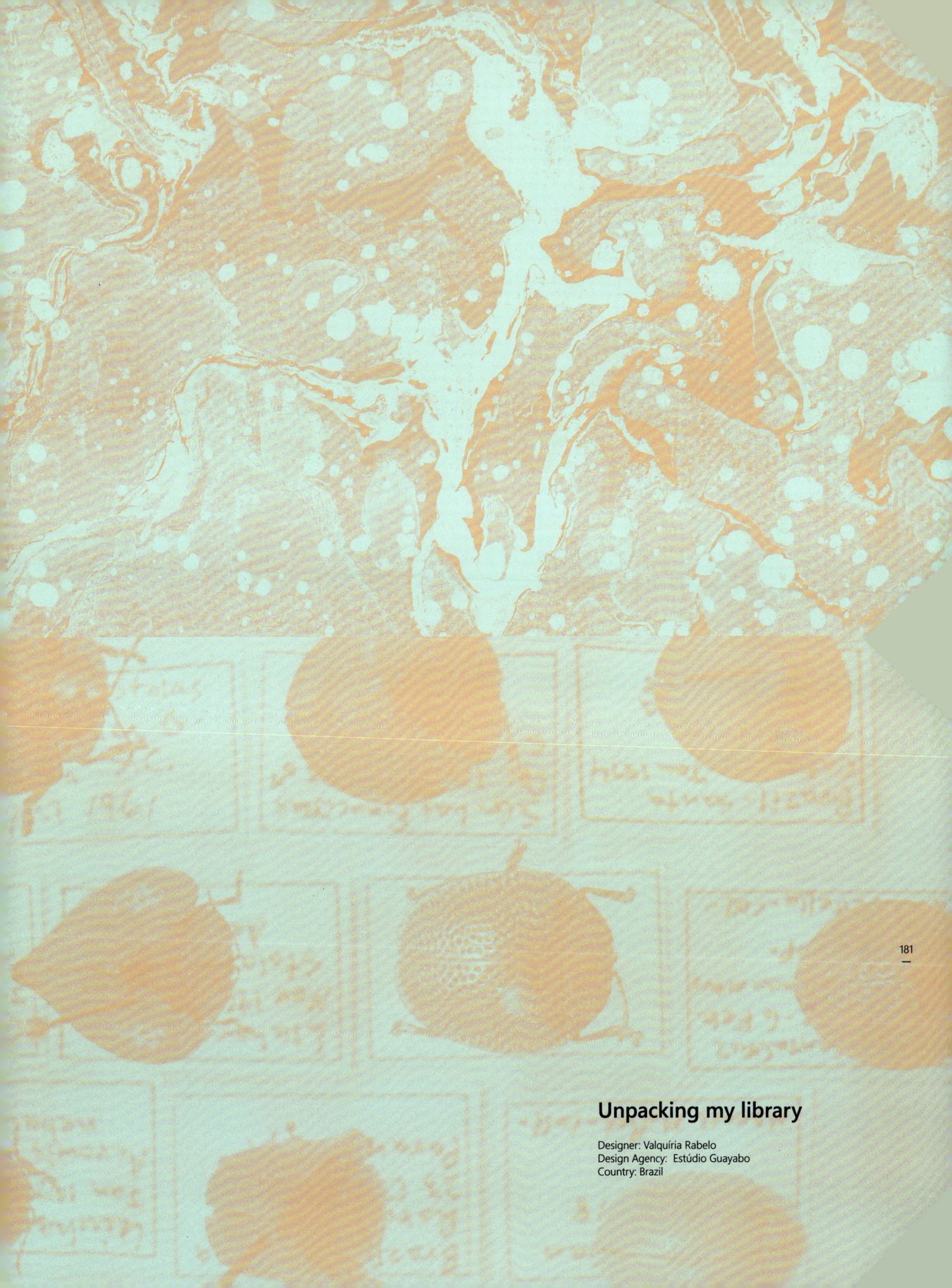

Unpacking my library

Designer: Valquíria Rabelo
Design Agency: Estúdio Guayabo
Country: Brazil

Tea-Hee

Designer: Jiani Lu
Country: Canada

Tea-Hee is a playful and lighthearted self-written, hand bound book designed as a personal, informal reference guide for tea lovers and enthusiasts alike. It introduces readers into the world of tea and its craft through three chapters that paint a picture on the culture and craft of tea making. It sets a friendly and approachable tone through inviting colors and organic lines; yet does not compromise the technical and instructional side of tea-making by involving a mechanical and systematic visual approach with hard-edged illustrations, and vector based infographics.

A remedy for sluggish mornings, a boost of energy for staying awake, a pick-me-up to power you through the day, black tea is among teas with its rich flavour, that it remains years on being produced in the West, the East, black tea has always been called the leaves. Whereas in the maroon colour of the infused drink. Like many which refers to produced from the leaves of the Camellia sinensis plant. What sepa-rates this tea from others is in the production process which involves a maximised oxidisation process that truly bring out the immersive flavours of the tea.

// CHAPTER ONE   TEA TYPES

01

" There is no trouble so great or grave that cannot be much diminished by a nice cup of tea. "

- Bernard-Paul Heroux

With thousands of variations, a spectrum of colours and a boundless palate of any day, there are perfect for any moment of any day. There should be no matter what mood you're in, whether you're in the mood for dark and rich flavours or fruity and light scents.

Tea-Hee

Designer: Jiani Lu
Country: Canada

MOMENTAUFNAHME

Designer: Kevin Kremer, Natalie Kennepohl, Laura Oster-
meier, Miriam Rieger
Design Agency: MEDIADESIGN Hochschule Munich
Country: Germany
Photographer: Kevin Kremer, Miriam Rieger

Client: Student Project
Series: 200 x 135 x 120 mmSingle Book: 120 x 185 mm
Theinhardt Grotesk: François RappoAdobe Garamond
Pro: based on Claude Garamond's workStempel Gara-
mond: based on Claude Garamond's work

This project aims to reflect the electric time before the
outbreak of World War I in 1914. It consists of eight in-
dividual books, each committed to a different topic of
that time ("Women's rights", "Decline of the male role
model", "The thrill of speed", "Virginia Woolf", "Sig-
mund Freud", etc.). Every book has a different graphic
appeal and includes artful features, such as different
materials, formats, hand lettering, etc. The project represents an outline of a fascinating, unfortunately often
overshadowed time.

Rituale, Mythen, Masken

erlebte der Krieg zwischen den Alten und den Modernen einen seiner Höhepunkte in Paris, anlässlich der Uraufführung eines Balletts des jungen russischen Komponisten Igor Strawinsky (1882 – 1971), der sich bereits mit zwei Ballettes, der Feuervogel (1910) und Patruschka (1911), einen Namen gemacht hatte.

human character changed.

MOMENTAUFNAHME

Designer: Kevin Kremer, Natalie Kennepohl, Laura Ostermeier, Miriam Rieger
Design Agency: MEDIADESIGN Hochschule Munich
Country: Germany
Photographer: Kevin Kremer, Miriam Rieger

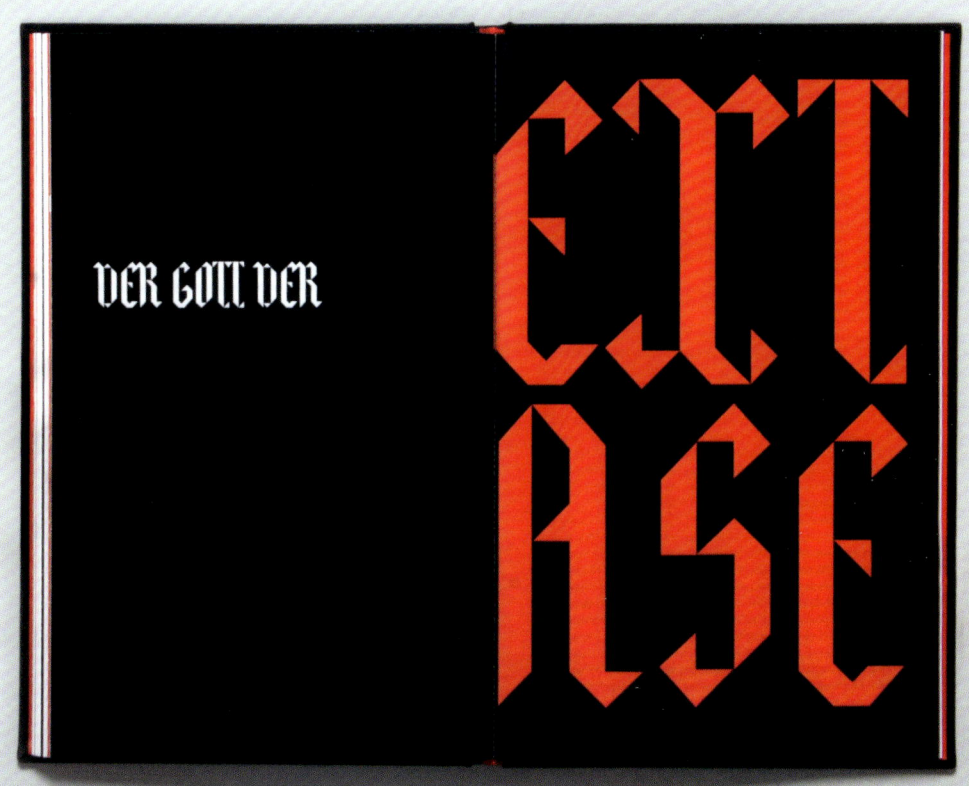

MOMENTAUFNAHME

Designer: Kevin Kremer, Natalie Kennepohl, Laura Oster
meier, Miriam Rieger
Design Agency: MEDIADESIGN Hochschule Munich
Country: Germany
Photographer: Kevin Kremer, Miriam Rieger

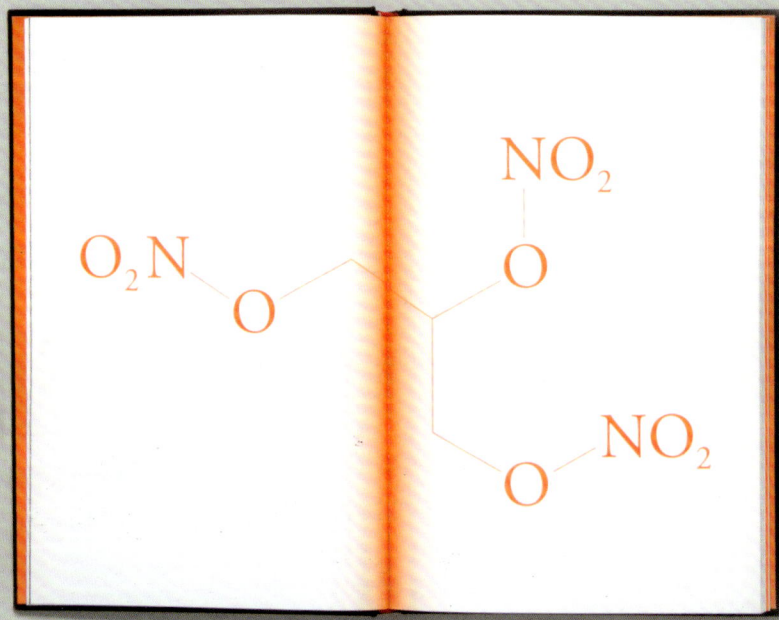

MOMENTAUFNAHME

Designer: Kevin Kremer, Natalie Kennepohl, Laura Ostermeier, Miriam Rieger
Design Agency: MEDIADESIGN Hochschule Munich
Country: Germany
Photographer: Kevin Kremer, Miriam Rieger

3. Der Geschäftsmann

ROPAS   EUROPAS

REICHSTER

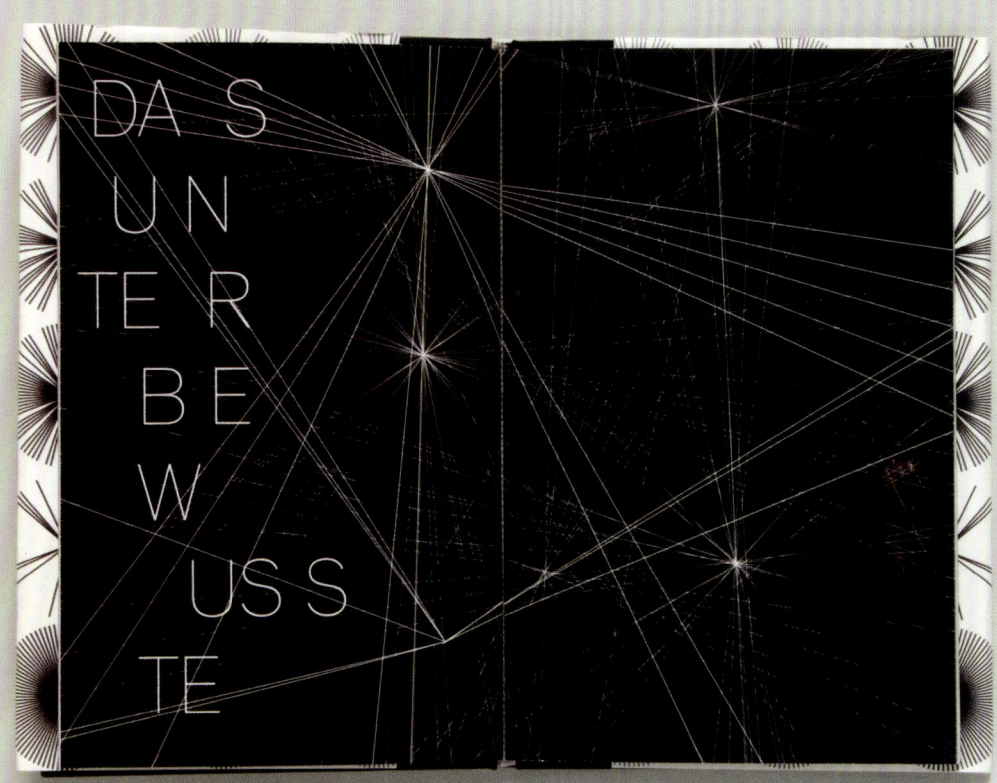

MOMENTAUFNAHME

Designer: Kevin Kremer, Natalie Kennepohl, Laura Oster-
meier, Miriam Rieger
Design Agency: MEDIADESIGN Hochschule Munich
Country: Germany
Photographer: Kevin Kremer, Miriam Rieger

›Die Frauen in meinem Geburtsort waschen jeden Montag, bügeln jeden Dienstag, gehen am Mittwoch aus, backen am Donnerstag, machen freitags sauber, gehen am Samstag auf den Mark und am Sonntag in die Kirche. Es gibt natürlich Ausnahmen, Hunderte von Ausnahmen, aber sie werden als exzentrisch und unweiblich angesehen.‹

0mm Photographic Hours

Designer: Kristine H. Kawakubo
Design Agency: KLUB
Country: Netherlands
Photographer: Kristine H. Kawakubo

Client: KLUB

The second issue of FN was locating into photography. It has been structured into four sections in selected prominent photographers. Each of selected artist has represent the individualize life attitude of a city and the relationship between their aesthetic impressions and city connection. Silence the moment of a city, a life style, documenting or documented by exposure moment. Through the second issue of FN, we would like to provide a transparent space, without distance of observation for the readers into the 'Hours'.

0mm Photographic Hours

Designer: Kristine H. Kawakubo
Design Agency: KLUB
Country: Netherlands
Photographer: Kristine H. Kawakubo

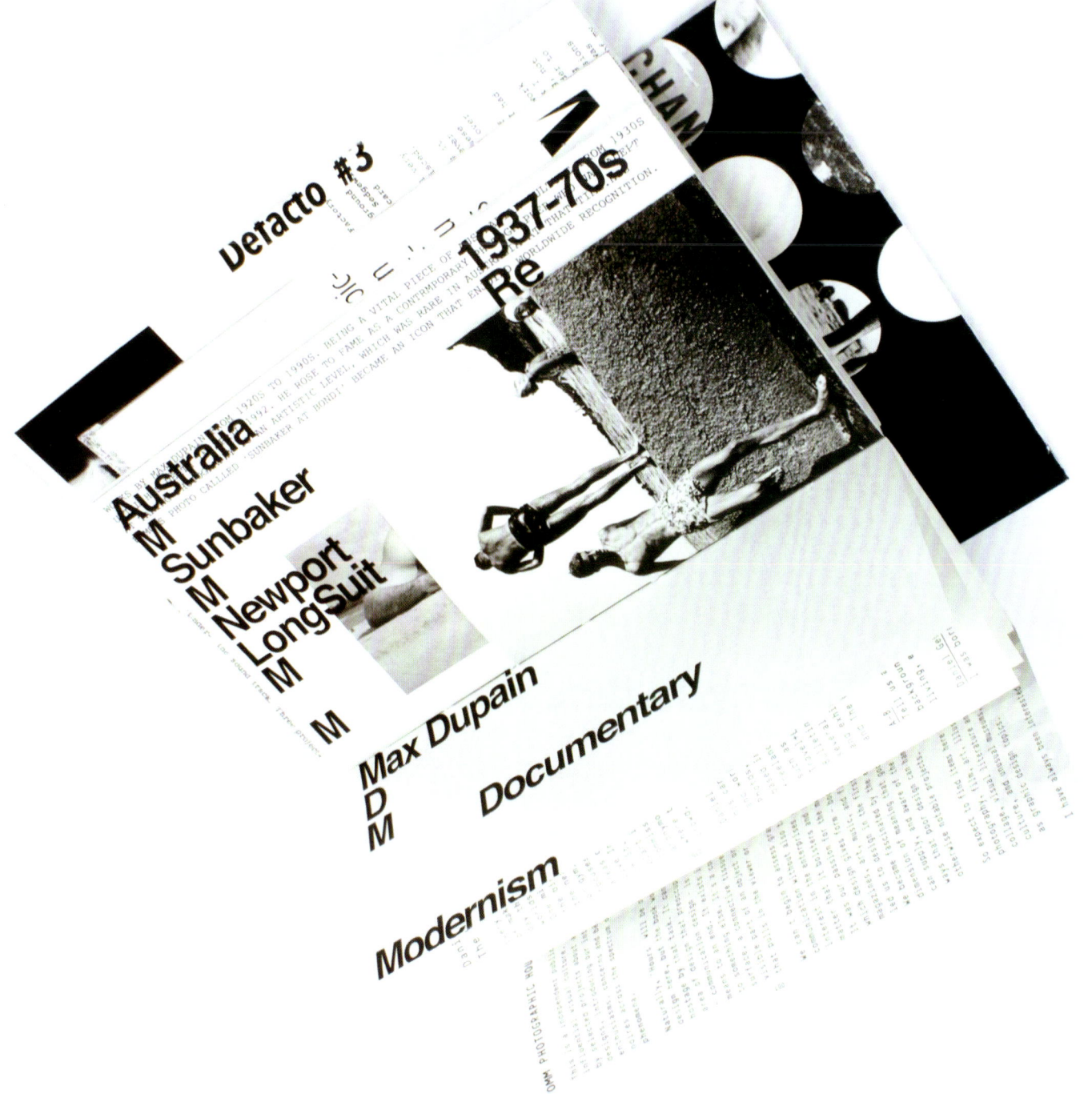

0mm Photographic Hours

Designer: Kristine H. Kawakubo
Design Agency: KLUB
Country: Netherlands
Photographer: Kristine H. Kawakubo

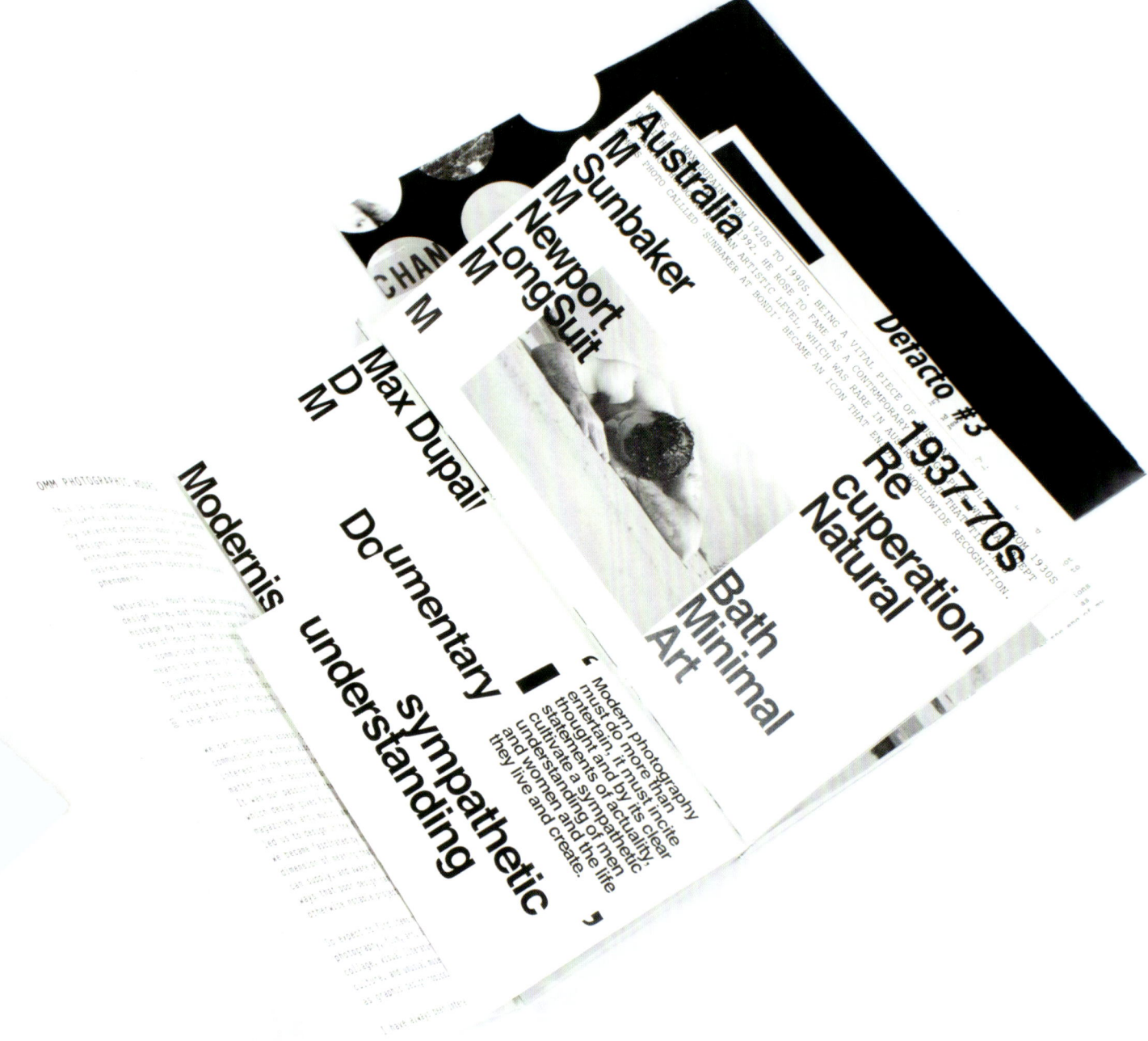

0mm Photographic Hours

Designer: Kristine H. Kawakubo
Design Agency: KLUB
Country: Netherlands
Photographer: Kristine H. Kawakubo

There's a television documentary about you called
*Vracim se do Zeme Labyrintu, or I'm Returning to
a Country of Labyrinth.* Was that how it felt for you,
returning to Prague after so many years, basically
half your life, in America?

I must say it was. You are very right, because when
I came here first I was lost looking for faces, which
I will recognise, but didn't recognise anybody. My first
days here were really for me very melancholy. I knew my few
old friends, but apart from those, most I had passed everyday in that sense, because I
was looking for faces, and had lost my memory
of streets, of people. And to start to get
to know the streets takes a little time. But now by age which
is friends of a half my age a quarter. My age which is
it's a nice because it keeps me young.

You don't want to see the bare reality of what happened. I took the
picture as the picture, not as the realistic story of what happened.

Detacto #3

First Next

Designer: Kristine H. Kawakubo
Design Agency: KLUB
Country: Netherlands
Photographer: Kristine H. Kawakubo

Client: Astudio

'FN' (First and Next) was inspired by the prominent historical manifesto 'First Things First 1964'. The concept of 'FN' is based on build debatable contemporary visual issues which relative into art, design, film, music, and public social issues and providing a groundbreaking version to the readers. As the first issue of FN, there was structured by the detailed introduction of the impacts of capitalism into creative industry and public in general.

critically
consumerism consumers
and materialism on fashion industry is

How to use visual imagery is

A Green Silence series
in Adbusters as
photography by
artist

First Next

Designer: Kristine H. Kawakubo
Design Agency: KLUB
Country: Netherlands
Photographer: Kristine H. Kawakubo

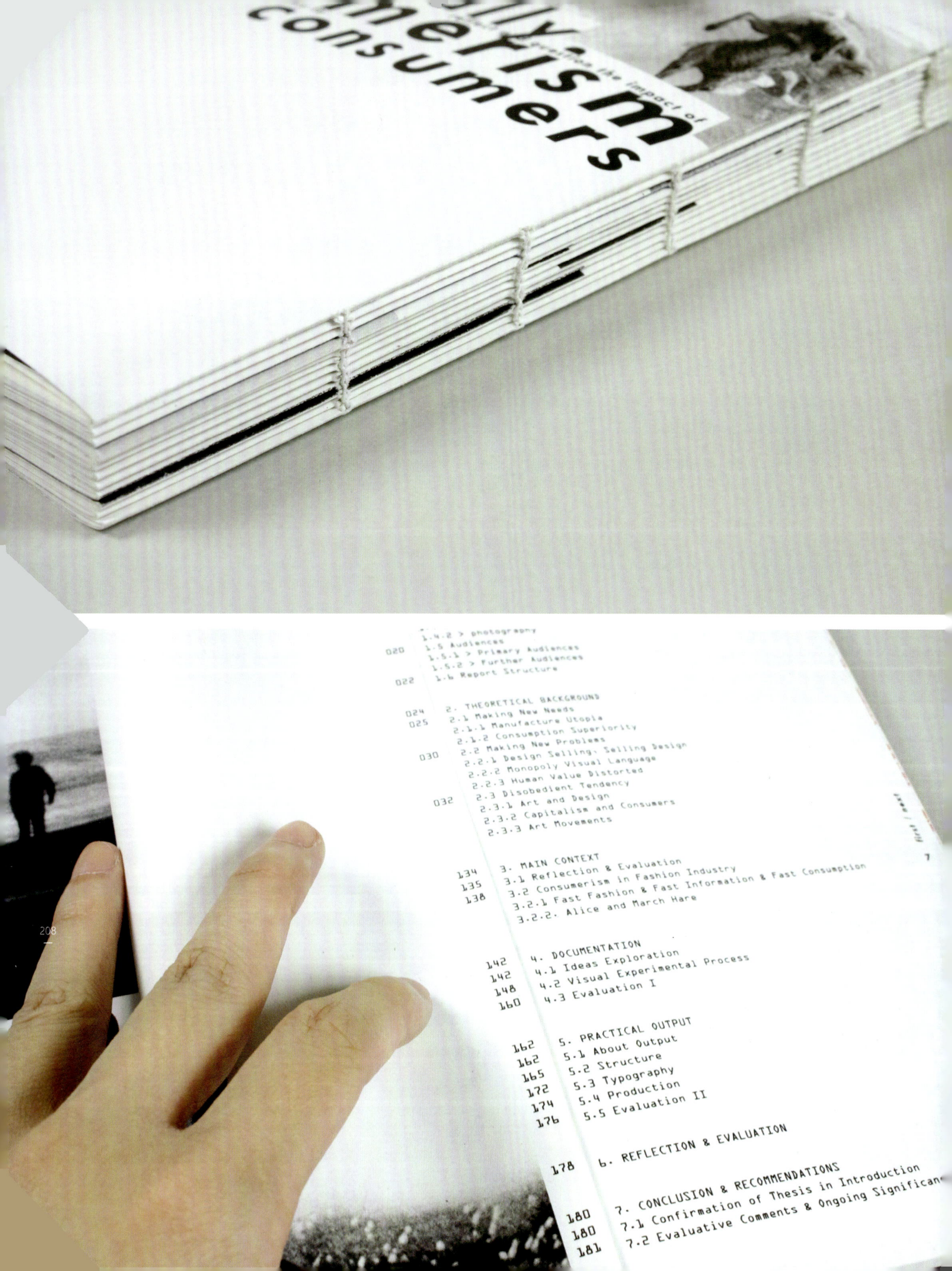

First Next

Designer: Kristine H. Kawakubo
Design Agency: KLUB
Country: Netherlands
Photographer: Kristine H. Kawakubo

The idea behind this series of photography (with model) was tried to revealing the fact that people have been dominated by mass culture (material / cloths) and lose the ability to think independently. However, more and more consumers have self-awareness and tried to resist this situation (ripping the material / cloths). It was conceptually present a more subjective viewpoint of the sequence of the definition of conceptual consumerism and the reality consumerism.

152

153

First Next

Designer: Kristine H. Kawakubo
Design Agency: KLUB
Country: Netherlands
Photographer: Kristine H. Kawakubo

TIFFANY & CO.

CUSTOMER COPY

TIFFANY & CO.

134

135

211

3 Main Context
3.4 Reflection & Evaluation

Capitaaliam culture organizes people as buyers of commodities and services. It is an economic and technico-scientific development that has also transformed the information and knowledge into commodities.
Jan van Toorn, 1998, p.154

In the previous unit 2, I had explored collage art and print methods. I was mainly base on using collage are to critic consumerism. In the experimental period, I did the collage into magazine, which was consisted with the images without models and I was using those collected material to be assemble into collage and implied into traditional print method - screen print, simultaneously. In the output of unit 2, I choose to present the magazine as my output rather than the screen print collage I. However, there are visually difficult to convey this idea of critic consumerism to the audience from this collage magazine. Because of, there was lack of a clear image and focus concept of each image. Therefore, the audience would difficult to follow what it meaning behind.

Printed FTN

Designer: Kristine H. Kawakubo
Design Agency: KLUB
Country: Netherlands
Photographer: Kristine H. Kawakubo

Client: KLUB

It was an experimental project about exploring the process of reproduction FTN (previous MA project: First Thing Next) by low-tech printing (risograph). It's interesting to observed the interaction between inks (colour management: hues, tones,...) and images (typography, complexity,...).

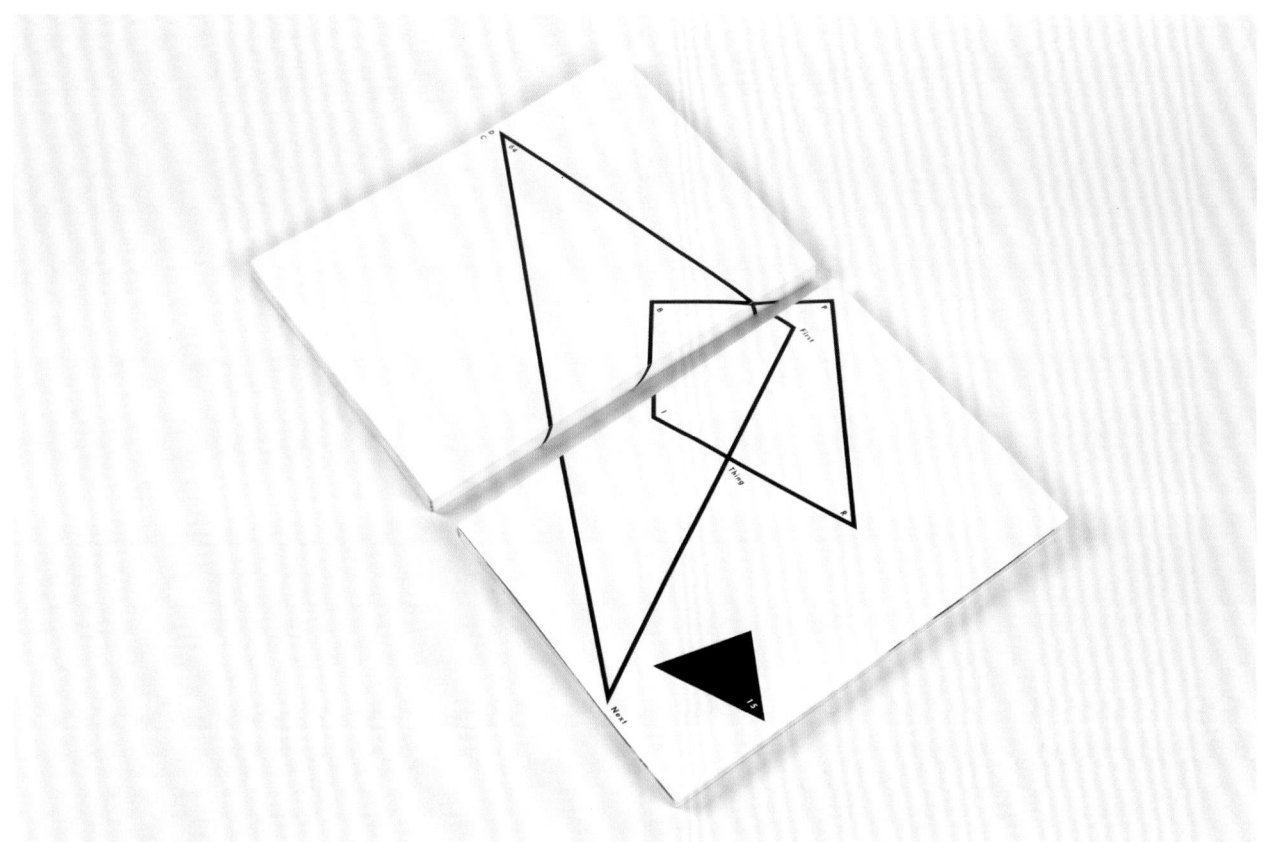

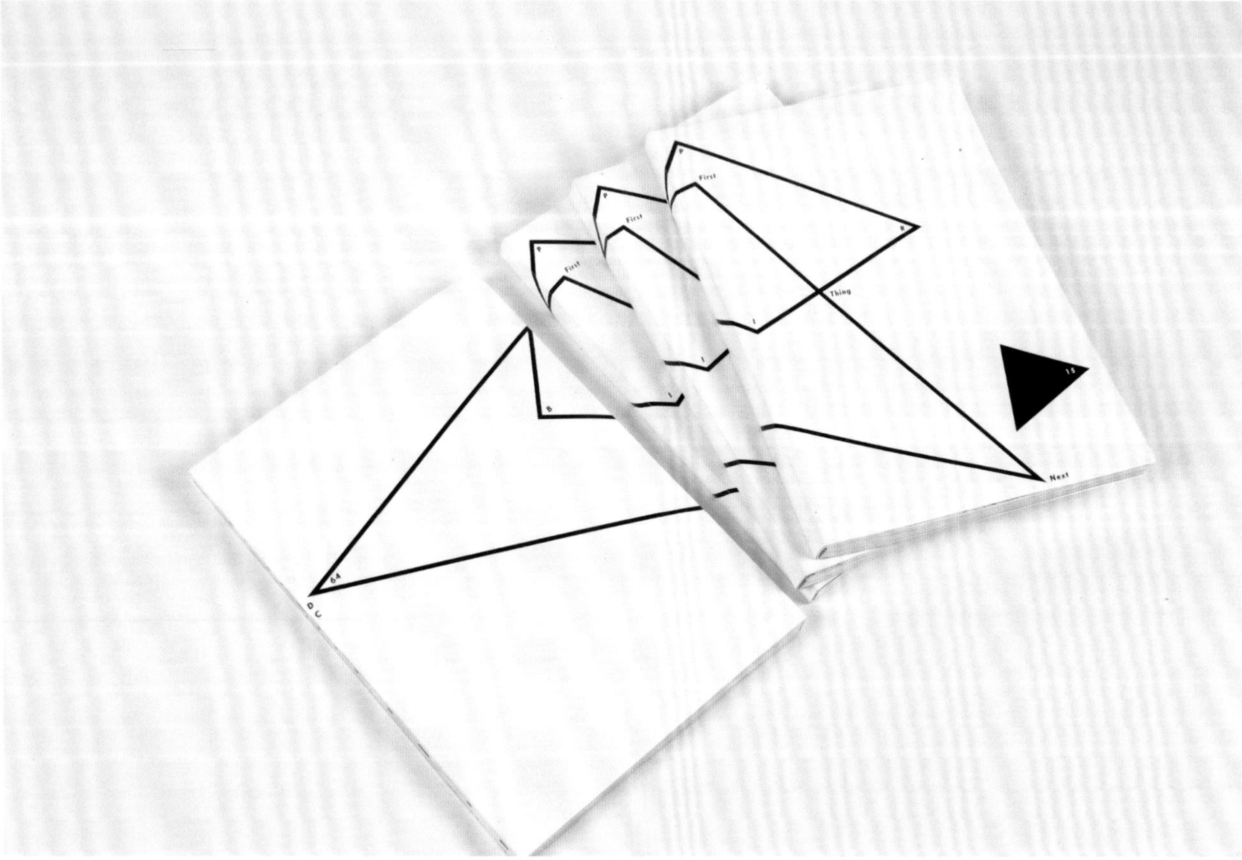

Printed FTN

Designer: Kristine H. Kawakubo
Design Agency: KLUB
Country: Netherlands
Photographer: Kristine H. Kawakubo

A Cheng

Designer: Xiao Ren / Zifei Li
Design Agency: One Thousand Times
Country: China

Client: Jiangsu Phoenix Literature and Art
Publishing / HTreading

The new edition of *Collected Works of A Cheng* is published by HTreading and Jiangsu Literature and Art Publishing House, including works of Three Kings (The Chess Master · The King of Children · The King of Trees) and other six works. Yang Kui is invited as the reviser. One Thousand Times is responsible for the visual design of the new edition of *Collected Works of A Cheng*.

In the perspective of font, Jin Nong's calligraphy is deemed to be able to accurately reflect A Cheng's literature works. Basing on the modern printing Song typeface and taking the structure of Jin Nong's calligraphy for reference, One Thousand Times designs a set of printing archaize font and applies the font on the cover of this set of books as the main visual element.

One Thousand Times adjusts the middle space and redraw the special strokes. Compare with the regular Song typeface, the archaize font has a higher barycentre and a looser middle space. Therefore, the designers conclude the features of the two fonts and highlight the peculiarities of Jin Nong's calligraphy in the design without changing the basic principles of regular Song typeface.

The regular Song typeface has a balanced right-and-left structure. The new typeface has a sloping structure with the left side lower than the right side. Meanwhile, in order to emphasize the style of handwriting strokes and woodcarving, the designers add a small hook and raising stroke to the regular vertical stroke, making the archaize font alike to Jin Nong's calligraphy.

When designing the whole collection, designers use the archaize Jin Nong Font to create the sense of consistency and highlight the blank in the sketch paintings. This effortless design coincide with A Cheng's literature style.

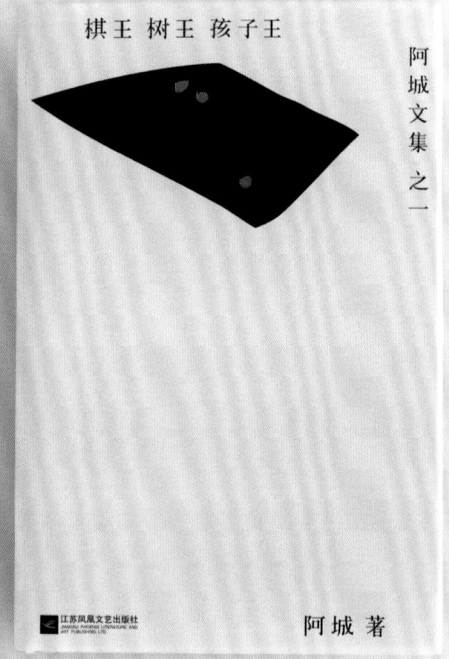

棋王 树王 孩子王

阿城文集 之一

阿城 著

江苏凤凰文艺出版社

文化不是味精

阿城文集 之六

阿城 著

江苏凤凰文艺出版社

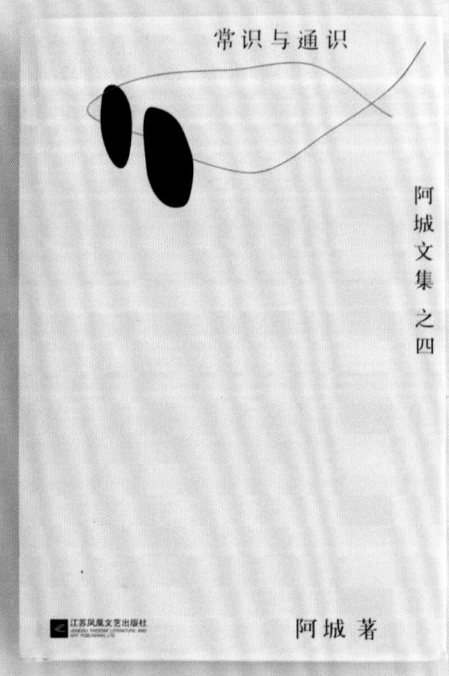

常识与通识

阿城文集 之四

阿城 著

江苏凤凰文艺出版社

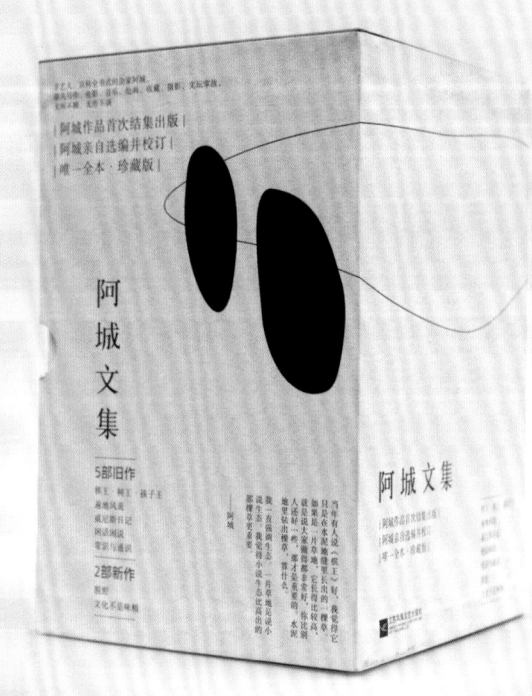

A Cheng

Designer: Xiao Ren / Zifei Li
Design Agency: One Thousand Times
Country: China

Da Hui Yuan Xing

Designer: Sha Zhu
Design Agency: One Thousand Times
Country: China

Client: Guangxi Normal University Press

Da Hui Yuan Xing is a collection of essays by artist Zhu Xinjian that composes of more than 60 essays and 160 entries of quotations and excerpts. This book is collected, edited and designed by One Thousand Times and is published by Guangxi Normal University Press Imaginist.

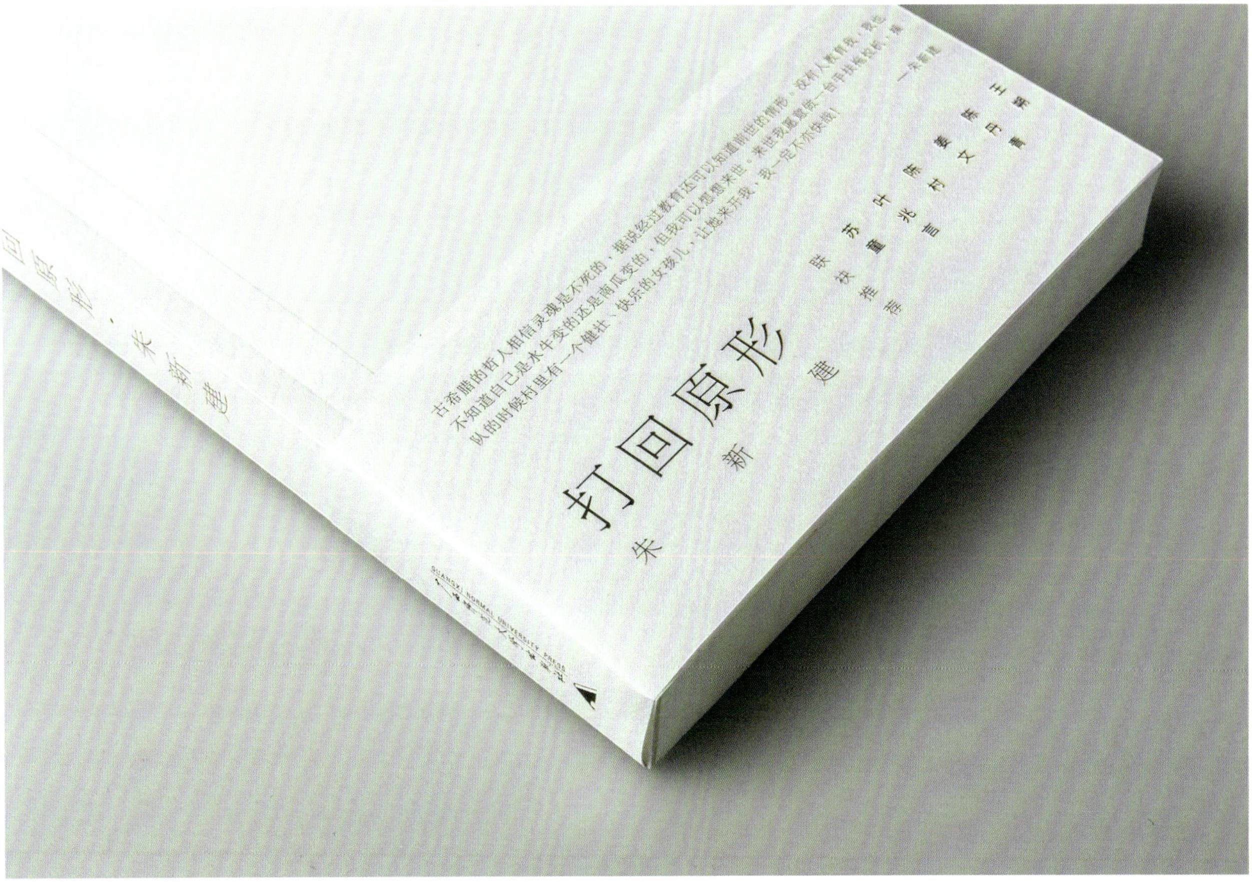
打回原形
朱 新 建

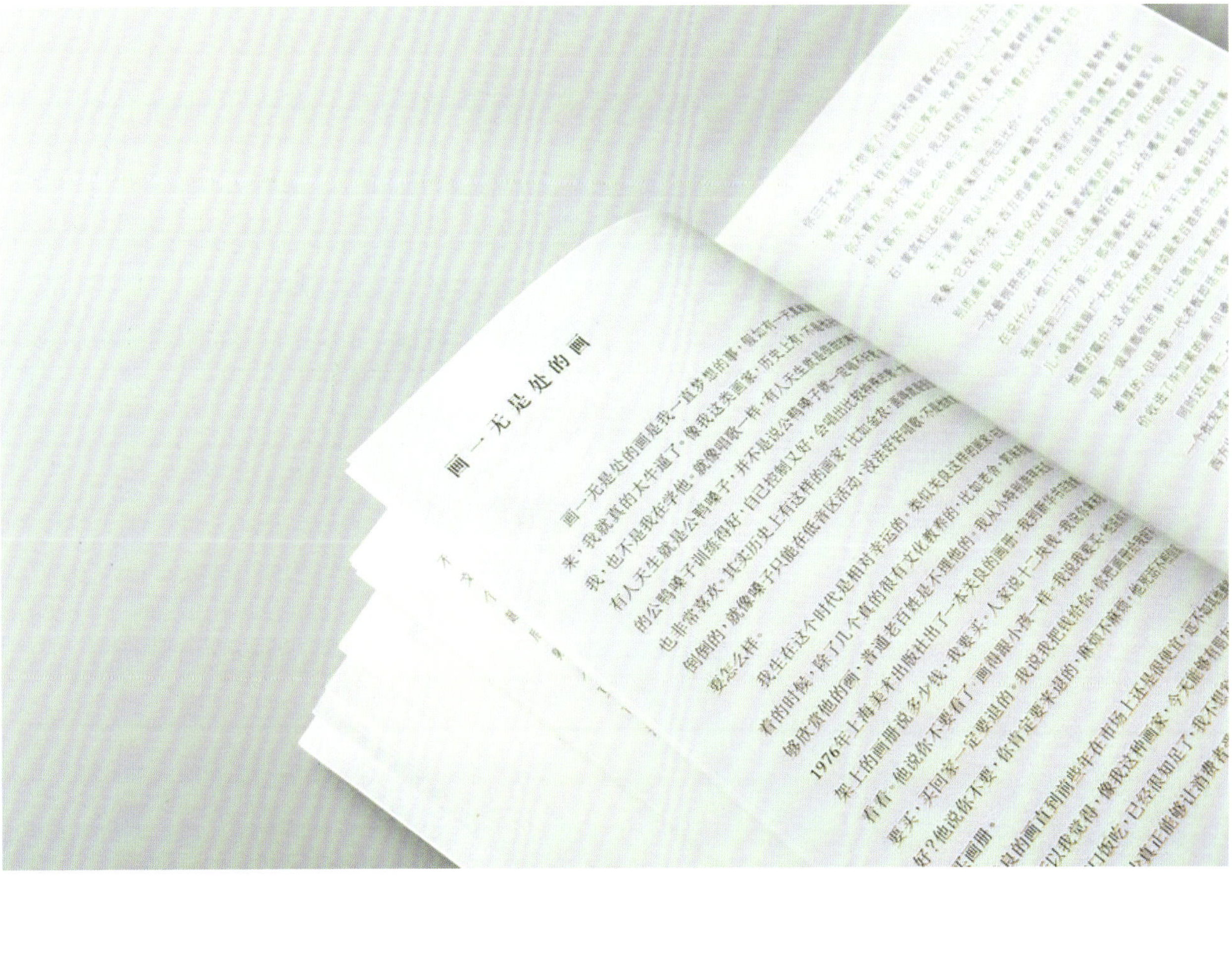
画一无是处的画

Ting branding and editorial designs

Designer: Mohamed Samir
Design Agency: Non
Design Director: Mohamed Samir
Country: United Arab Emirates

Client: Personal work

The Ting series is focusing on organic and abstract. It is exploring the living creatures motion and the relation between it and the human behavior. Both graphical interpretation and photography are being used in all the magazine versions. It includes also sections about the traditional visual art subjects like typography but with a new graphical interpretation.

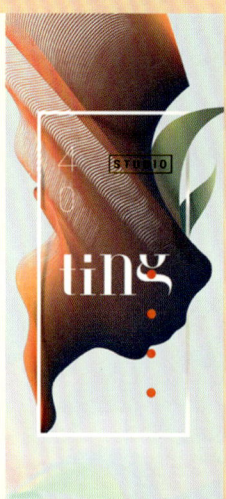

—Welcome to ting

31 January 2015
Christopher Robbins
3636 Bifford Drive,
London SE1 4SS
UK

Dear Marius,

On the Graphics List the other day, I got the strangest request, for a dummy letter! Surely a letter is easy enough to fake, and not something I would have thought needed special dummy text. Perhaps I am ignorant, but I kind of assumed it was a joke. Except that it wasn't very funny. Unless I'm just too ignorant to understand it. Is there some sort of official dummy letters? I certainly find that "lorem ipsum" stuff incredibly useful in large documents, so I assume it could be used for a letter and the designer (corporate funster, whatever) of course would have to add his or her own date and name and address.

I usually take the time to write utter bollocks a la automatic writing or something as short as a letter. As long as it doesn't have the word "bollocks" in it, it amuses me and helps prepare myself for the job at hand.

Ting branding and editorial designs

Designer: Mohamed Samir
Design Agency: Non
Design Director: Mohamed Samir
Country: United Arab Emirates

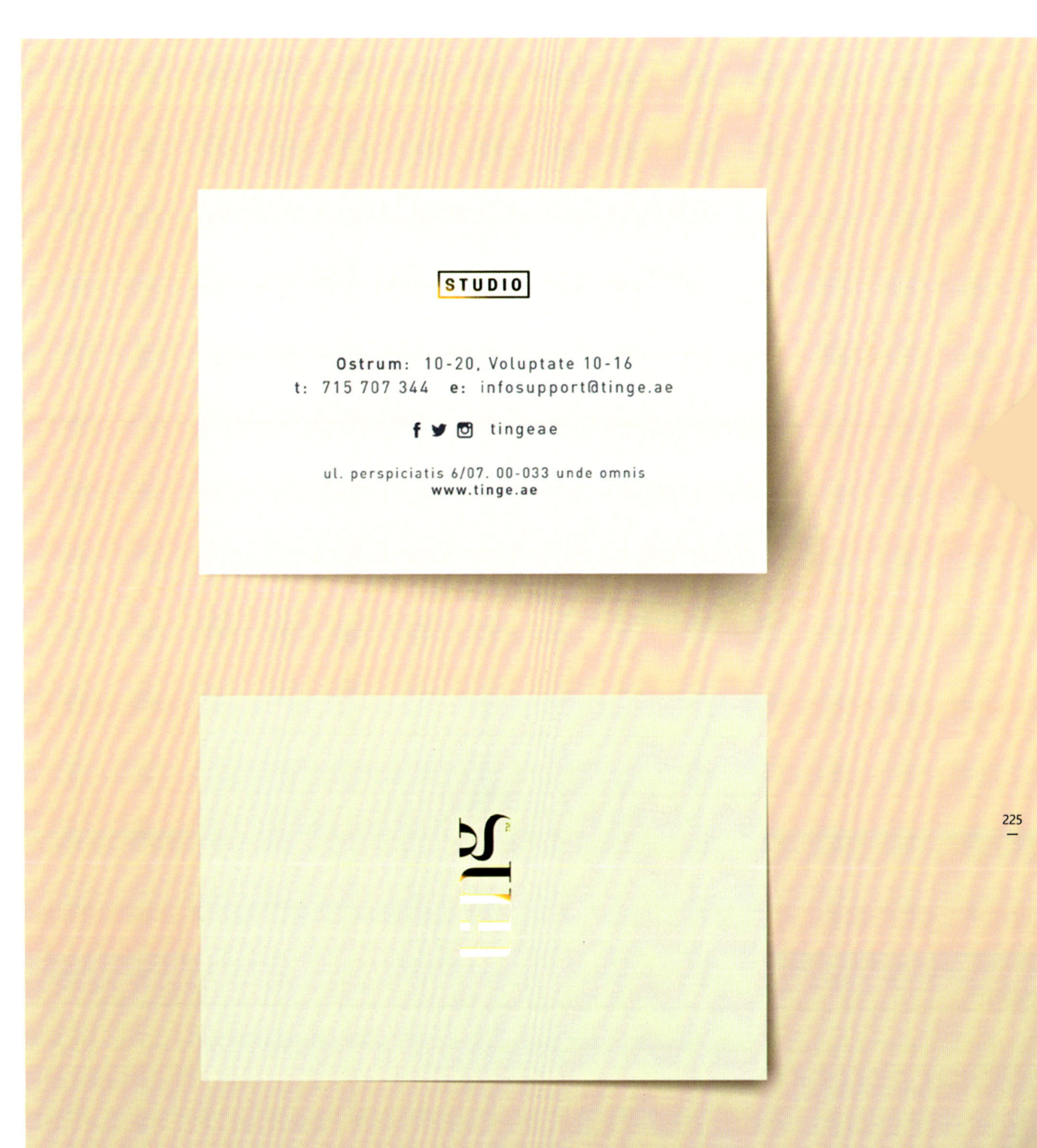

— Language
of flowers

Tinge Studio Magazine | Flowers & Human Section | Meanings & feelings

Red roses are given as a
symbol of love, beauty, and
passion.

Their symbolism in dreams
has also been discussed,
with possible interpreta-
tions including "blossoming
potential".

27

28

Ting branding and editorial designs

Designer: Mohamed Samir
Design Agency: Non
Design Director: Mohamed Samir
Country: United Arab Emirates

— We are
Butterflies

Tinge Studio Magazine | Butterflies & Human Section | Chinese dream

The Taoist philosopher,
Zhuangzi, once had a dream
about being a butterfly that flew
without care about humanity;
however; when he awoke and
realized that it was just a dream,
he thought to himself, "Was I
before a man who dreamt about
being a butterfly, or am I now a
butterfly who dreams about being a man?"

two butterflies
flying together
symbolize love

226
—

23

24

—Gesa-mtkunst-werk

The conscious act of artistically addressing all the senses with regard to a total experience made a resounding debut in 1849 when Richard Wagner conceived of a Gesamtkunstwerk, or an operatic work for the stage that drew inspiration from ancient Greek theater in its inclusion of all the major art forms.

Generally, the term Installation art is applied to interior spaces,

Attitude in photography

The reactions of artists and writers have contributed significantly to perceptions of photography as fine art. Prominent painters, such as Francis Bacon and Pablo Picasso, have asserted their interest in the medium: I have discovered photography. Now I can kill myself. I have nothing else to learn. - Pablo Picasso; I have always been very interested in photography. I have looked at far more photographs than I have paintings. Because their reality is stronger than reality itself. - Francis Bacon.

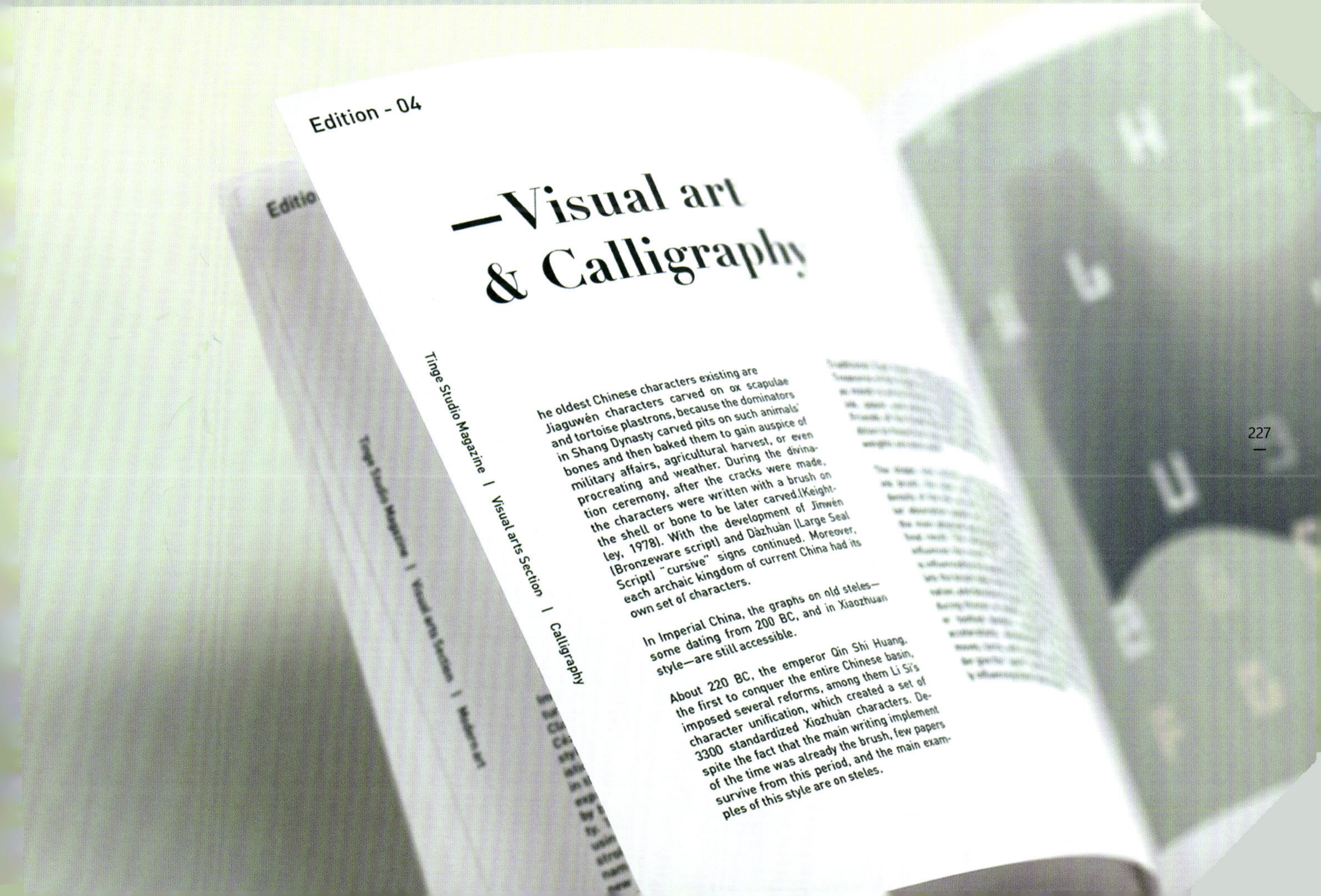

—Visual art & Calligraphy

The oldest Chinese characters existing are Jiaguwén characters carved on ox scapulae and tortoise plastrons, because the dominators in Shang Dynasty carved pits on such animals bones and then baked them to gain auspice of military affairs, agricultural harvest, or even procreating and weather. During the divination ceremony, after the cracks were made, the characters were written with a brush on the shell or bone to be later carved.(Keightley, 1978). With the development of Jinwén (Bronzeware script) and Dàzhuàn (Large Seal Script) "cursive" signs continued. Moreover, each archaic kingdom of current China had its own set of characters.

In Imperial China, the graphs on old steles—some dating from 200 BC, and in Xiaozhuan style—are still accessible.

About 220 BC, the emperor Qin Shi Huang, the first to conquer the entire Chinese basin, imposed several reforms, among them Li Si's character unification, which created a set of 3300 standardized Xiozhuăn characters. Despite the fact that the main writing implement of the time was already the brush, few papers survive from this period, and the main examples of this style are on steles.

(Po)nowoczesne losy obrazów

Designer: Tomek Głowacki
Design Agency: Poważne Studio
Country: Poland
Photographer: Poważne Studio

Client: Lodz Film School

The book includes two different esseys about photography. It
has two covers, upsite down to each other, with two ways of
reading.

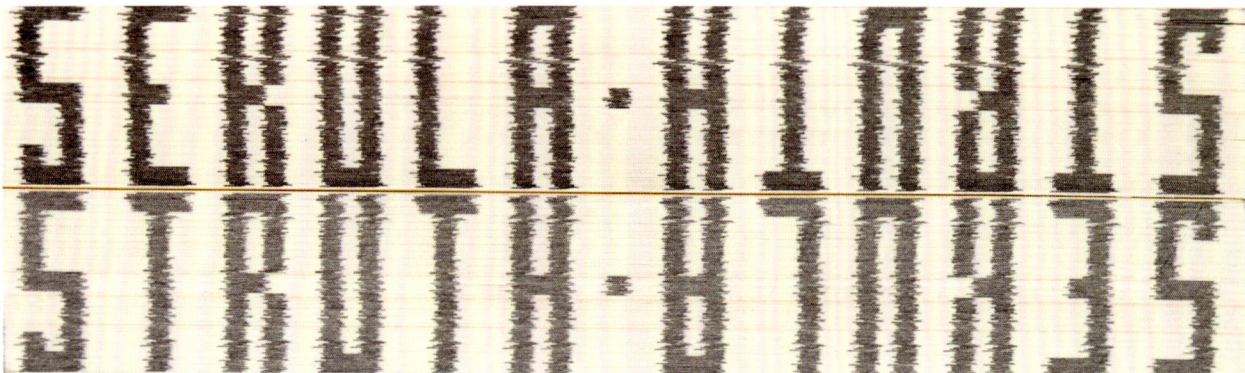

Untitled Slide Sequence (1972)

Fotografia między archiwum a opowieścią. Materializm Allana Sekuli

1. Artyści jako krytycy

Powodem, dla którego Allan i ja zaczęliśmy pisać – o naszej praktyce artystycznej i o sztuce w ogóle – było to, że nikt inny nie pisał o rzeczach, które wydawały się nam istotne.

Martha Rosler[6]

W sztuce po drugiej wojnie światowej, to minimaliści jako pierwsi trudnili się krytyką artystyczną[7]. Brali aktywny udział w teoretycznych debatach wokół kształtu i charakteru minimalizmu i do pewnego stopnia samodzielnie ten kształt i charakter ustanowili. Ten typ samoświadomości stał się później obowiązującą praktyką, zwłaszcza w dobie konceptualizmu, którego pojawienie się i najintensywniejsza obecność przypadła na czas studiów Sekuli. W kontekście amerykańskim szukanie genealogii w minimalizmie jest o tyle istotne, że, jak argumentuje Hal Foster, ruch ten otworzył drogę dla krytyki instytucjonalnej i feministycznej w sztuce lat 70. i 80[8]. Konceptualizm jest zaś niezbędny, ponieważ to w ramach związanych z nim praktyk na ścianach galerii pojawiły się zestawienia tekstu i obrazu, stanowiące podstawową formę wypowiedzi artystycznej Sekuli. Liz Kotz dowodzi, że właśnie połączenie fotografii z językiem było najważniejszym osiągnięciem

6 Martina Pachmanová, Martha Rosler: Subverting the Myths of everyday life [wywiad], [w:] tejże, Mobile Fidelities. Conversations on Feminism, History and Visuality, „n.paradoxa" 2006, vol. 19 [numer specjalny], s. 100, URL: http://web.ukonline.co.uk/n.paradoxa/pachmanova.htm [dostęp: 25.05.2008].
7 Mam tu na myśli zwłaszcza Donalda Judda oraz, w mniejszym stopniu, Roberta Morrisa.
8 Por. Hal Foster, Istota minimalizmu, [w:] tegoż, Powrót Realnego, przeł. Małgorzata Sugiera, Mateusz Borowski, Kraków 2010, s. 59-95.

26

27

Sleepwalk and Workers (2002-2007)

Gabinet kolekcjonera

Miejsce Obrazów. O fotografiach muzealnych Thomasa Struth

10. Thomas Struth, National Gallery 1 (London 1989, 184.0 x 196.0 cm, dzięki uprzejmości artysty.

Fish Story (1988–1995) Middle Passage

Panorama. Ocean Atlantycki.

(Po)nowoczesne losy obrazów

Designer: Tomek Głowacki
Design Agency: Poważne Studio
Country: Poland
Photographer: Poważne Studio

Ecce Animalia

Designer: Alicja Kobza
Design Agency: Poważne Studio
Country: Poland

Client: Centre of Polish Sculpture In Orońsko

The catalogue and branding for the exhibition Ecce Animalia in
Centre of Polish Sculpture in Oronsko.

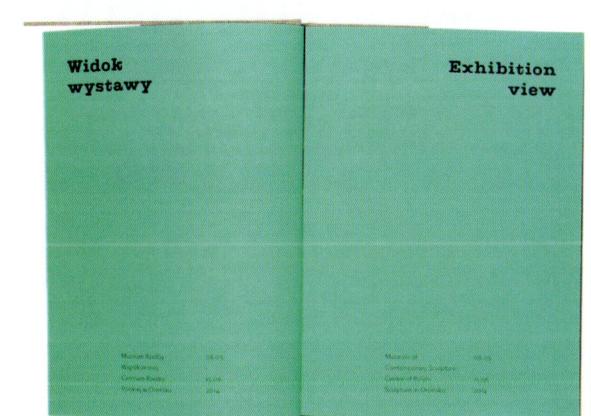

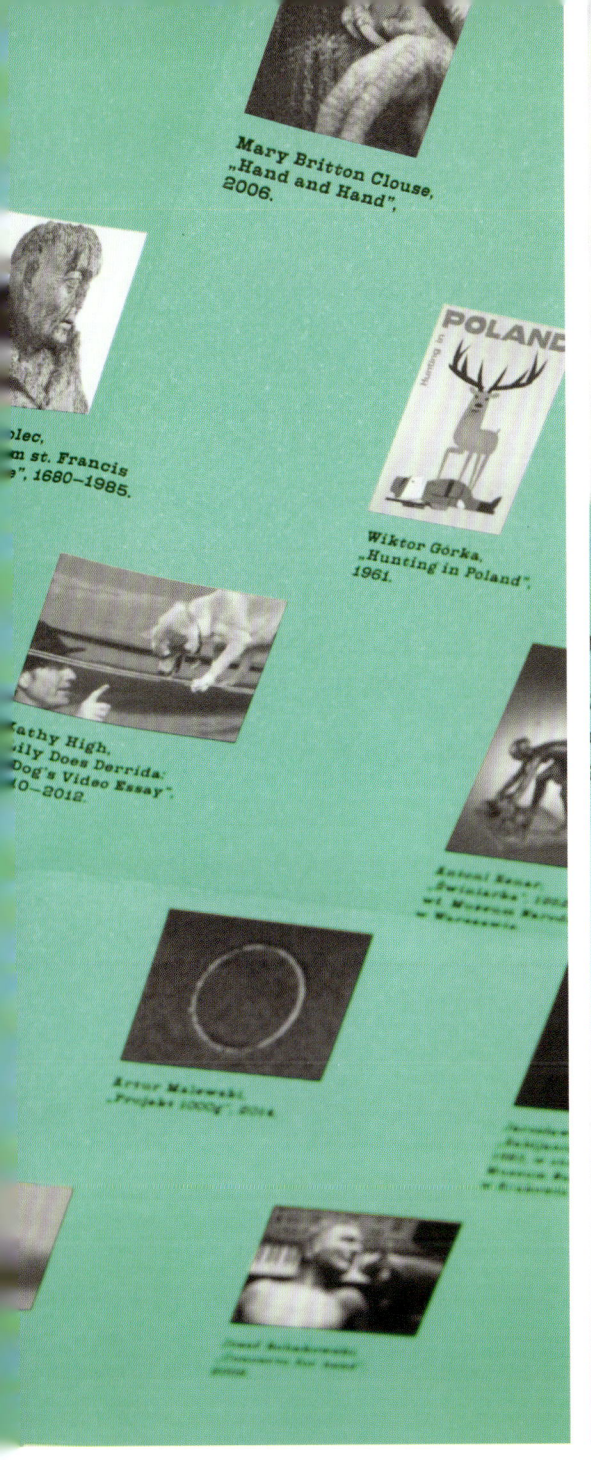

Mary Britton Clouse,
„Hand and Hand",
2006.

...olec,
...m st. Francis
...", 1680—1985.

POLAND

Wiktor Górka,
„Hunting in Poland",
1961.

...athy High,
...ily Does Derrida:
...Dog's Video Essay",
...0—2012.

...Antoni Kenar,
...Świniarka... 195...
...wł. Muzeum Narod...
...w Warszawie.

Artur Malewski,
„Projekt 1000g", 2014.

...zeto Castellano,
„Study of Hunting
Dogs in Blue", 2012.

Józef Gott,
„Lisica z młodymi
i upolowanym łabędziem",
...ok. 1798—1860,
...Muzeum Narodowe
...Warszawie.

Museum
of Contemporary   15.06.
Sculpture, Centre   2014
of Polish Sculpture
in Orońsko

opening: 8th March, 2 PM

Ecce animalia is an international exhibition focusing on animal subjectivity and
individuality as well as the relationships
between people and animals.

CURATED BY:

Dorota Łagodzka
and Leszek Golec

cooperation: Anna Barcz, IBL PAN

Animals have functioned in human image-ma...
ing since prehistoric rock paintings and the e...
liest carvings on tusks and antlers. That is w...
they are one of the first subjects in the hist...
of art. In later epochs animals appeared wi...
traditional iconography as symbols, attrib...
decorations, landscape elements, in hu...
scenes and in still-life paintings. Rarely di...
appear because of their importance or fo...
own sake.

More recently art has undergone a s...
animal turn – and also, more broadly, i...
and society – sometimes related to th...
of posthumanism. A new approach t...
in art which began in the 1960s a...
manifested a growing interest in...
living creatures rather than symbol...
number of animal images, and n...
presenting animals. Artists now e...
issues connected with animal su...
dividuality and the complexity...
between people and other an...
pates in the animal stud...
a part of it – critical...
approach to an...
artistic issues.

...nied by inte...
...ce entitled
...e Fall of...
...rganized...
...ch of...
...wi...
...4.

Ecce Animalia

Designer: Alicja Kobza
Design Agency: Poważne Studio
Country: Poland

Monograph of Museum of Art in Lódz

Designer: Alicja Kobza, Małgorzata Frąckiewicz, Tomek Głowacki
Design Agency: Poważne Studio
Country: Poland
Photographer: Poważne Studio

client: Muzeum Sztuki in Łódź

Design for the two-volume publication summerizing activity of the Museum of Art in Łódź from the
beginning of its existence.

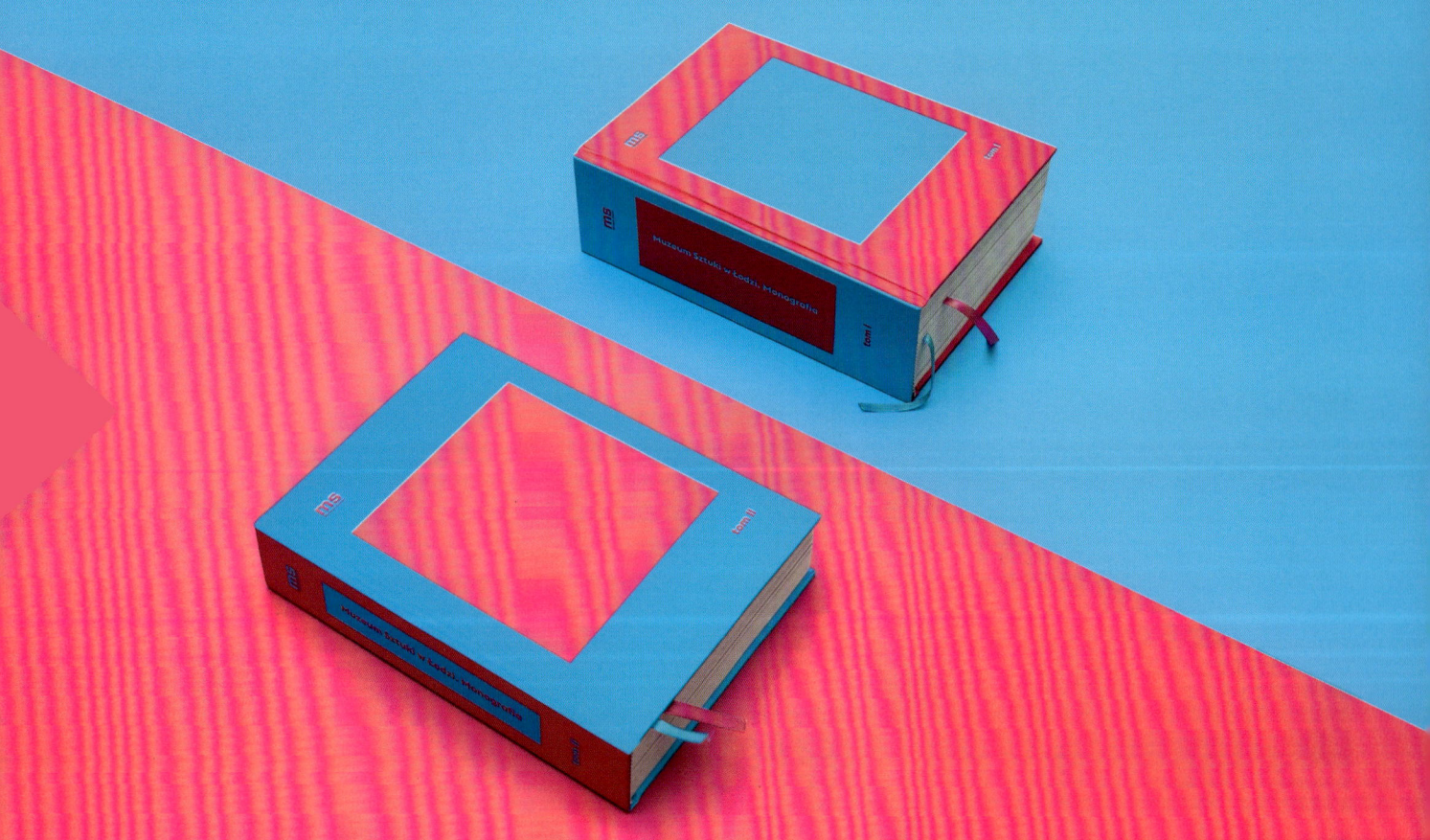

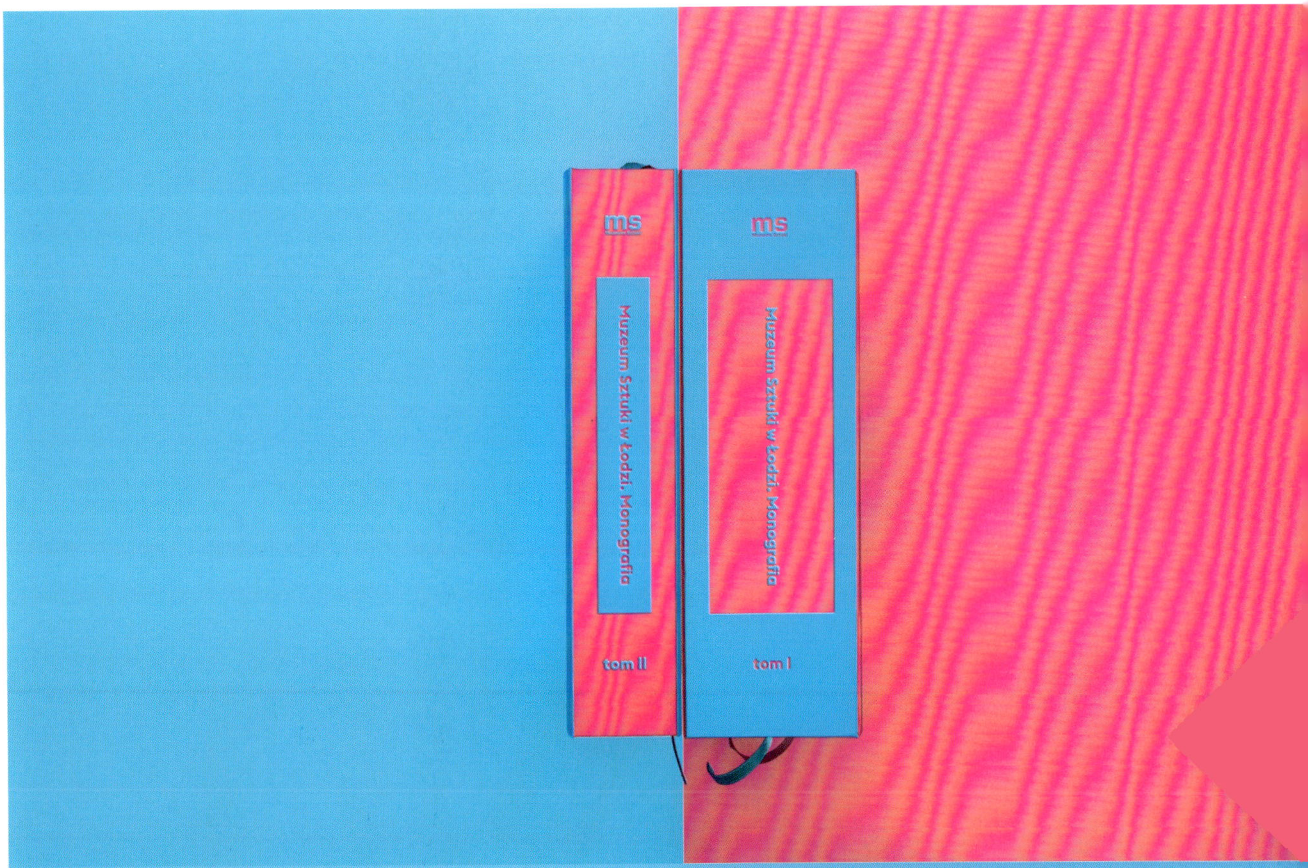

ms

Muzeum Sztuki w Łodzi. Monografia

Muzeum Sztuki w Łodzi. Monografia

tom II

tom I

**Rozdział
2**

Marcin Szeląg, Jan Szczepański, Janina Ładnowska, Mariam Minich,
Magdalena Ziółkowska, Tadeusz Kantor, Marta Madejska, Andrzej Szczerski,
Ryszard Stanisławski, Paweł Polit / Agnieszka Szewczyk, Marysia Lewandowska
Marta Leśniakowska, Magdalena Moskalewicz, Daniel Muzyczuk, Adam Mazur

Monograph of Museum of Art in Lódz

Designer: Alicja Kobza, Małgorzata Frąckiewicz, Tomek Głowacki
Design Agency: Poważne Studio
Country: Poland
Photographer: Poważne Studio

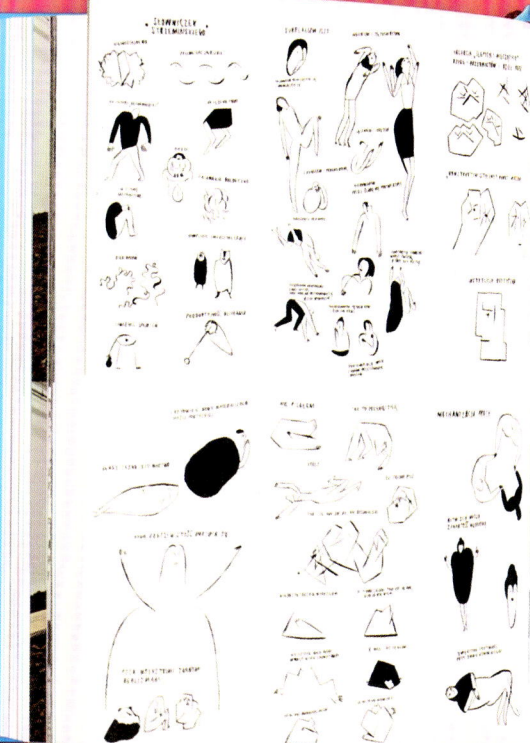

kariery, procesu sądowego, utraty reputacji i możliwości tworzenia sztuki. W instalacji Zadana artysty prezentowanej w Archiwum Państwowym na Placu Wolności Sawicka wydobyła fragment tekstu Kobro o obowiązkach sztuki: „Zadaniem sztuki jest współdziałanie w kierunku zwycięstwa wyższych form organizacji". W nagraniu słychać męski głos korygujący głos kobiety, mówiącej po polsku z rosyjskim akcentem, co przypomina dodatkowo o nierównej pozycji artystki jako kobiety wobec jej męża i innych mężczyzn w patriarchalnym społeczeństwie. W serii fotomontaży Sawickiej, przedstawiających rzeźby Kobro na klatkach schodowych modernistycznych bloków, jej twórczość znajduje fikcyjny dom, zastosowanie i uspołecznienie, jakiego nigdy nie zaznała w swoim życiu jako radykalna artystka i wyemancypowana kobieta. Natomiast w wyniku krytycznej lektury wybranych tekstów, m.in. Aspektów rzeczywistości Władysława Strzemińskiego zaproszona również do realizacji nowej pracy Agnieszka Piksa stworzyła dla nich wizualny, komiksowy kontrapunkt. Skupiła się na fragmentach, w których autor krytykuje surrealizm i jednocześnie zdradza dogłębną znajomość piętnowanych nieracjonalnych, indywidualistycznych, bezproduktywnych impulsów i wyparć, jakie przetworzył ten nurt sztuki, a nawet pewną nimi fascynację. Wybrane pasaże wskazują także na militarną polemiczność i stanowczość sądów Strzemińskiego. Rysunki Piksy nie ilustrują tekstów, lecz wydobywają z nich wątki dla autora drugoplanowe lub przez niego nieuświadamiane. Do wybranych fraz [na przykład „Surrealizm jest dążeniem skrętem i kurczem pragnieniem kierowanym przez ślepą grę protoplazmy"] wykonała rysunki, w których upodmiotowiona, wcielesniona forma walczy z apodyktycznością i surową precyzją tekstów. W ten sposób Piksa wydobyła w postawie Strzemińskiego szczeliny, pęknięcia, obsesyjne zapętlenia, pomyłki, emocje, wskazując na fantazmatyczne aspekty jego projektu budowy zdyscyplinowanego, racjonalnego i funkcjonalnego życia przy pomocy sztuki. Kontrapunktem dla aktualizujących historyczne źródła projektów Sawickiej i Piksy, prezentowanych w Archiwum Państwowym, były prace Nevin Aladağ, Josefa Daberniga, Romana Ondaka i Ruth Oppenheim, operujące wymykającymi się definicjom, ambiwalentnymi przepływami afektów wywołanych

Renegocjacje historii

Jakub Woynarowski, Agnieszka Rejniak-Majewska

Bartolina Busca-Pé...e o Zé!

Designer: João Brandão Ferreira
Design Agency: Atelier d'alves
Country: Portugal

Client: Susana Cardoso Ferreira

"Bartolina Busca-Pé... E o Zé!" is a 200-page story, therefore it could not be conceptualized like a picture book, in which the illustration follows, almost literally, the story and takes centre stage. That was our starting point. So the end product is not a picture book, rather it is a book with pictures—but also with letters, words, and shapes that coexist on the same level. The illustration does not unveil Bartolina's world, it hints at it so that the readers can imagine and build it themselves. Characters are never represented as a whole, many times being portrayed through actions and emotions, and even then only partially, via nondescript elements such as legs, eyes, and mouth. A scare is a giant mouth screaming, the fear of the dark is a black spread... And the text has its own surprises in store, for instance when type is used to emphasise a noise, a gesture or a state of mind. Reading this book requires going beyond the words on the page to interpret the shapes they form and the images they reveal.

de surpresa

de descoberta

Bartolina Busca-Pé...e o Zé!

de aventura

Ação emocionante com muita dificuldade em atravessar.

As aventuras são missões, sair do país e ex p lor ar o mundo. É fazer coisas novas, perigosas ou divertidas.

Viagem para lutar contra monstros, salvar pessoas, etc. Quando alguém nunca fez uma coisa m mas um dia faz.

aluca

Designer: João Brandão Ferreira
Design Agency: Atelier d'alves
Country: Portugal

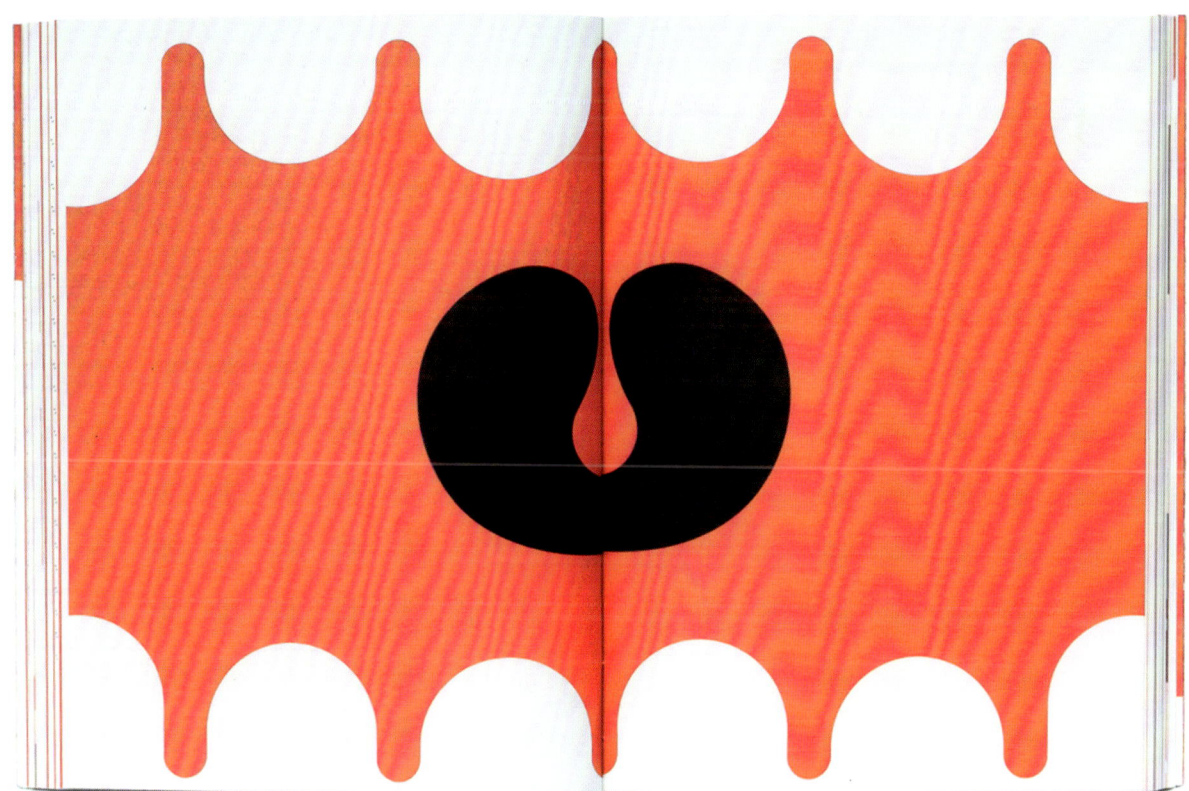

de vergonha

— Olá, Bartolina! — saudou o dono da Herdade dos Vitorinos, aparecendo à porta de casa mal ela saltou da bicicleta.

— Olá, senhor Manuel Vitorino.

— Já preparei a encomenda dos teus pais. Podes ir dar a tua voltinha, que eu trato de arrumar tudo no cesto da bicicleta.

— Obrigada!

A Bartolina foi primeiro visitar as galinhas, depois deu um salto à pocilga, passou algum tempo no curral, a mimar os cabritinhos, e foi sentar-se na cerca, a olhar para os cavalos. Mas era um olhar sem ver. Não conseguia parar de pensar na tristeza da pobre Violante. Tinha de haver maneira de a ajudar. Mas como? Estaria a escapar-lhe algum pormenor importante?

— Olá, Bê!

A Bartolina voltou a cabeça e só não caiu do poleiro abaixo porque entrelaçara as pernas nas traves.

— Zê?! Seguiste-me? — perguntou em tom de acusação.

— Não, eu venho aqui muitas vezes passear e conversar com

114

Encontro

4

de ideia

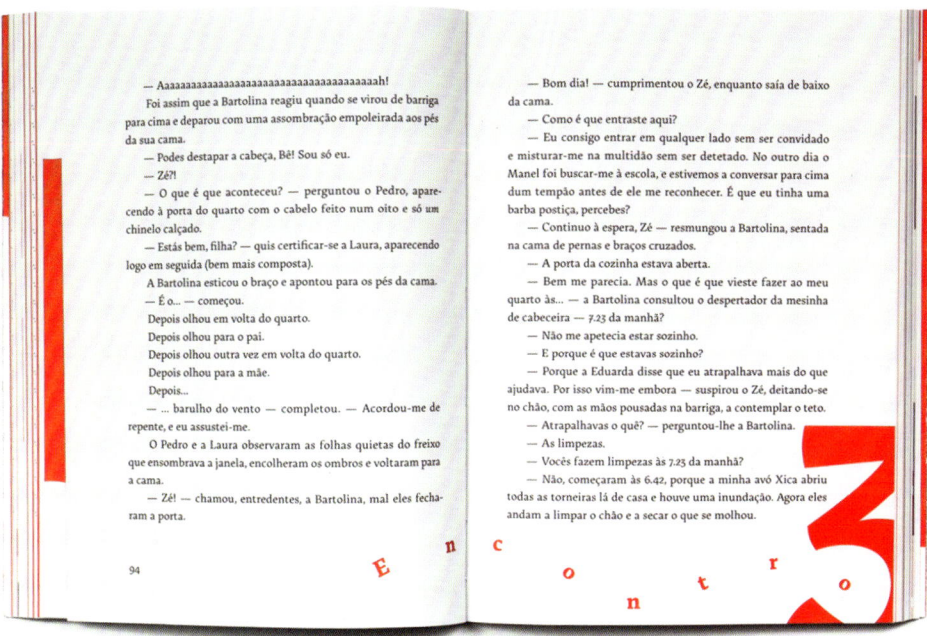

Bartolina Busca-Pé...e o Zé!

Designer: João Brandão Ferreira
Design Agency: Atelier d'alves
Country: Portugal

Bartolina Busca-Pé...e o Zé!

Designer: João Brandão Ferreira
Design Agency: Atelier d'alves
Country: Portugal

É encontrar uma coisa que chama a atenção. É algo que pode estar escondido debaixo da terra ou numa gruta. É ver o que p rdemos. É uma coisa que não estava lá e depois está.

É inventar uma coisa nova e ficar muito contente. É algo que acontece depois de uma aventura. É aprender.

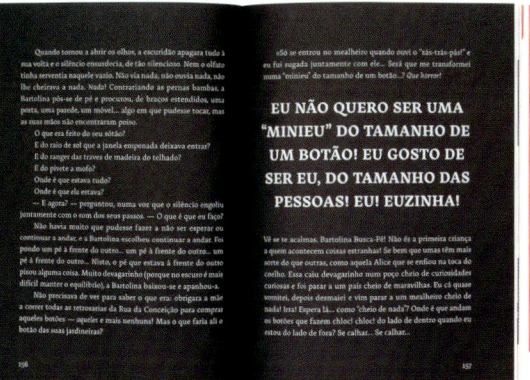

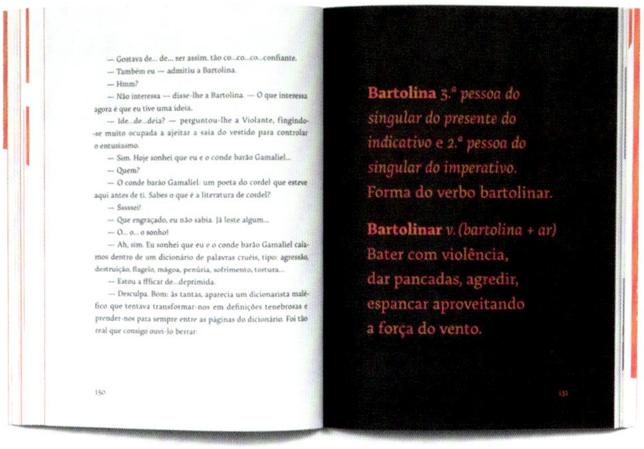

London Studio Visits: Thank You

Designer: Harry Lee, Matthew Caldwell, Harry Ingrams, Tom Austin
Design Agency: N/A
Country: UK
Photographer: Harry Lee

Client: Falmouth University

Over the course of 3 days in November, 62 Falmouth Graphic Design students visited 27 design studios in London. Tasked with the theme of circles, all 62 students photographed found circles in everyday objects and environments. These circles then created tube stops, on our very own circle-line from London to Falmouth. The book was sent to all the studios we visited, as a small thank you for their time.

Thank you

A+B
AKQA
The Allotment
B&B
BBH
Bisqit
The Brand Union
Carter Wong
d.studio
Design Bridge
Dragon Rouge
Hat-Trick
JKR
Johnson Banks
Lewis Moberly
Magpie Studio
Mother
MSL Group
Open Agency
The Partners
Pentagram
Purpose
Skype
Springetts
Turner Duckworth
Unreal
ustwo

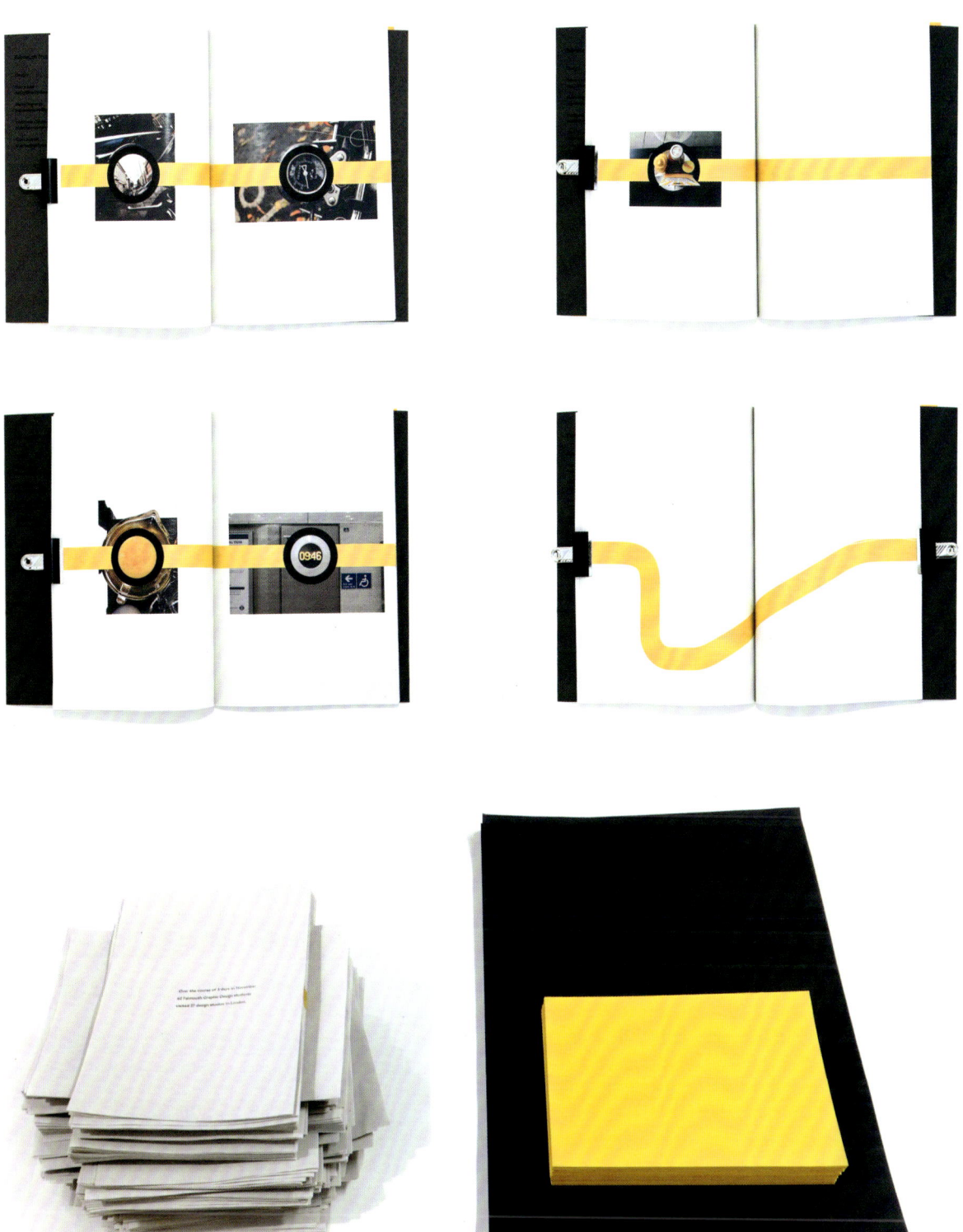

London Studio Visits: Thank You

Designer: Harry Lee, Matthew Caldwell, Harry Ingrams, Tom Austin
Design Agency: N/A
Country: UK
Photographer: Harry Lee

there's more to sharks

Great White Lies

Designer: Harry Lee
Country: UK

Great White Lies

Designer: Harry Lee
Country: UK

Client: Self Initiated

A publication aimed to combat the myths associated with sharks in the media by educating the masses on their true nature.
The newspaper format was specifically chosen as certain newspapers are often to blame for these over exaggerated shark headlines, but the layout purposely abandons the traditional rules.
7 misconceptions about sharks are stated and proved wrong using research shown with images and informal text.

4

attacks are common

10000* **2900***

340*

130*

40*

30*

13*

6*

5*

If your idea of 'common' is along the lines with being struck by lightning – twice, then yes.

Put it this way, consider the amount of people who enter the water all around the world each year – it's in the billions. On average, there are around 70 shark attacks each year, of which about 5 are fatal. Realise that the media accentuates these attacks, leading to the perception of them being common.

*average number of related deaths per year

3

all sharks are the same

To state that sharks are all the same is more ridiculous than saying humans are **all identical.**

Scientifically speaking, sharks are a group of fish characterised by a skeleton constructed purely by cartilage, five to seven gill slits on the sides of the head, and pectoral fins that are not fused to the head.

There are around 400 different species of shark, each with a different diet, habitat and behaviour.

Sizes can range from the six inch cigar shark, to the 45 foot whale shark. Over half of these species are less than 3 foot long. And of these 400 shark species, only 3 have been involved with a number of human fatalities; Bull, Tiger and Great White – the famed Hammerhead has never had a confirmed human kill.

255
—

misconception

a view or opinion that is incorrect
because based on faulty thinking
or understanding.

Sharks have been wrongly portrayed in the media,
leading to many having the wrong impression.
The real problem is this false image is affecting
them in real life.

The following pages aims to highlight these
misconceptions and destroy them.

Great White Lies

Designer: Harry Lee
Country: UK

Great White Lies

Designer: Harry Lee
Country: UK

we ~~should~~ **fear them**

Yes, sharks are deadly. It has something to do with their razor-sharp teeth.

But whilst it's wise to avoid waters heavily populated with sharks, encounters are rare and fatalities from attacks are even rarer.

THEY DON HUNT

There's a reason they look freakish when they go in for a bite – and it's not to ramp up the fear factor for their prey. The shark's eyes roll back to expose tough carriage as protection, turning them white. The teeth-baring move is the result of muscles pushing the jaw forward whilst the skin around the mouth is held back. As the jaw is constructed of cartilage it's pretty flexible, so moving it back and forth is no big deal. When swimming normally the jaw recedes, making the shark more streamlined.

It begs the question: why do w this irrational fear of sharks? They don't hunt us, we're unli even have an encounter in our

The answer simply lies with our understand unfortunately only know what the media te often than not is skewed to portray sharks a

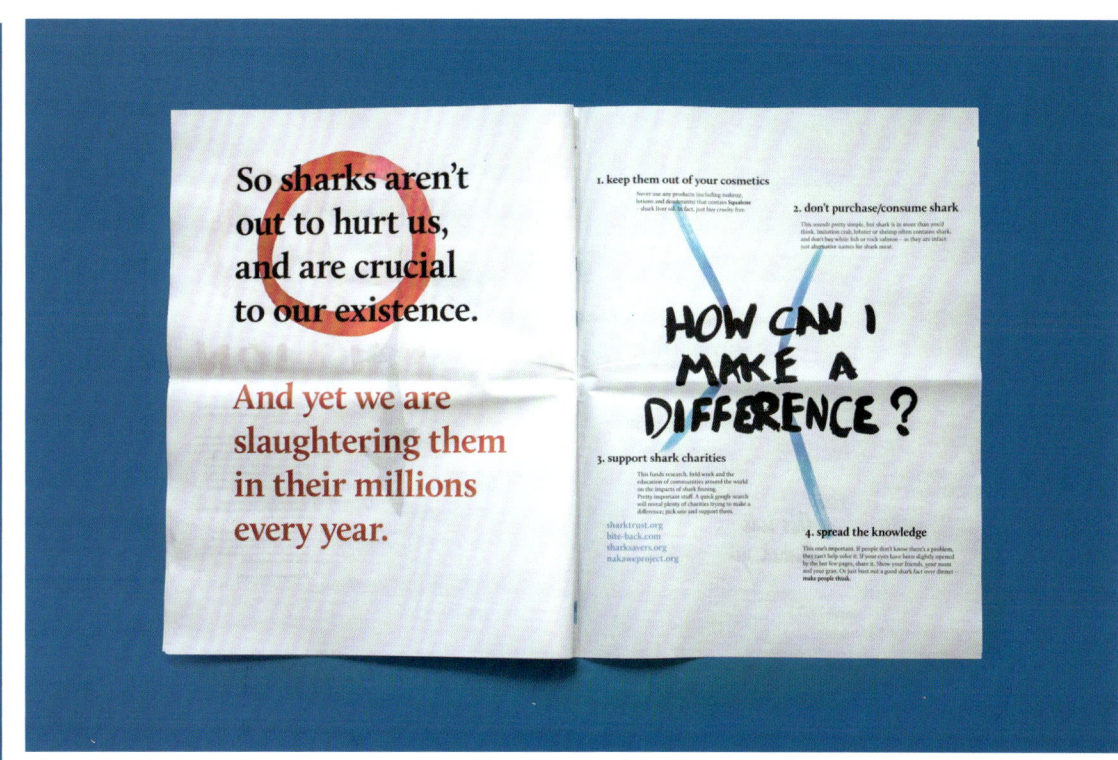

So sharks aren't out to hurt us, and are crucial to our existence.

And yet we are slaughtering them in their millions every year.

1. keep them out of your cosmetics

Never use any products (including makeup, lotions and deodorants) that contain **Squalene** - shark liver oil. In fact, just buy cruelty free.

2. don't purchase/consume shark

This sounds pretty simple, but shark is in more than you'd think. Imitation crab, lobster or shrimp often contains shark, and don't buy white fish or rock salmon - as they are infact not alternative names for shark meat.

HOW CAN I MAKE A DIFFERENCE?

3. support shark charities

This funds research, field work and the education of communities around the world on the impacts of shark finning. Pretty important stuff. A quick google search will reveal plenty of charities trying to make a difference; pick one and support them.

sharktrust.org
bite-back.com
sharksavers.org
makeaweproject.org

4. spread the knowledge

This one's important. If people don't know there's a problem, they can't help solve it. If your eyes have been slightly opened by the last few pages, share it. Show your friends, your mum and your gran. Or just bust out a good shark fact over dinner - make people think.

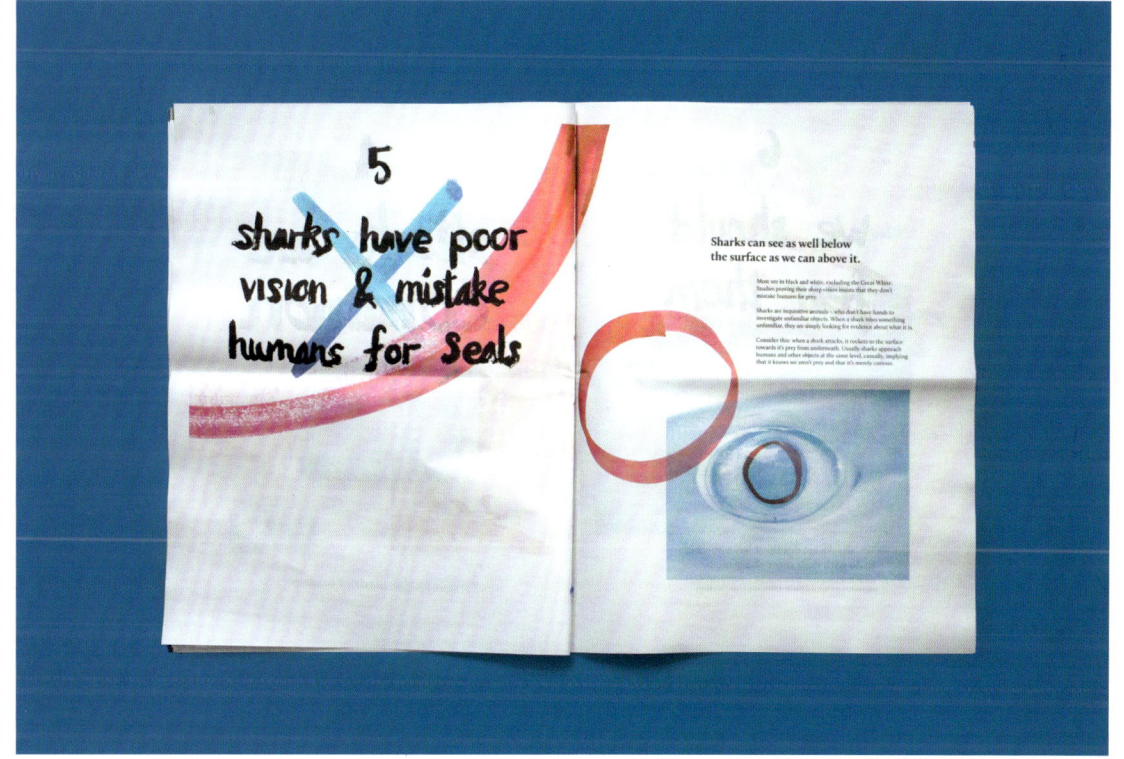

5

sharks have poor vision & mistake humans for seals

Sharks can see as well below the surface as we can above it.

Most are in black and white, excluding the Great White. Studies proving their sharp vision means that they don't mistake humans for prey.

Sharks are inquisitive animals - who don't have hands to investigate unfamiliar objects. When a shark bites something unfamiliar, they are simply looking for evidence about what it is.

Consider this: when a shark attacks, it rockets to the surface towards it's prey from underneath. Usually sharks approach humans and other objects at the same level, casually, implying that it knows we aren't prey, and that it's merely curious.

Stitch

Designer: Harry Lee, Harry Ingrams
Design Agency: Harry & Harry
Country: UK
Photographer: Jonathan Vivaas Kise

Client: Jets Presents

"Stitch" is an exhibition of fashion with the aim of showcasing upcoming talent outside of London.
A 72-page catalogue was produced featuring the collections and was given on the night to all who attended, for reference during and after the show. We took the challenge of creating a unique composition for each designer, to show details of the garments and keep it visually interesting.

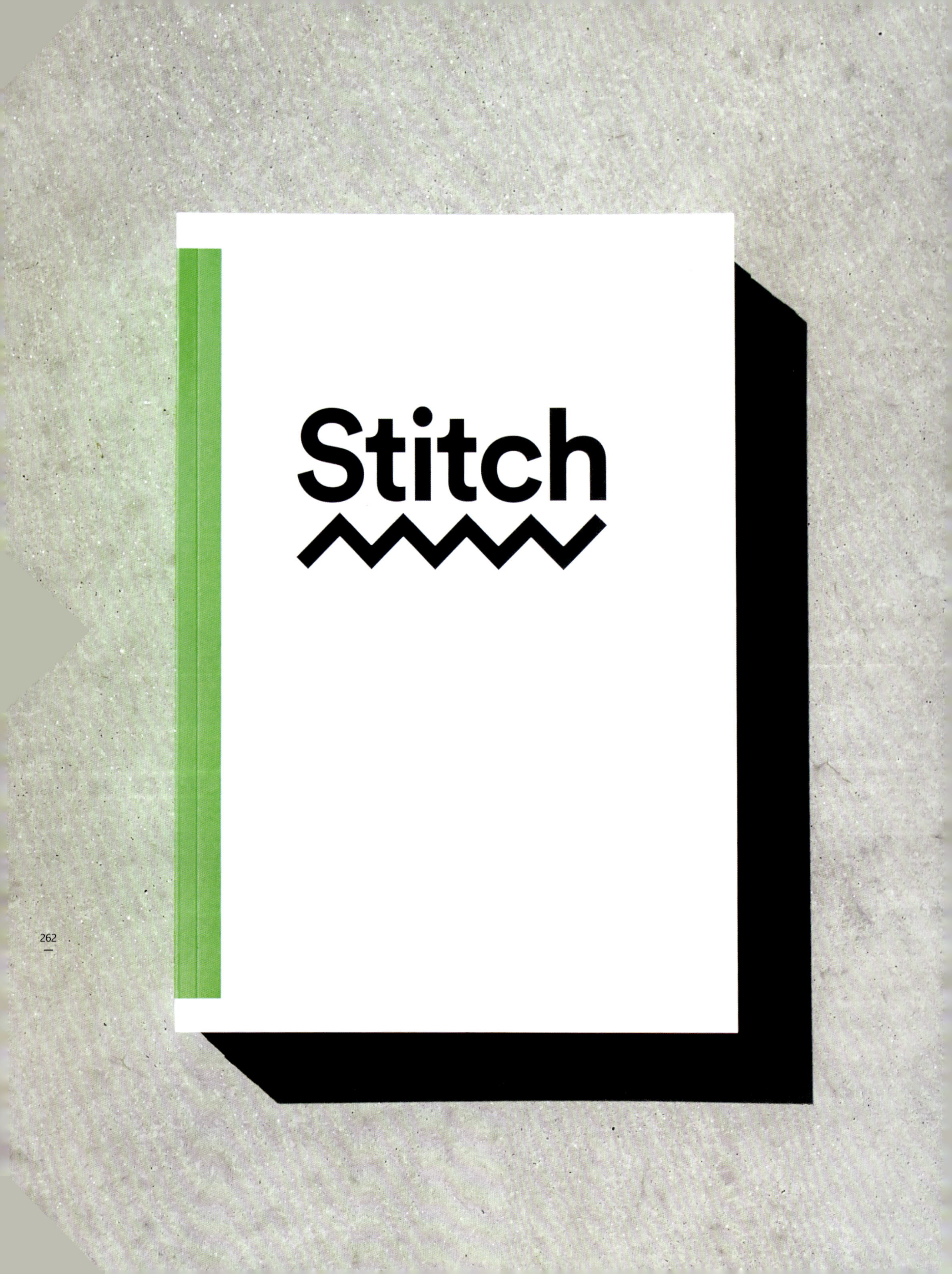
Stitch

Stitch

Designer: Harry Lee, Harry Ingrams
Design Agency: Harry & Harry
Country: UK
Photographer: Jonathan Vivaas Kise

Stitch

Designer: Harry Lee, Harry Ingrams
Design Agency: Harry & Harry
Country: UK
Photographer: Jonathan Vivaas Kise

Envelhecimento e Ino-vação Social　Ageing and Social Innovation

Designer: Ana Simões
Design Agency: White Studio
Country: USA
Creative Director: Eduardo Aires
Photographer: Jorge Almeida

This is a book that gathers the conferences, projects and workshops that took part during the event Envelhecimento e Inovação Social / Ageing and Social Innovation, for which White Studio designed also the visual identity.

The goal of the graphic concept for this event was to create a strong and positive image. We started with a skin metaphor, creating a pattern from the small wrinkles that form as years go by, that can also be a metaphor for interconnectivity, communication and partnership The Strong yellow colour was chosen to bring freshness, binding all the materials into a complete and strong visual identity.

In the book, the texts are treated in a very neutral and simple way, to assure a comfortable and focused reading. Some fun is brough inside from the colour of the cover and the overall image. We use yellow inside in titles, tables and graphic or typographic details.

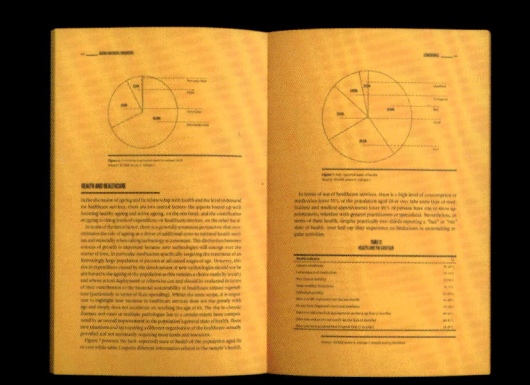

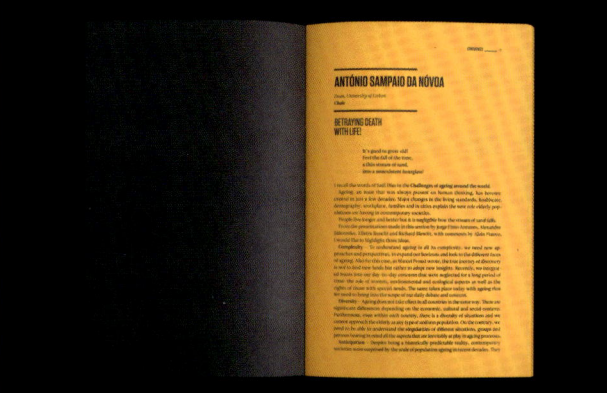

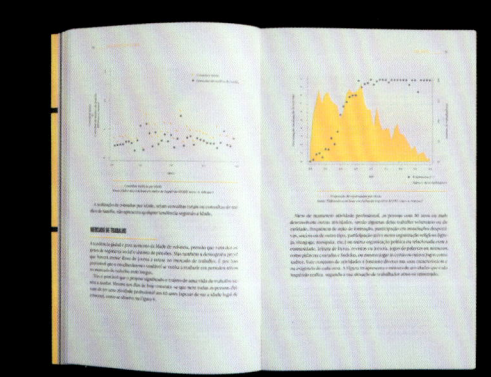

ENVELHECIMENTO ATIVO:
UM DESAFIO
PARA O INDIVÍDUO
E PARA A SOCIEDADE

Envelhecimento e Ino-
vação Social   Ageing
and Social Innovation

Designer: Ana Simões
Design Agency: White Studio
Country: USA
Creative Director: Eduardo Aires
Photographer: Jorge Almeida

Dong chang

Designer: Dongchang
Design Agency: Dongchang
Country: China

"Dongchang" the name comes from the right part of the first name of the two founder " 陳 "and" 張 "," 東 "and" 長 ".

随风 · Kite

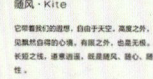
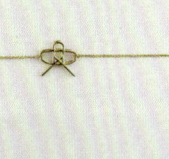

它带着我们的畅想，自由于天空，高度之外，
见到然然自得的心情。有限之外，也是无根，
长短之线。逐素逍遥，就是随风。随心。随
性。

Kites, flying with our imagination. Beside
the sky,there is a peace contented mind.
Limited or unlimited. The length of the
line is the freedom of mind, following the
wind, the heart and the nature.

关 于 童 兵

About Dongchang

童兵，坚持探索中国首饰设计新
方向的设计师品牌。

童兵认为饰物是精神的外沿，能
够借用饰物解读内心；通过外物，
反观内己。

小文，首饰设计师，毕业于巴黎
Ecole BJOP 珠宝学院。与毕业
于广州美术学院平面设计师张槊
共同创立设计师品牌童东兵。

Dongchang Jewelry, exploring for the new direction of
Chinese jewelry style

Dongchang believes that jewelry can tell.it tells about
spirit , tell us who we are , what we think or what you
want to be. By jewelry we can see what is deep inside
our heart . it's the outward expression of peoples
world view and values. Understand yourself through
surroundings .

Wen , after graduated from Ecole BJOP in Paris.
She started Dongchang Jewelry Atelier with shuo
Zhang,who is a graphic designer , studied visual
communication in Guangzhou Academy of Fine Arts.

Dong chang

Designer: Dongchang
Design Agency: Dongchang
Country: China

Dong chang

Designer: Dongchang
Design Agency: Dongchang
Country: China

每次感性的灵光一现与理性的规划拓展都是我们成长的节点。我们分享了这些谨献给那些在心底里为梦想留有一席空间，并默默坚持的理想者们，前进的路上我们共勉。

every step we've moved forward.every collection we've made out with every perceptual inspiration and rational planning thereafter.We want to share these with those who are also working on dreams rooted inside their hearts.Coz we are not alone on the way to dreams.

Dong chang

Designer: Dongchang
Design Agency: Dongchang
Country: China

4th Greater China Illustration Awards

Design Agency: Toby Ng Design
Creative Director: Toby Ng
Designer: Toby Ng, Ronald Cheung
Country: Hong Kong, China

Client: Hong Kong Society of Illustrators

The 4th Greater China Illustration Awards, organised by the Hong Kong Society of Illustrators whose aim is to elevate the standard of illustrations of the Greater China region to an international level through competition and observation.

Based on their theme 'A Vibrant Transformation A Meticulous Masterpiece', we designed their identity and all the printed matter related to the Awards. The design, comprised of a set of 4 graphics, depicts a small colour-coded triangle that radiates into a big triangle through a variety of patterned organic lines. The small triangle represent the illustrator's hand / pen / brush and the big triangle, with its various organic, hand crafted line patterns symbolises creativity and possibilities.

Four colours and four patterns created a colour code to distinguish the different award categories and sections; these were used in the small triangles to reinforce the competition's award identity.

The 4th
Greater China
Illustration
Awards
第四屆中華區插畫獎

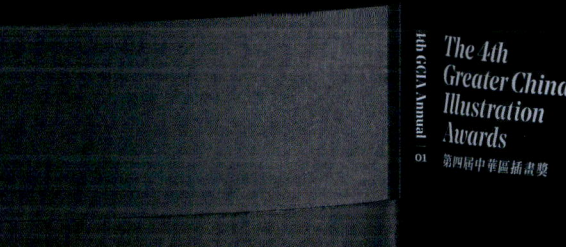

4th GCIA Annual
01

The 4th
Greater China
Illustration
Awards
第四屆中華區插畫獎

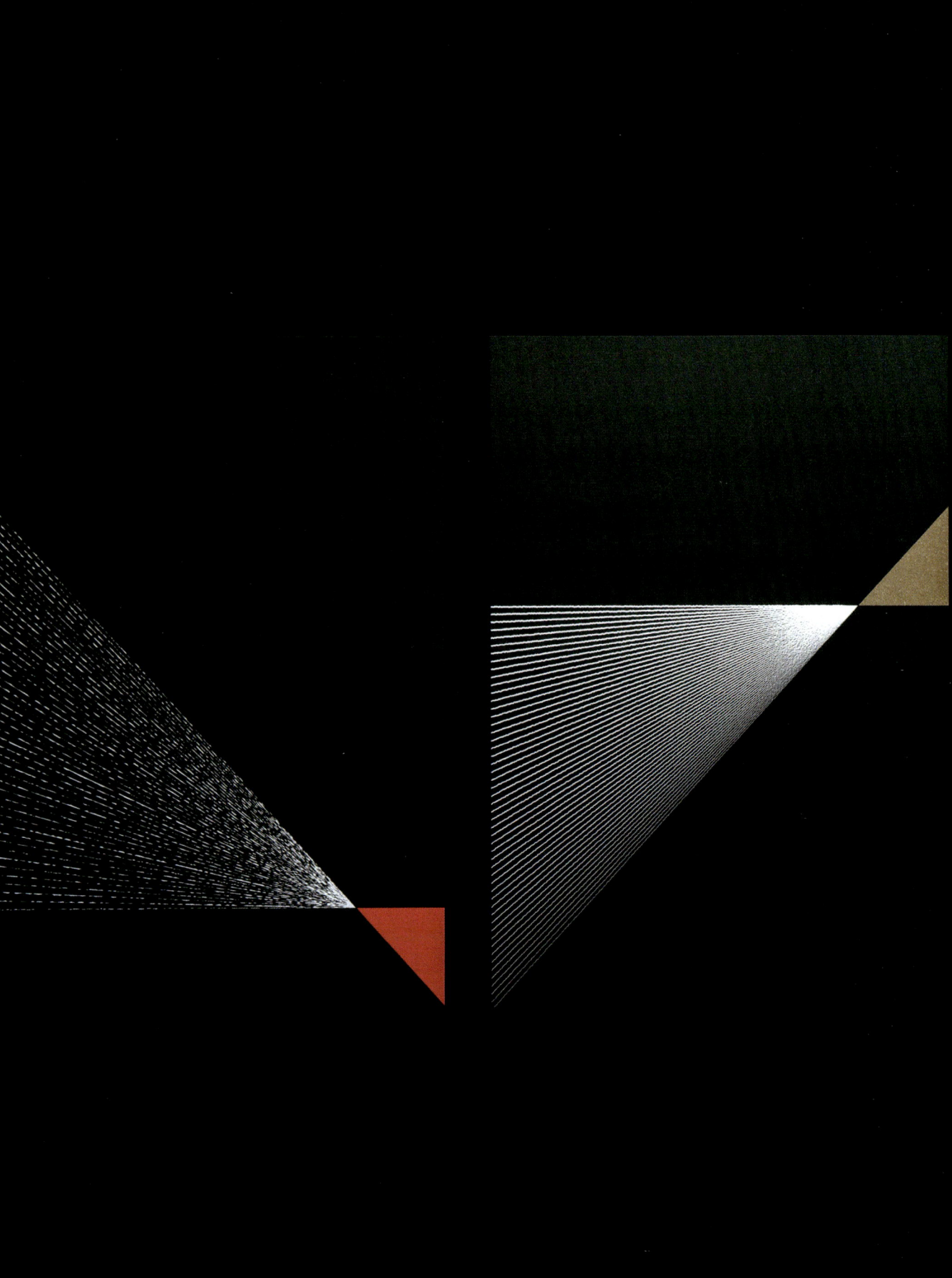

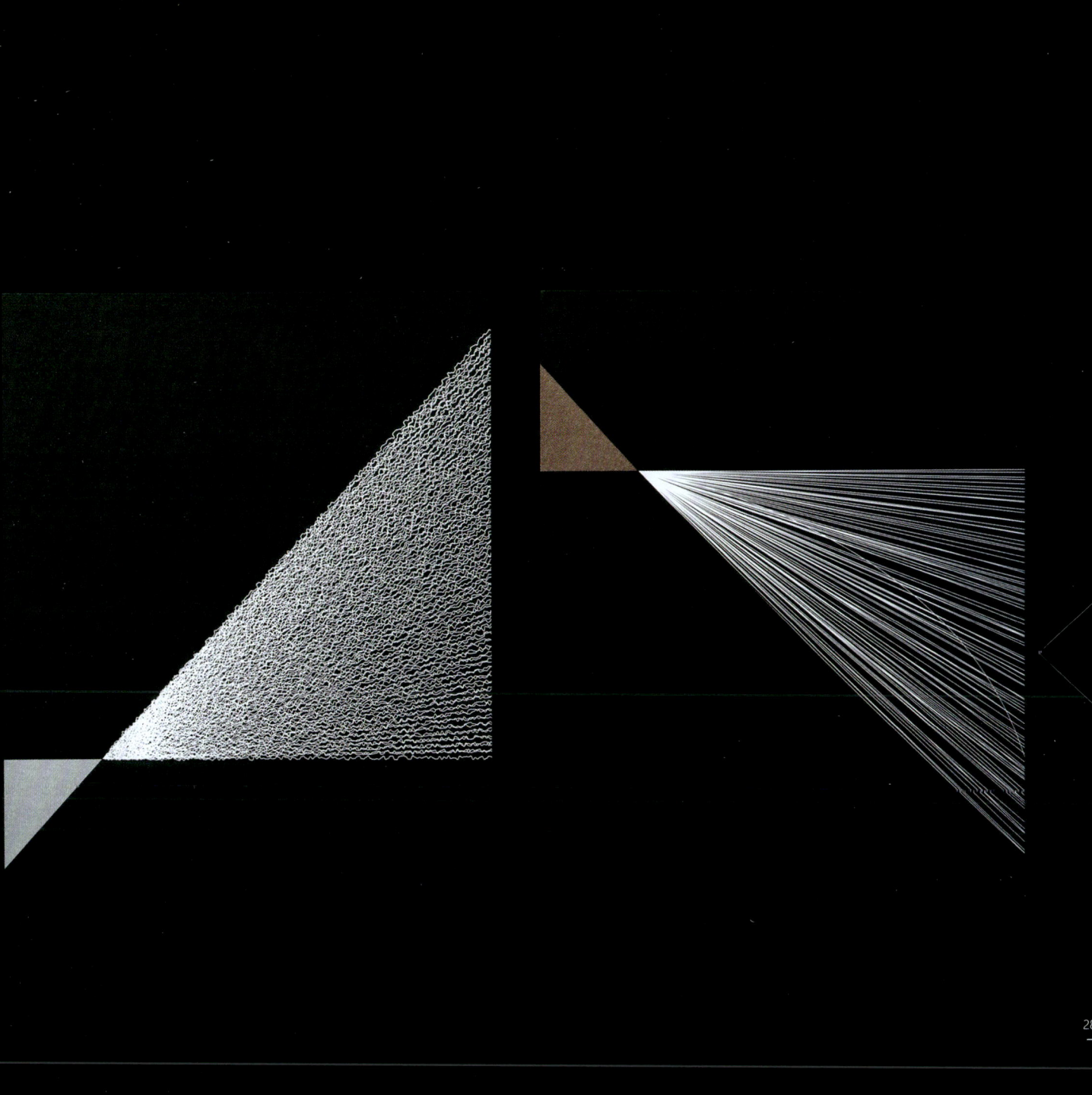

4th Greater China
Illustration Awards

Design Agency: Toby Ng Design
Creative Director: Toby Ng
Designer: Toby Ng, Ronald Cheung
Country: Hong Kong, China

The 4th
Greater China
Illustration
Awards

第四屆中華區插畫獎

Presentation Ceremony
頒獎典禮

2016.04.15
Friday 星期五

Atrium, Innocentre
72 Tat Chee Avenue, Kowloon Tong
九龍塘達之路72號創新中心中庭

Roving Shows
巡迴作品展

1st Show 第一場

2016.04.15–18

Chamber 2, Innocentre
72 Tat Chee Avenue, Kowloon Tong
九龍塘達之路72號創新中心2號展廳

2nd Show 第二場

2016.05.16–06.15

Exhibition Area, 5/F, Youth Square
238 Chai Wan Road, Chai Wan
香港柴灣道238號青年廣場5樓展覽區

3rd Show 第三場

2016.06.20–26

Exhibition Gallery, 1/3
Core C, Cyberport 3
數碼港三座C座3樓展覽廊

4th Show 第四場

2016.07.28–08.05

Gallery A
Jockey Club Innovation Tower, PolyU
香港理工大學賽馬會創新樓展覽廳A

5th Show 第五場

The details of the 5th show will
be announced, please stay tuned
for updates on our website
即將公佈詳情，請留意網站消息

Enquiry 查詢

Hong Kong Productivity Council
香港生產力促進局

Mr. Leung 梁先生
addisonleung@hkpc.org
+852 2788 5764

For more details 詳情請瀏覽
www.gciawards.org

Designed by Toby Ng Design

The 4th
Greater China
Illustration
Awards
第四屆中華區插畫獎

The 4th
Greater China
Illustration
Awards
第四屆中華區插畫獎

Presentation
Ceremony
頒獎典禮

15.4.2016

4th Greater China
Illustration Awards

Design Agency: Toby Ng Design
Creative Director: Toby Ng
Designer: Toby Ng, Ronald Cheung
Country: Hong Kong, China

4th Greater China
Illustration Awards

Design Agency: Toby Ng Design
Creative Director: Toby Ng
Designer: Toby Ng, Ronald Cheung
Country: Hong Kong, China

評語 Comment

Mr. Steve SIMPSON

我認為這件作品真的非常出色，在很多方面都相當出色，技巧、構圖、技巧、戲劇、故事、用色。年輕本身就是美好的事物，祝好運。

I thought this collection of work was absolutely wonderful. It works on many levels - technique, composition, story, color and there is also a little humor. Young here is a beautiful thing, good luck.

創作理念 Concept

長輪專輯Blur相隔7年生
於2015年推出最新大碟
The Magic Whip（英式 魔魔）
邀請香港漫畫家江記（KongKee）
為之創作 一本漫畫
在中讓城旅們將香港江記的故事
描述，在記的創作之靈感來
香港既既統也非未
既傳統最也將以非古亦有集

In 2015, London band Blur released their new album The Magic Whip after a ten-year hiatus. Hong Kong comics artist KongKee was invited to create a comic book that tells how Hong Kong became the tour for Blur. KongKee's work often depicts the contradictions in Hong Kong, where the traditional meets the avant-garde and the old meets the futuristic.

The Pavilia Hill

Design Agency: Toby Ng Design
Creative Director: Toby Ng
Designer: Toby Ng, Ronald Cheung
Country: Hong Kong, China

Client: New World Development

The Pavilia Hill is a luxury bespoke residence in the heart of Hong Kong and curated by Cultural Entrepreneur Adrian Cheng under New World Development's The Artisanal Movement.
The design pays tribute to nature and artisanship. Its interior and landscape designs are all based on Wabi-Sabi, a Japanese aesthetic and worldview centred on the acceptance of transience and imperfection.
Based on the principles of Wabi-Sabi, we designed a visceral and texturally rich book to reflect the serenity of the main feature of this residence, the Tranquil Zen gardens by Japanese Zen priest and landscape architect Shunmyo Masuno.
A raw stone texture was chosen for the book's hard cover, to resemble the special stone sculptures' sublime presence in The Pavilia Hill. In addition, by deploying various printing methods in combination with a selection of 10 types of texturally rich fancy paper, the final effect created a striking visual impact and sensual experience for readers of the book.

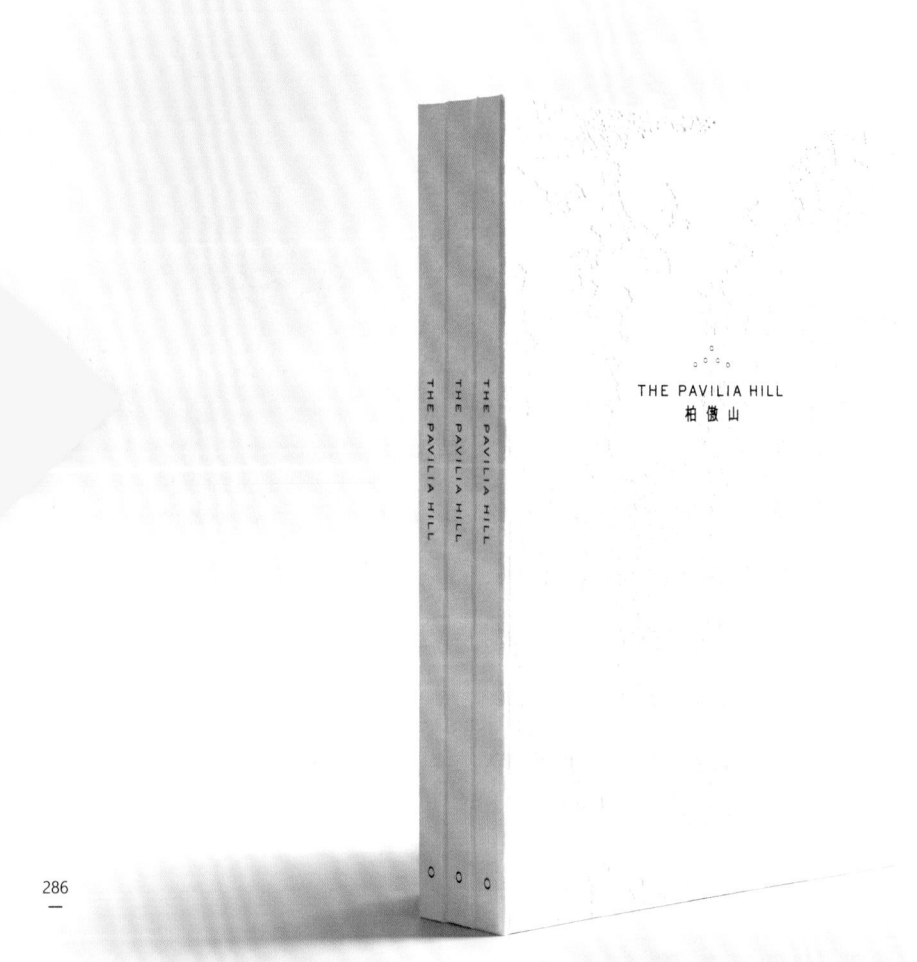

THE PAVILIA HILL
柏傲山

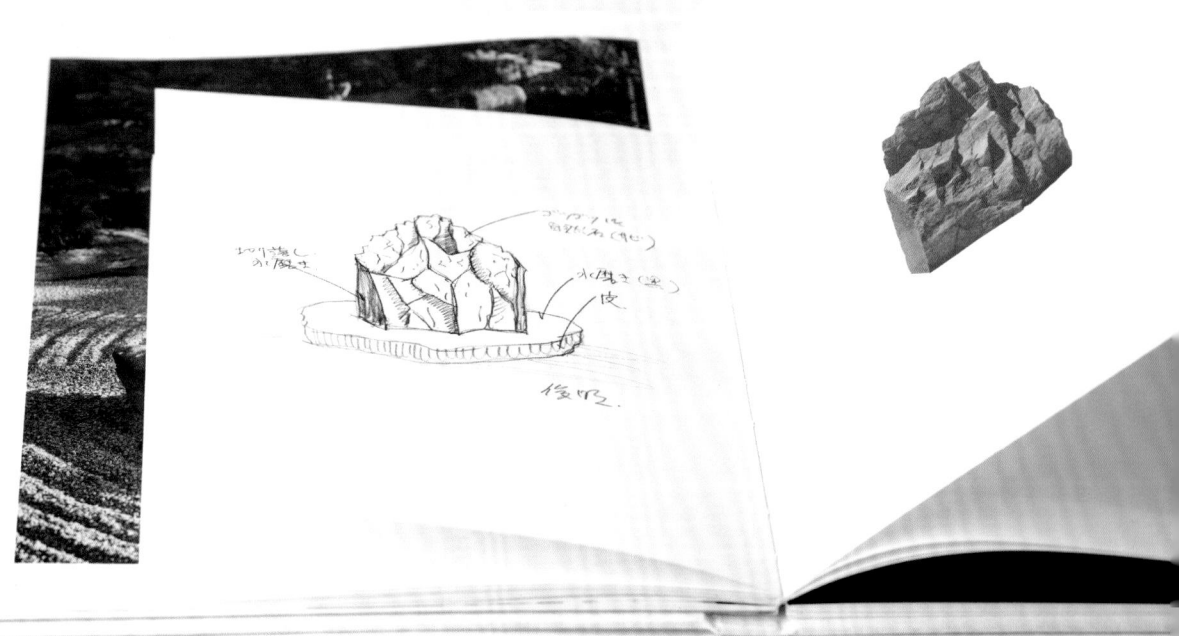

The Pavilia Hill

Design Agency: Toby Ng Design
Creative Director: Toby Ng
Designer: Toby Ng, Ronald Cheung
Country: Hong Kong, China

289

SEEKING – ZEN GARDEN

山 *Mountain*

水 *Water*

有 *Existence*

清 *Purity*

音 *Sound*

I've used natural materials that will age in their own original and beautiful ways.

Koichiro Ikebuchi's choice of natural
oak wood flooring provides a soothing texture
and a grain pattern that graces the sole
of your feet.

It is a reminder of the human qualities that
THE PAVILIA HILL stands for.

At the Heated Pool and the Pool Spa,
the reflective surface of the water glistens.

An abundance of natural light fills the
space, allowing the gold leaf decoration to
dance and shimmer in unison.

It is an artful play of light and shadow.

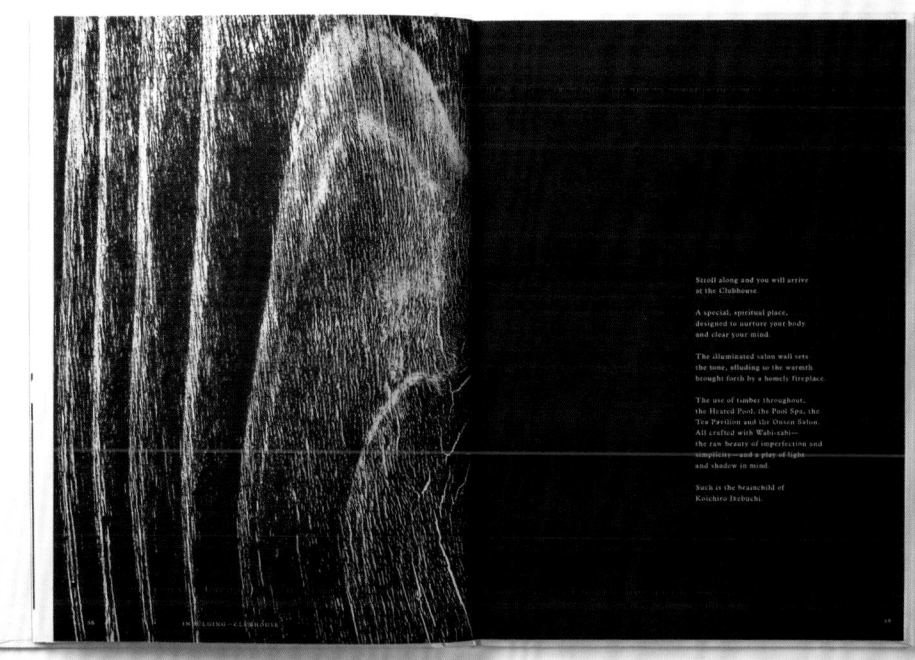

Stroll along and you will arrive
at the Clubhouse.

A special, spiritual place,
designed to nurture your body
and clear your mind.

The illuminated salon wall sets
the tone, alluding to the warmth
brought forth by a homely fireplace.

The use of timber throughout,
the Heated Pool, the Pool Spa, the
Tea Pavilion and the Onsen Salon.
All crafted with Wabi-sabi—
the raw beauty of imperfection and
simplicity—and a play of light
and shadow in mind.

Such is the brainchild of
Koichiro Ikebuchi.

Catching Moonbeams

Design Agency: Toby Ng Design
Creative Director: Toby Ng
Designer: Toby Ng, Fibi Kung
Country: Hong Kong, China

Client: Antalis Hong Kong

The light of the moon was chosen as a metaphor for Antalis paper printing effects project to promote their black, grey and sliver paper. The project is presented in a set of two volumes within a specially designed moon-textured case. The whole set is designed to capture the concept of 'Catching Moonbeams', highlighting the ephemeral and illusory nature of light, darkness, colours. Its effects take the reader in the first volume, 'The Dark Side of the Moon', from black, a place where there is no reflection from the light of the sun, to the second volume, 'By the Light of the Silvery Moon', where the experience of light and silver are subtly illustrated.

'The Dark Side of the Moon' is an experiential journey – both visceral and texturally rich. As readers touch and feel the different paper textures and printing effects, they are taken step by step to the moon. Finally, with man's first step on the moon, the impossible becomes possible, the dream comes true through the prints and textures – we can touch the moon!
In the 2nd volume, 'By the Light of the Silvery Moon', we continue to catch moonbeams in a simple paper sample booklet showcasing Antalis' black to grey and silver papers.

CATCHING MOONBEAMS

293
—

Catching Moonbeams

Design Agency: Toby Ng Design
Creative Director: Toby Ng
Designer: Toby Ng, Hibi Kung
Country: Hong Kong, China

Catching Moonbeams

Design Agency: Toby Ng Design
Creative Director: Toby Ng
Designer: Toby Ng, Fibi Kung
Country: Hong Kong, China

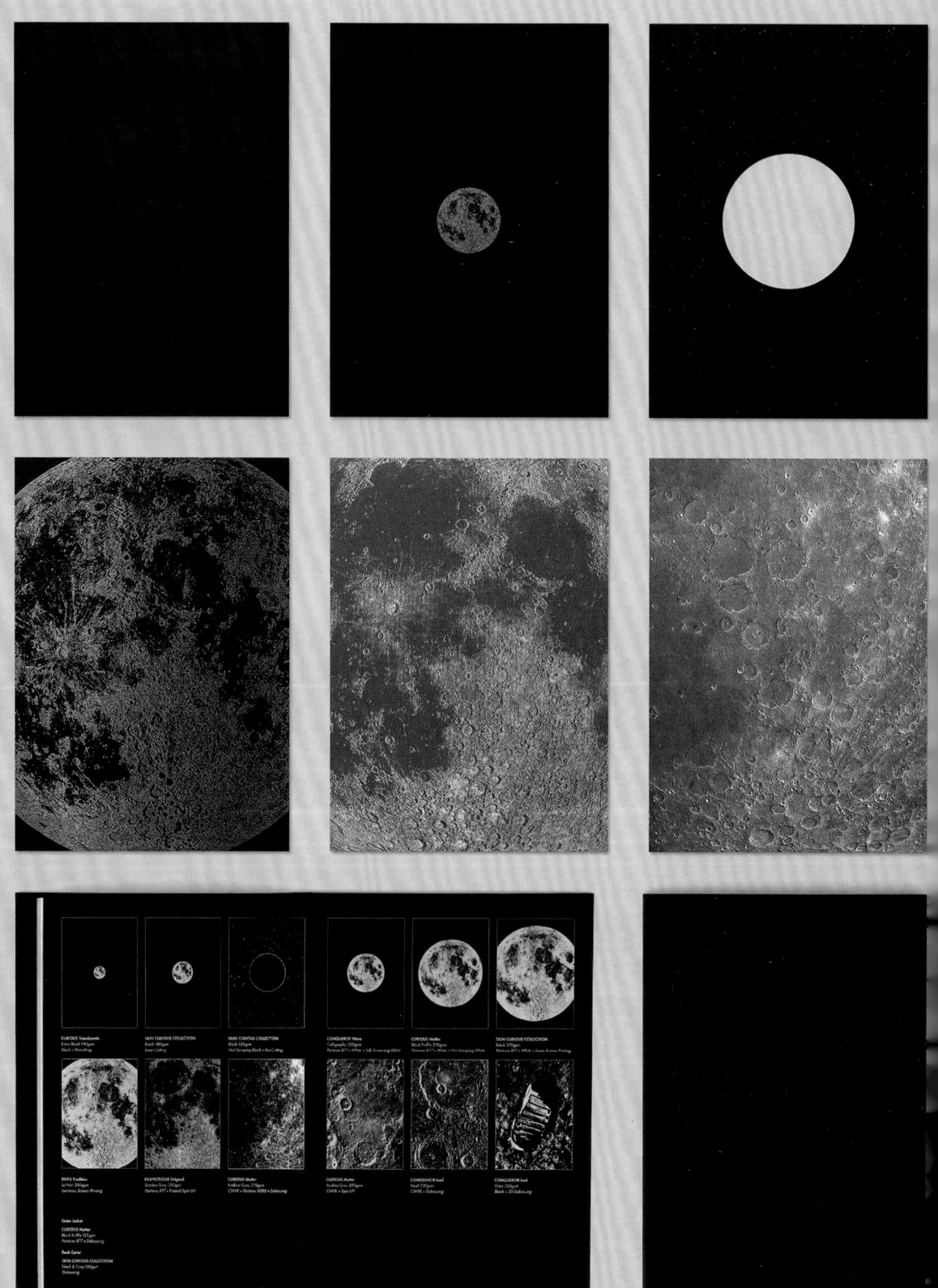

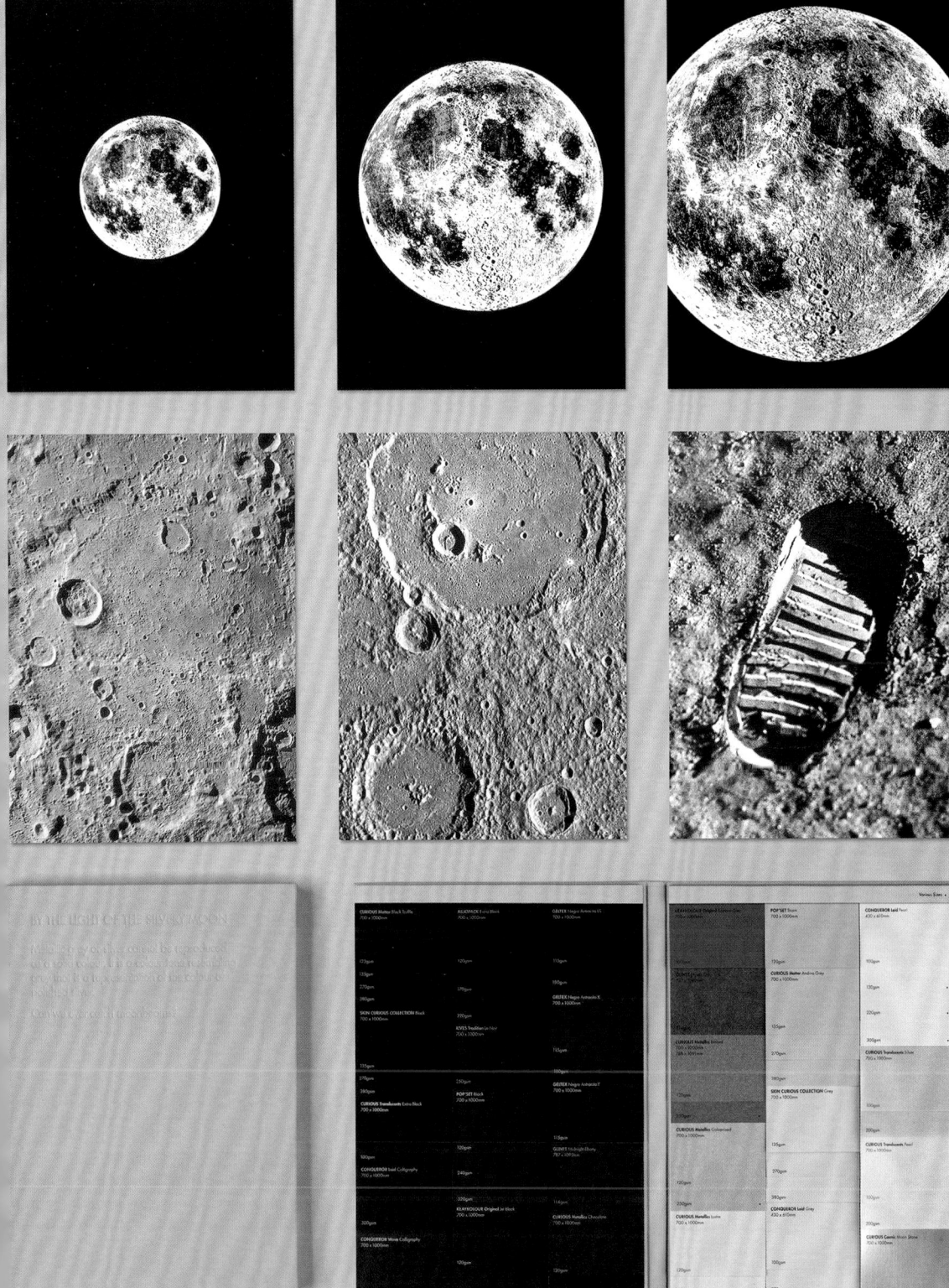

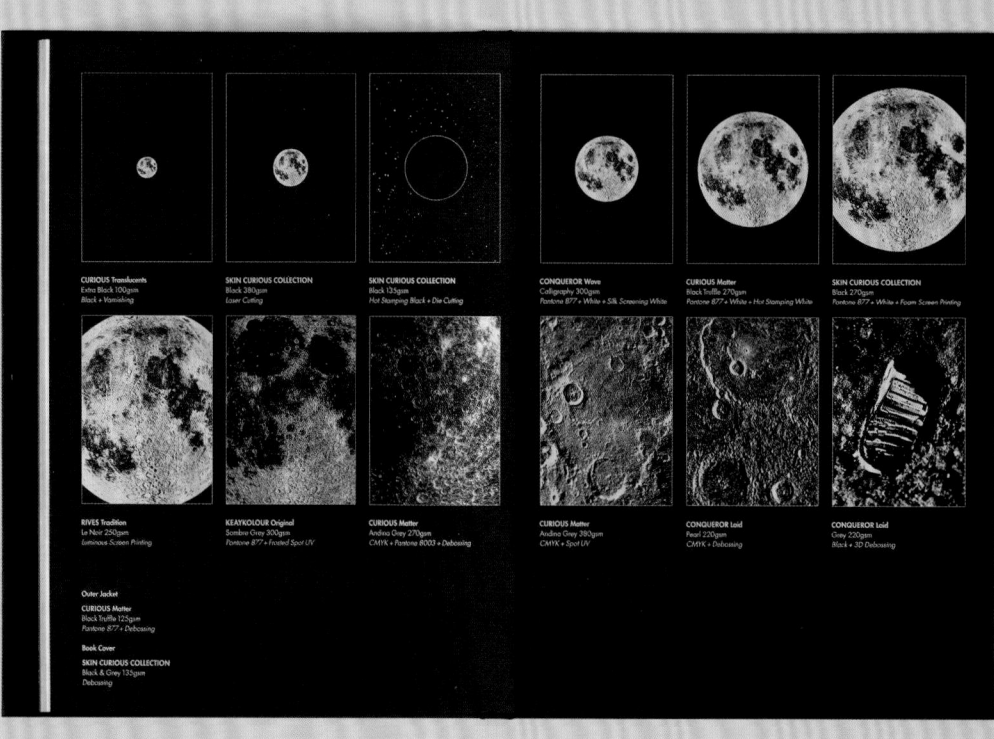

CURIOUS Translucents
Extra Black 100gsm
Black + Varnishing

SKIN CURIOUS COLLECTION
Black 380gsm
Laser Cutting

SKIN CURIOUS COLLECTION
Black 135gsm
Hot Stamping Black + Die Cutting

CONQUEROR Wove
Calligraphy 300gsm
Pantone 877 + White + Silk Screening White

CURIOUS Matter
Black Truffle 270gsm
Pantone 877 + White + Hot Stamping White

SKIN CURIOUS COLLECTION
Black 270gsm
Pantone 877 + White + Foam Screen Printing

RIVES Tradition
Le Noir 250gsm
Luminous Screen Printing

KEAYKOLOUR Original
Sombre Gray 300gsm
Pantone 877 + Frosted Spot UV

CURIOUS Matter
Andina Gray 270gsm
CMYK + Pantone 8003 + Debossing

CURIOUS Matter
Andina Gray 390gsm
CMYK + Spot UV

CONQUEROR Laid
Pearl 220gsm
CMYK + Debossing

CONQUEROR Laid
Grey 220gsm
Black + 3D Debossing

Outer Jacket
CURIOUS Matter
Black Truffle 125gsm
Pantone 877 + Debossing

Book Cover
SKIN CURIOUS COLLECTION
Black & Grey 135gsm
Debossing

Catching Moonbeams

Design Agency: Toby Ng Design
Creative Director: Toby Ng
Designer: Toby Ng, Fibi Kung
Country: Hong Kong, China

TYPEFACES ENDOWED WITH EXTRAORDINARY FEATURE

Designer: Yang Liu, Jianing Yuan
Design Agency: Y&Y
Country: China
Art Director: Jianing Yuan
Creative Director: Yang Liu
Photographer: Jianing Yuan

"Typefaces Endowed with Extraordinary Feature" is divided into two parts in English and Chinese, the both sides of the book are regarded as home page, one side is Chinese character and other one is English letter that offer new reading experience for readers. On the design of cover, we used cortical PU material with exquisite stamping pro-cess to have done perfect effect. The book has two versions, including red one and black one, particu-larly, for preventing soft cover from upwarping and damaging in process of carry, we thread rubber band through book as lace. What's more, spray color on fore-edge bring into correspondence with color, whole book and rubber band.

TAKE ME AWAY PLEASE. Package Design

Designer: Yang Liu, Jianing Yuan
Design Agency: Y&Y
Country: China
Art Director: Jianing Yuan
Creative Director: Yang Liu
Photographer: Jianing Yuan

302

The inspiration derives from labeling meat products, and in light of it, we made the redesign on label of product. As you see, original information on label has been replaced with all kinds of one for the book, and for highlight real effect, the part of commodity has been processed with UV technology like preservative film used as package of the goods in shop. What's more, in order to correspond to the theme, fore-edge of the book is processed by spray color. It's worth noting that, on the aspect of binding forms, we choose paperback and book jacket instead of too complicated technique, since let the book become succinct and clear, like meat packing on sale in supermarket, is what we pursued.
(The cover picture comes from Albert Martinez, Marc Navarro.)

TAKE ME AWAY PLEASE 2

TAKE ME AWAY PLEASE 2
Chocolate, Perfume, Cheese, Coffee,Butter, Juice, Milk, Flour, Bacon, Spices, Soap, Cream, Jewelry, Umbrellas, Tea, Bread, Candy, Oil......
ISBN 978-988-77705-5-8
DESIGNERBOOKS
TAKE ME AWAY PLEASE

TAKE ME AWAY PLEASE. 2
Package Design

Designer: Jingqi Han
Design Agency: Y&Y
Country: China
Art Director: Jianing Yuan
Creative Director: Yang Liu
Photographer: Jianing Yuan

The combination of rose pink with chocolate is featured as the book on deign. As you go through the whole cover, you will find that the main color of the book is romantic rose pink, appearance of a picture is divided by gold geometric graphics and lines, the visual effect characterized by sweet packaging is represented with the image of chocolate, and with the integration of UV and gilding, the whole style appears to be delicacy and flexible. Furthermore, with edge processing of fore-edge on the book, it's obvious that consumers' eyesight is easily attracted by its texture, which leads them to "take it away".

DEEP SPACE IN DARK TONE

Designer: Qinghong Sun
Design Agency: Y&Y
Country: China
Art Director: Jianing Yuan
Creative Director: Yang Liu
Photographer: Jianing Yuan

What "Deep Space in Dark Tone" shows to you is the application of dark one in space design. On the whole, in order to echo with unique temperament of dark space in content, we take advantage of dark black to express the cover of book. Through the combination between graphics, moreover, readers can clear all walks of life involved in various works, and with the exquisite gilding technology, elegant visual sense has also become obvious in readers' eyes. In particular, black piping design makes an integration of various tones of the book, and this comfortable touch will have made readers have good reading experience.

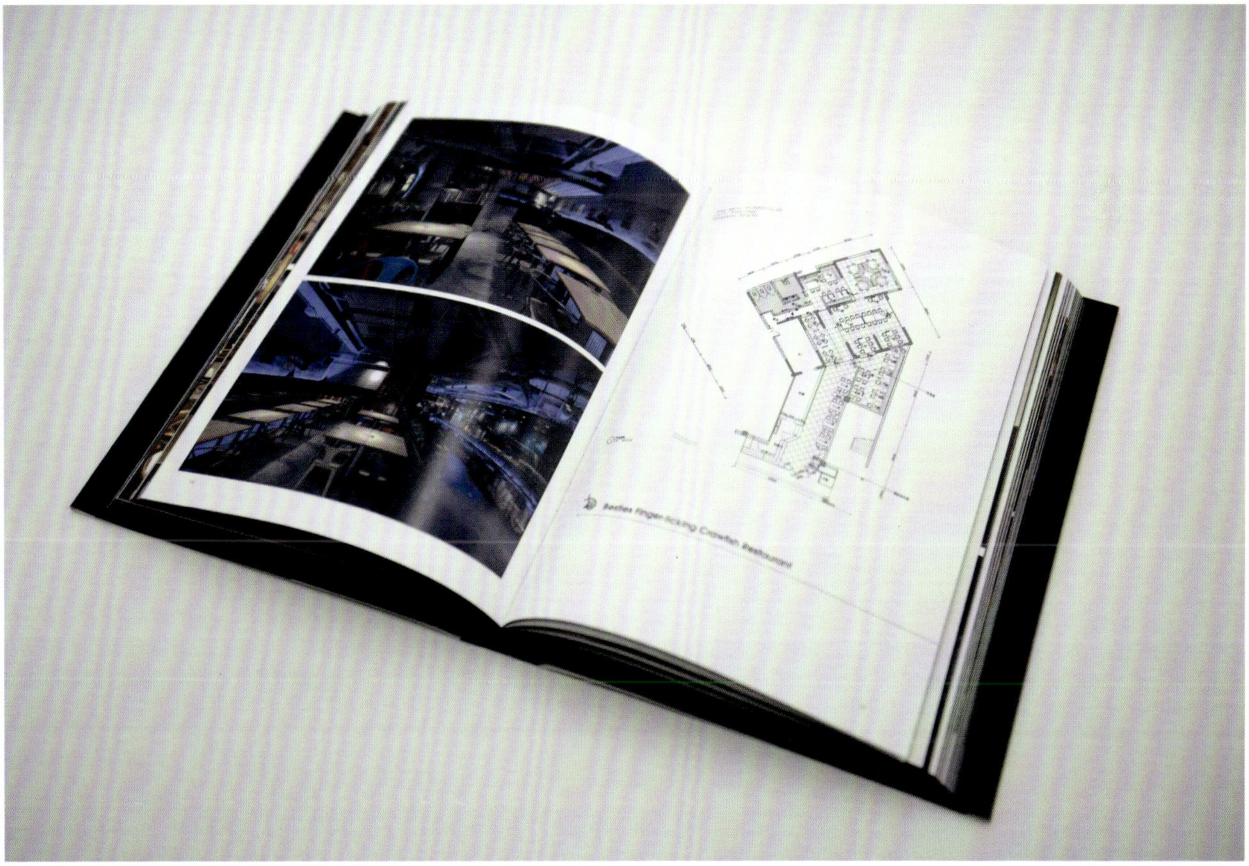

In and between boxes: Atelier Peter Fong

MY WORLD MY ORIGINALITY 4

Designer: Qinghong Sun
Design Agency: Y&Y
Country: China
Art Director: Jianing Yuan
Creative Director: Yang Liu
Photographer: Jianing Yuan

The book collects a range of case, from many designers around world, related to classic commercial space, in which you have an opportunity to appreciate a variety of personality shops in all walks of life. As you see, we make corresponding icon design for all kinds of shop so that readers are able to get to know property of different shop. More interesting, the whole graphic of shop on the cover is composed by the way of building like toy bricks. Simultaneously, your eyesight, in vast ocean of books, will have been attracted by fluorescent orange cover with hot laser gold.

SUPER HAND MADE CRAET 2

Designer: Heng Zhang
Design Agency: Y&Y
Country: China
Art Director: Jianing Yuan
Creative Director: Yang Liu
Photographer: Jianing Yuan

"Super Hand Made Craft 2" assembled a series of outstanding works in the hands of manual creators around the world, based on the it, the design of this book is more prone to interesting through highlight the theme of hand-made. As you see, this vivid and interesting stereo scene was created by carving the name of the book characterized by third dimension, and the cover of which has auxiliary foil made by some tools related to hand-made, such as texture background of linen as well as tape. Simultaneously, the design on bar code has also filled with elements catering to the theme of book. On craft, we made use of locking wire on hardcover and UV on text which increase its layered.

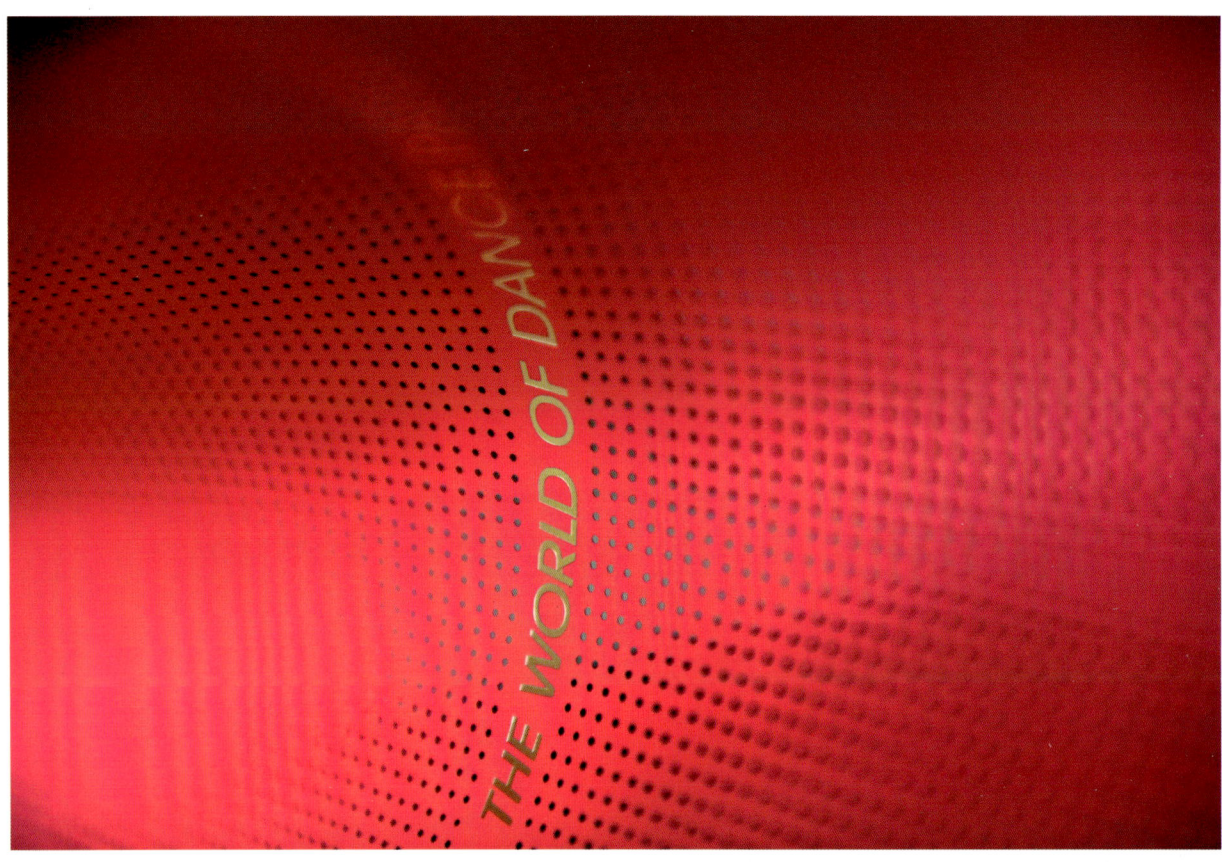

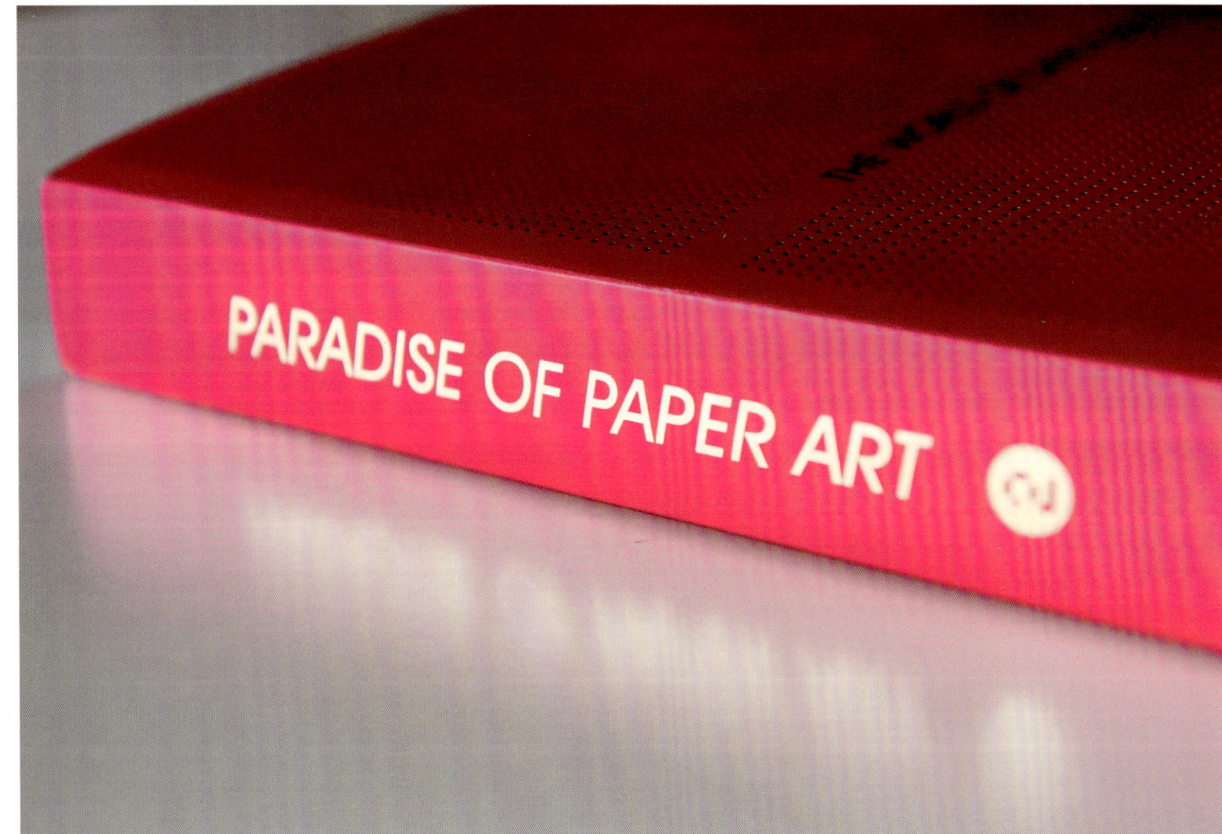

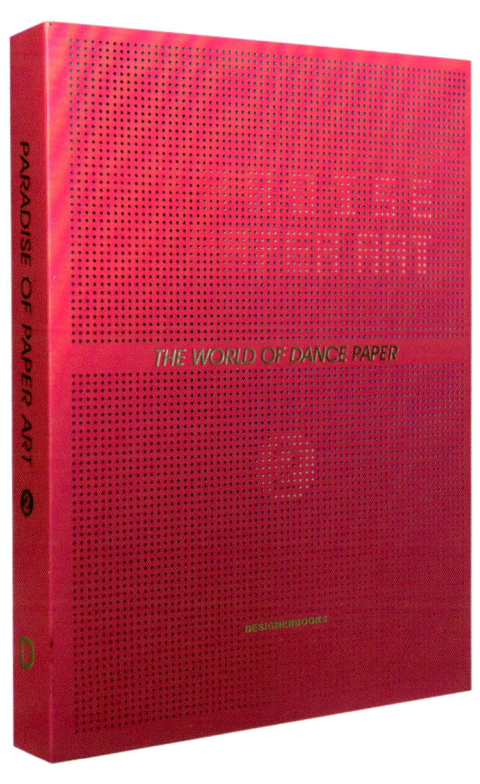

PARADISE OF PAPER ART 2
THE WORLD OF DANCE PAPER

Designer: Jianing Yuan, Yang Liu
Design Agency: Y&Y
Country: China
Art Director: Jianing Yuan
Creative Director: Yang Liu
Photographer: Jianing Yuan

On the whole, the book jacket is characterized by dazzling rose red, while inside cover is followed in the main color of series one and kept end-to-end arrangement by sequential process. Under laser engraving, the book jacket presents several regular holes, and title on the cover can be penetrated through them. Texts on the book jacket, moreover, highlight its theme as well with gilding and soft color.

Book about the Book

Designer: Tamás MARCELL
Design Agency: Marcell Studio
Creative Director: Tamás MARCELL
Country: Hungary
Photographer: István ORAVECZ

Client: Moholy-Nagy University of Art and Design Budapest. Doctoral School

ABSTRACT In my disserta I set out to answer the question of what kind of changes, problems, novel theoretical and conceptual approaches are presented by the spread of digital technology in design graphics, especially in the field of book design. How will the toolbox of artistic expression and presentation, developed over many centuries within the profession, be transformed by the disappearance of analogue technology? My chosen theme is centred on the book, which in universal cultural history not only represents a medium for the imparting of knowledge and beliefs, but has also been the most defining field of graphics throughout the centuries-long history of graphic design. In my analysis, I studied how the book, both as a vehicle for content and as a visual platform, has been transformed in the light of technology. My project reflects, in the form of physical and virtual presence, on the processes described below, and is entitled ORIGO. The title is a symbolic reference to shi_ing and change. The starting point marking out new directions. Although the process of virtualisation is not a single, distinct moment in time, in my view this is certainly a defining period in the several-thousand-year history of the book, during which it loses all its unique characteristics. Its spatiality, function, tactility and substance. My aim was to visually present two books that impart identical content, namely the work by Imre Kner entitled Könyv a könyről (Book about the Book). As a consequence of the special forms of presentation, which at times contradict and at others corroborate each other, they reflect on each other's strengths or weaknesses. They serve to demonstrate the fundamental similarities and differences between virtual and corporeal (digital/online) content in terms of presentation, functionality and graphic design.

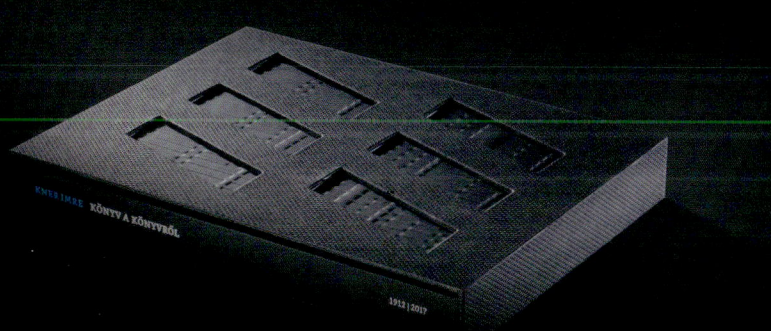

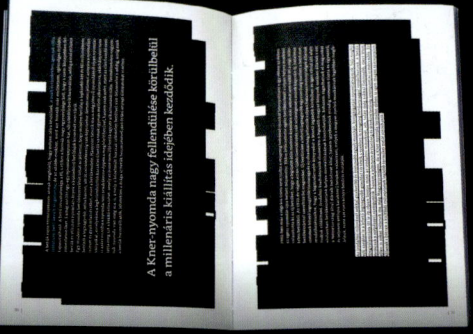

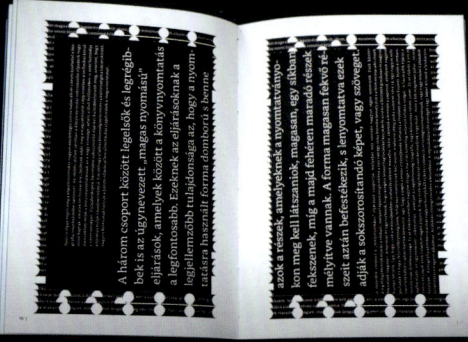

Book about the Book

Designer: Tamás MARCELL
Design Agency: Marcell Studio
Creative Director: Tamás MARCELL
Country: Hungary
Photographer: István ORAVECZ

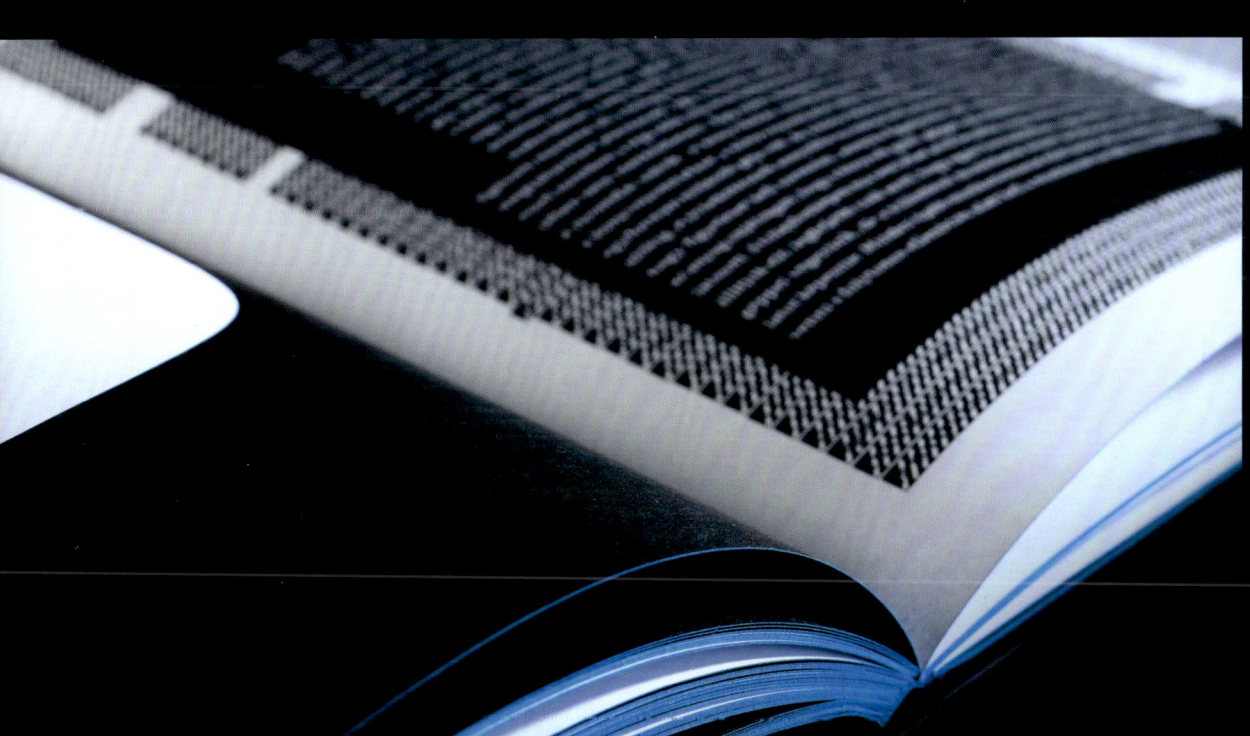

BE_MYSELF, ART
BOOK PORTFOLIO

Designer: Wu, Mu-Chang & Yang, Shi-Ching
Design Agency: Freelance
Country: Taiwan, China
Photographer: Wu, Mu-Chang

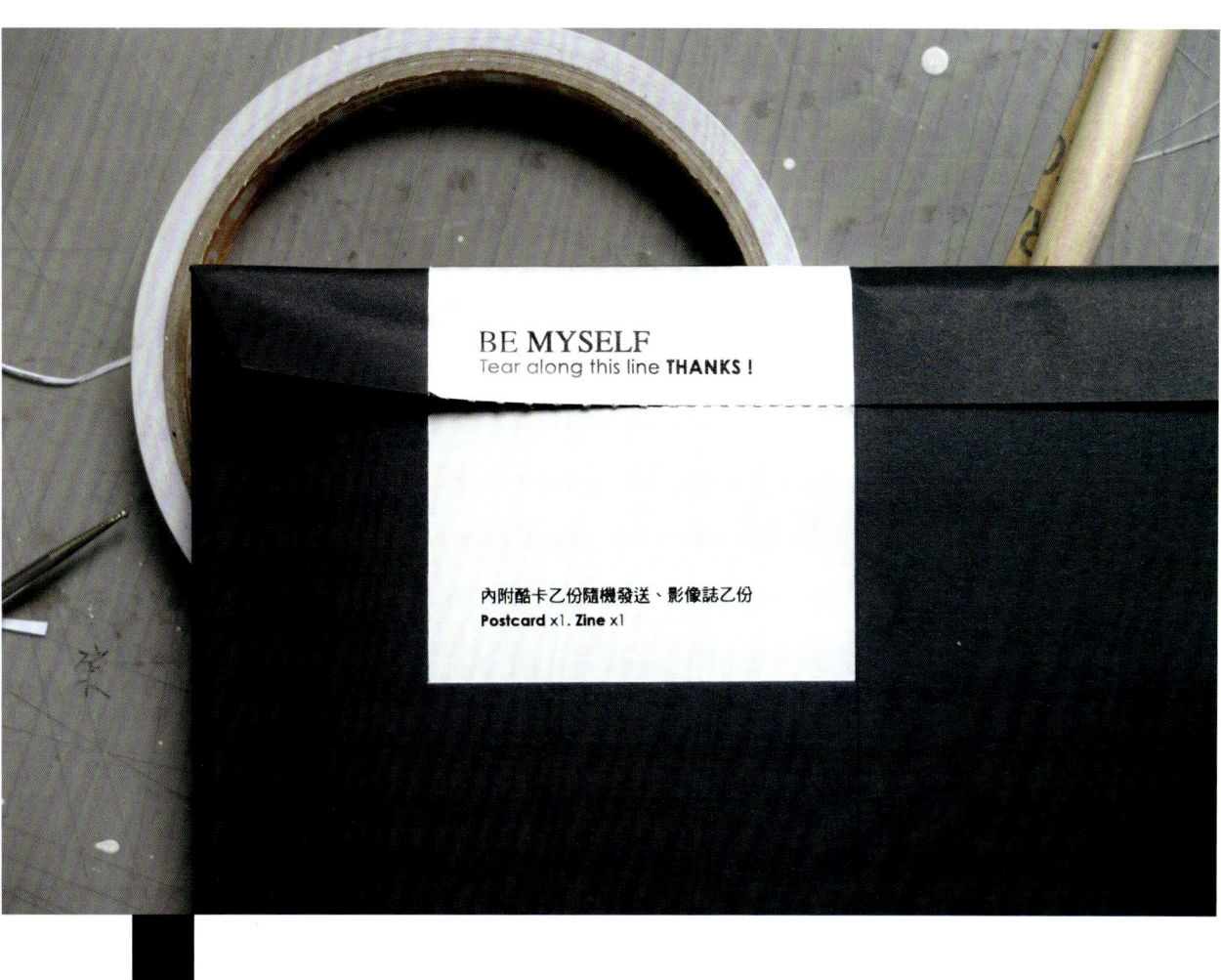

BE_MYSELF, ART
BOOK PORTFOLIO

Designer: Wu, Mu-Chang & Yang, Shi-Ching
Design Agency: Freelance
Country: Taiwan, China
Photographer: Wu, Mu-Chang

Client: K.S.U-Mixed Media Studio
Others: Designer: Liou,Zih-Yu; Dai,Yi-Jing; Shu,Bo-Yen

Be My Self_ Art Book is a Portfolio in the form of a zine without any complicated binding methods. Instead, Murphy Wu emphasizes the details of the packaging method. It probably is a more complicated and more wasted way of package method than usual. However, their team prefers the buyer will value the package and the book inside and to allow who touch it for the first time could intensely sence the tension of visual and the stimulation on their fingertips.

BE_MYSELF, ART
BOOK PORTFOLIO

Designer: Wu, Mu-Chang & Yang, Shi-Ching
Design Agency: Freelance
Country: Taiwan, China
Photographer: Wu, Mu-Chang

Book design and visual identity of Beijing Xuannan Culture Museum

Designer: Dongming Tian, Chen Xing, Xiang Li
Design agency: Stones Design
Art Director: Dongming Tian
Country: China
Photographer: He Li, Jiang Bian

Client: Beijing Xuannan Culture Museum
Other: The Red Dot Award Communication Design

Beijing Xuannan Culture Museum, founded in the 400-year history of Changchun Temple in the Ming dynasty, is the epitome of the history and culture of the south of Beijing. The overall design and editing of the Beijing Xuanan Culture Museum, in accordance with the order of time and space, leading readers to "push" the mountain gate, enter the museum, and visiting the exhibition halls. The overall design style is striving to integrate Chinese traditional culture and modern sense. It uses a bright red color throughout the long run, and symbolizes some traditional graphics. The book uses a variety of paper and printing technology, such as, using rice paper to print the manuscript which was written by Li Dazhao in prison, collecting ancient books and rare books, etc. Not only has the sense of history, but also enriches the reader's visual and tactile experience. The cover adopts the inner pages of the ancient books and rare books and map it according to the grid. The essence of Chinese cultural history is conveyed by Chinese characters. The shell (letter box) adopts the inclined cut, both sides of the spine have bronzing titles. The name can be found if leave it on the bookshelf casually. Protection of books is easier for readers to read and receive.
The overall visual system uses the concept of book covers, carrying out the graphical characters all the time. The symbol is transformed by the three characters 'Xuan, Nan, Bo'.

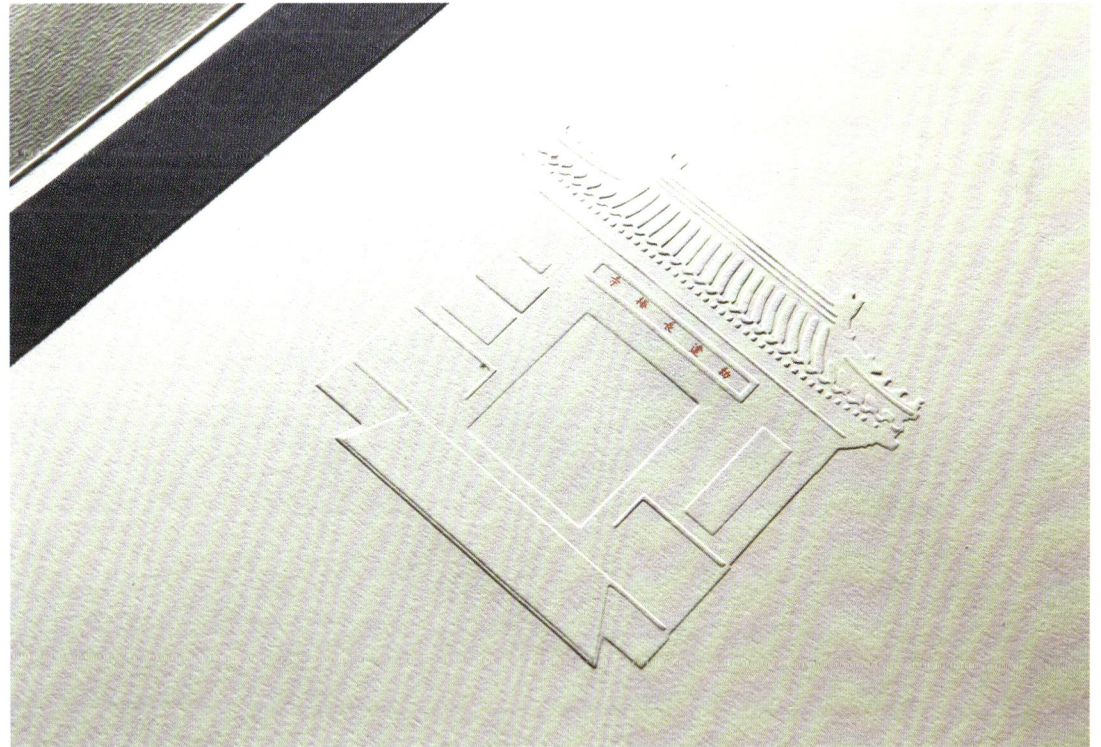

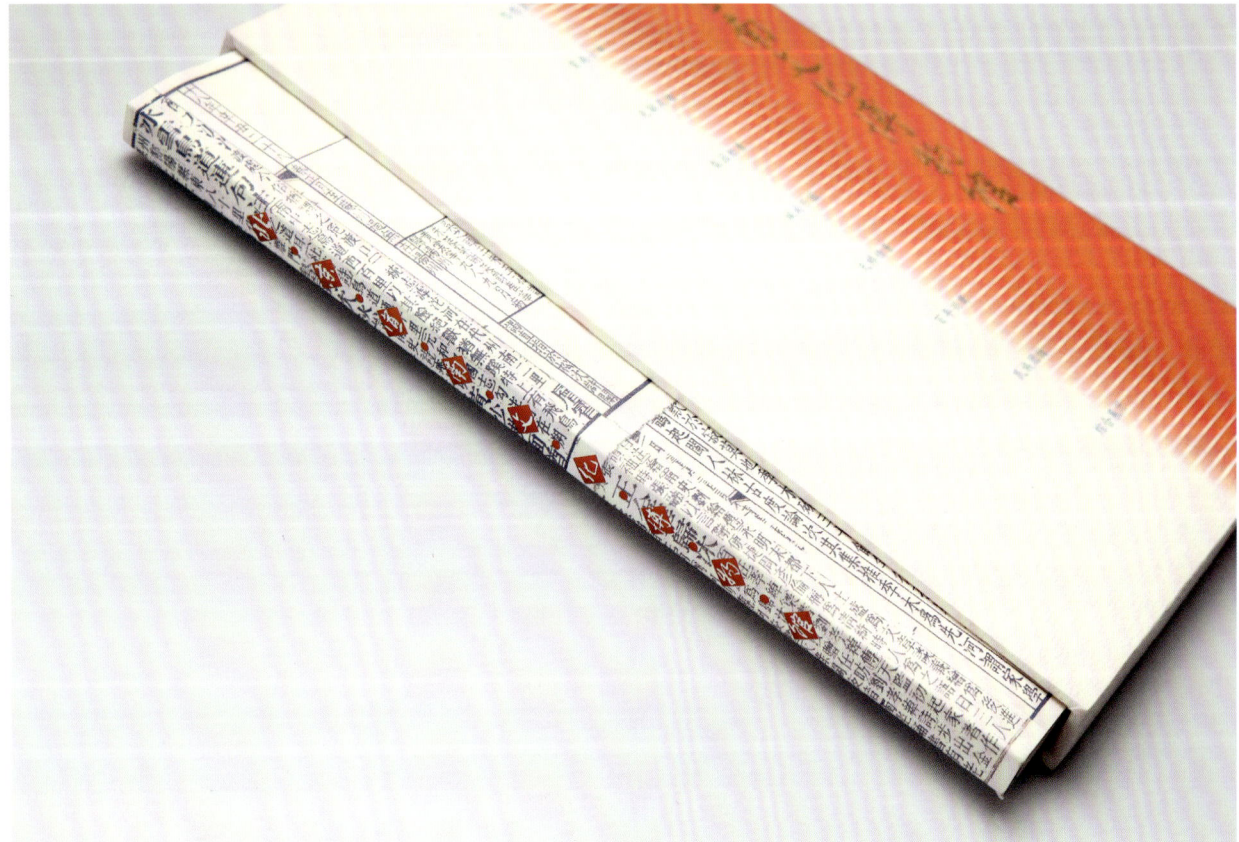

Book design and visual identity of Beijing Xuannan Culture Museum

Designer: Dongming Tian, Chen Xing, Xiang Li
Design agency: Stones Design
Art Director: Dongming Tian
Country: China
Photographer: He Li, Jiang Bian

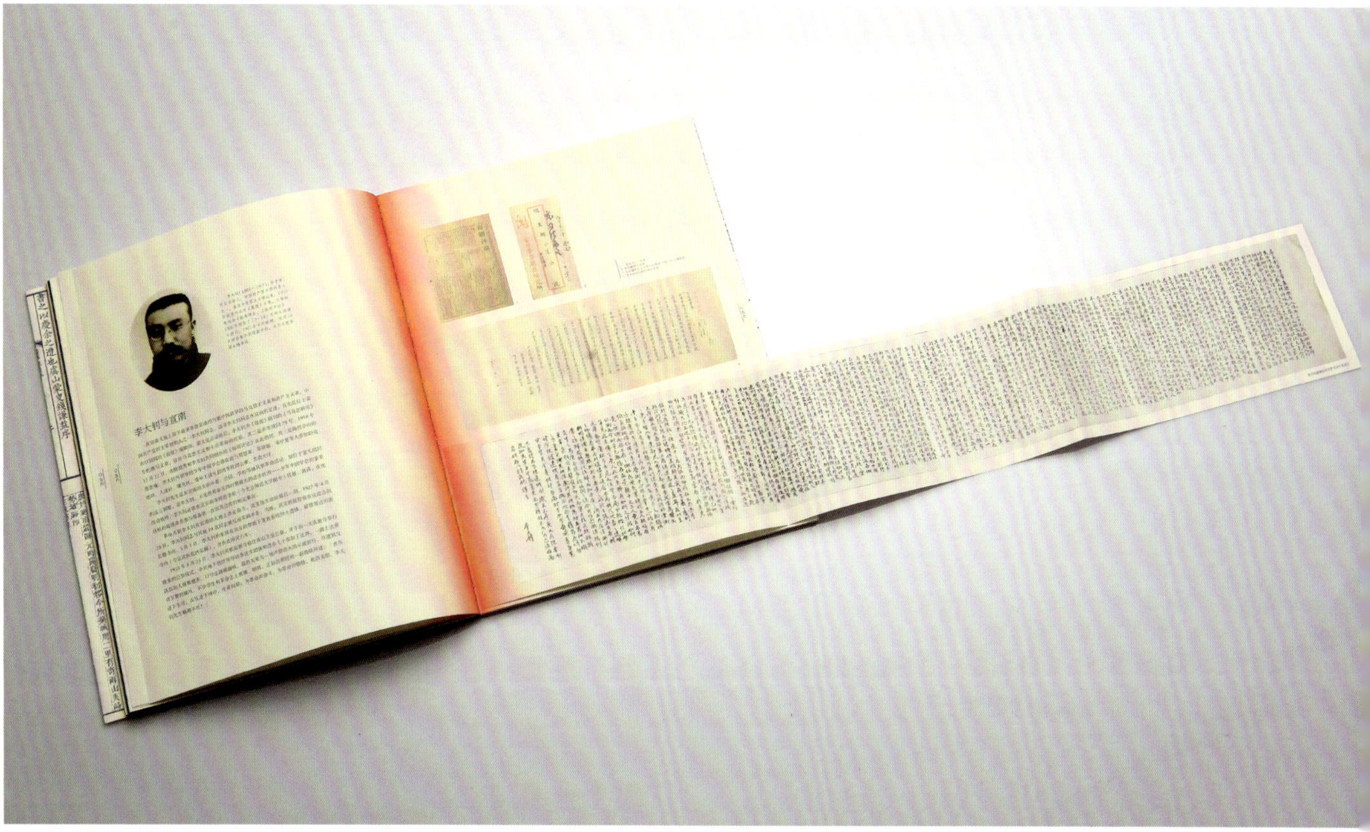

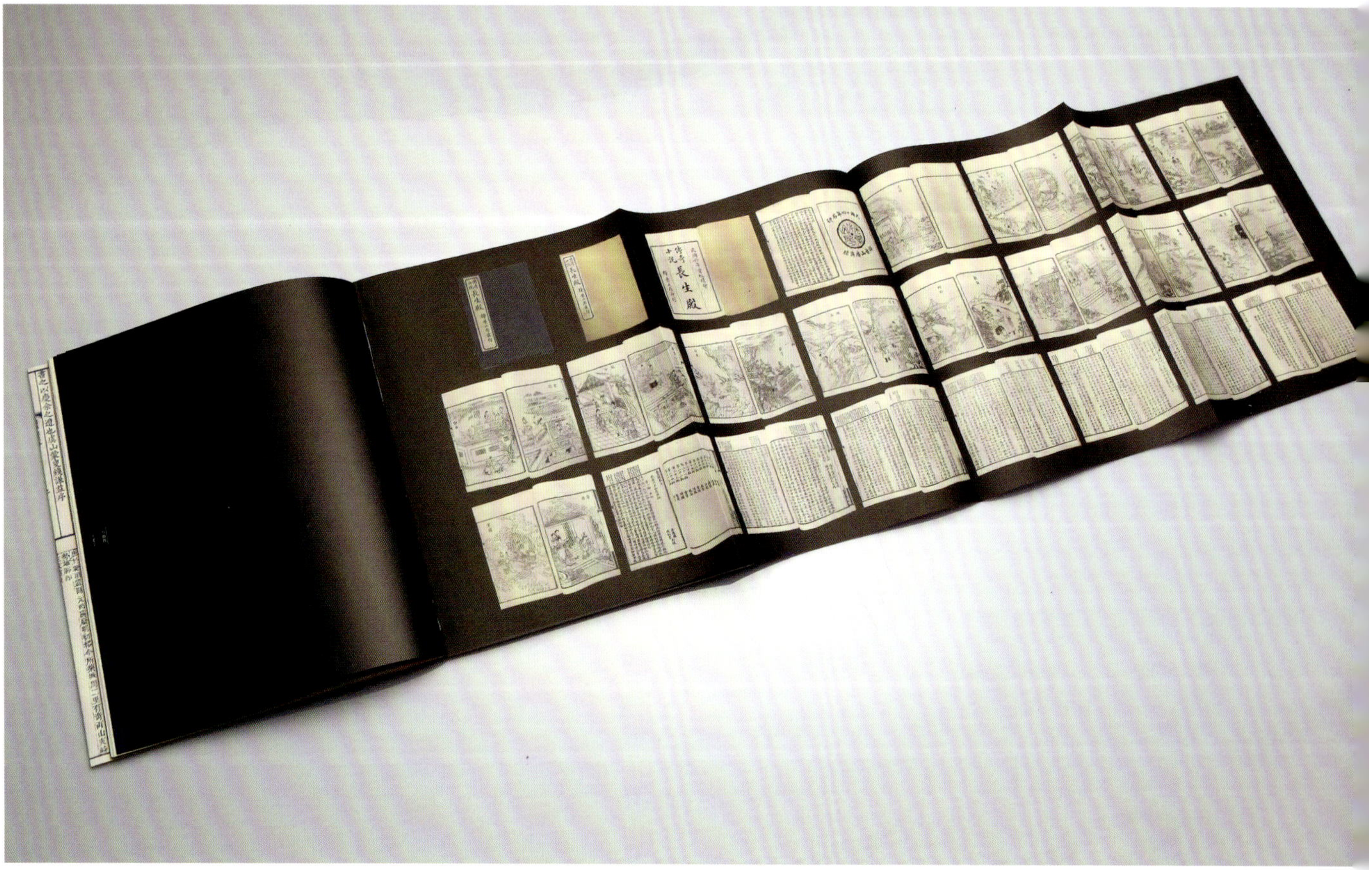

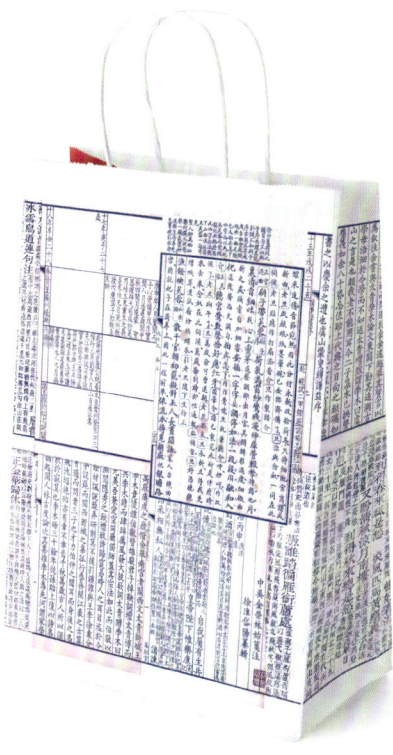

Book design and visual identity of Beijing Xuannan Culture Museum

Designer: Dongming Tian, Chen Xing, Xiang Li
Design agency: Stones Design
Art Director: Dongming Tian
Country: China
Photographer: He Li, Jiang Bian

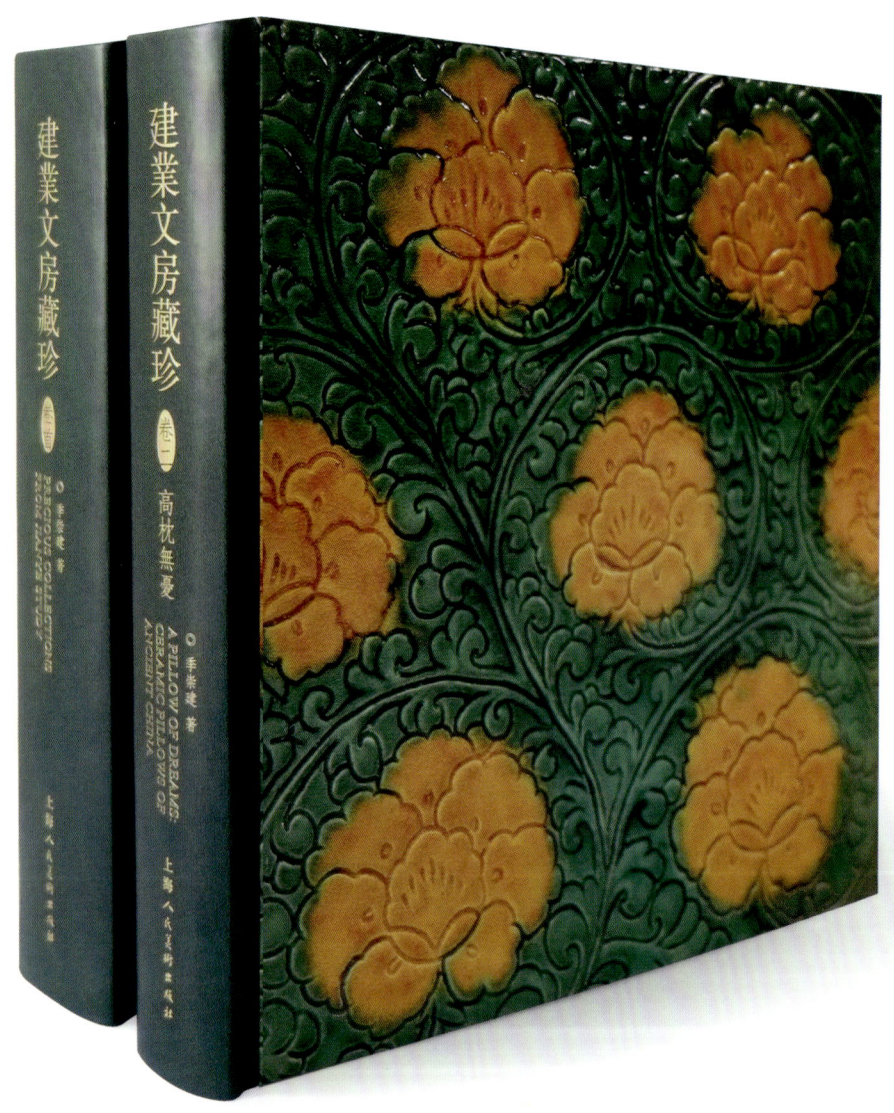

There are two volumes in the series of PRECIOUS COLLECTIONS FROM JIANYE STUDY producted by Shanghai Chongyuan Auction Co.,LTD:

PRECIOUS COLLECTIONS FROM JIANYE STUDY
A PILLOW OF DREAMS:CRRAMIC PILLOWS OF ANCIENT CHINA

Designer: Chenxue Zhao
Country: China

The Publisher: Shanghai People's Fine Arts Publishing House
Printing Company: Artron(Shanghai)Color Printing Co.,LTD.
Size: 290 × 290 mm

The series of books and pictures vividly illustrate the beauty of ancient Chinese traditional art. The collection includes sculptures, bronze, ceramics, jade objects and more than 100 pieces of ancient Chinese artworks. The porcelain pillow category is a separate book. It is a collection of porcelain pillow works from the Jin dynasty to the Song dynasty, mainly composed of characters, animals and flowers and birds. With its unique perspective and vivid annotations, it shows the exquisite craftsmanship of ancient Chinese people, as well as the art of calligraphy, painting and so on.

Painting process: Hardfaced hardcover is used for book binding design, the cover and the back cover of the Buddha and the porcelain pillow local pattern use full plate concave and convex technology which make the book totally presents almost the realistic texture of the reducer itself. The spine of the book is decorated with gold and gilding.

There are two volumes in the series of PRECIOUS COLLECTIONS FROM JIANYE STUDY producted by Shanghai Chongyuan Auction Co.,LTD:

PRECIOUS COLLECTIONS FROM JIANYE STUDY
A PILLOW OF DREAMS:CRRAMIC PILLOWS OF ANCIENT CHINA

Designer: Chenxue Zhao
Country: China

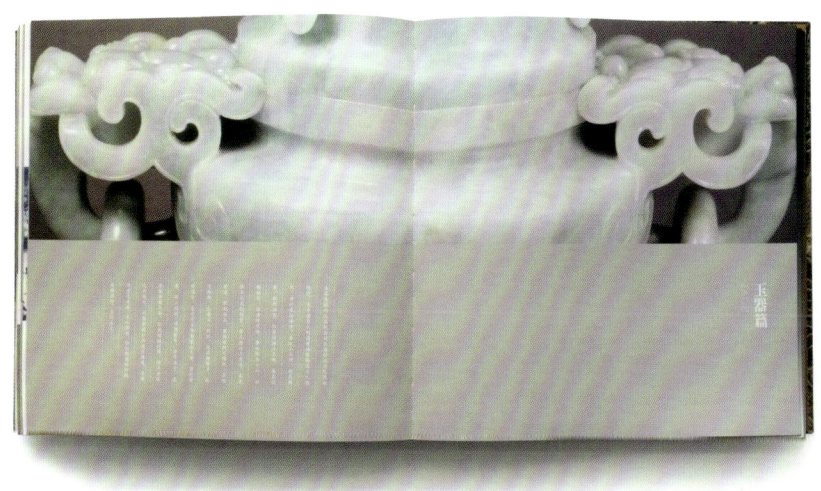

There are two volumes in the series of PRECIOUS COLLECTIONS FROM JIANYE STUDY producted by Shanghai Chongyuan Auction Co.,LTD:

PRECIOUS COLLECTIONS FROM JIANYE STUDY
A PILLOW OF DREAMS:CRRAMIC PILLOWS OF ANCIENT CHINA

Designer: Chenxue Zhao
Country: China

Monk Hanmo from Eastern Fujian

Designer: Hanxian Huang
Design agency: Wisdom Beijing International Cultural Development Co.,LTD.
Country: China

Client: Buddhist Association of Fuan City

Buddhist texts are simple and concise which make readers happy and make the hearts full of light. The first page of the book seems to feel the light in the heart, the whole book reveals a clean and pure design style.

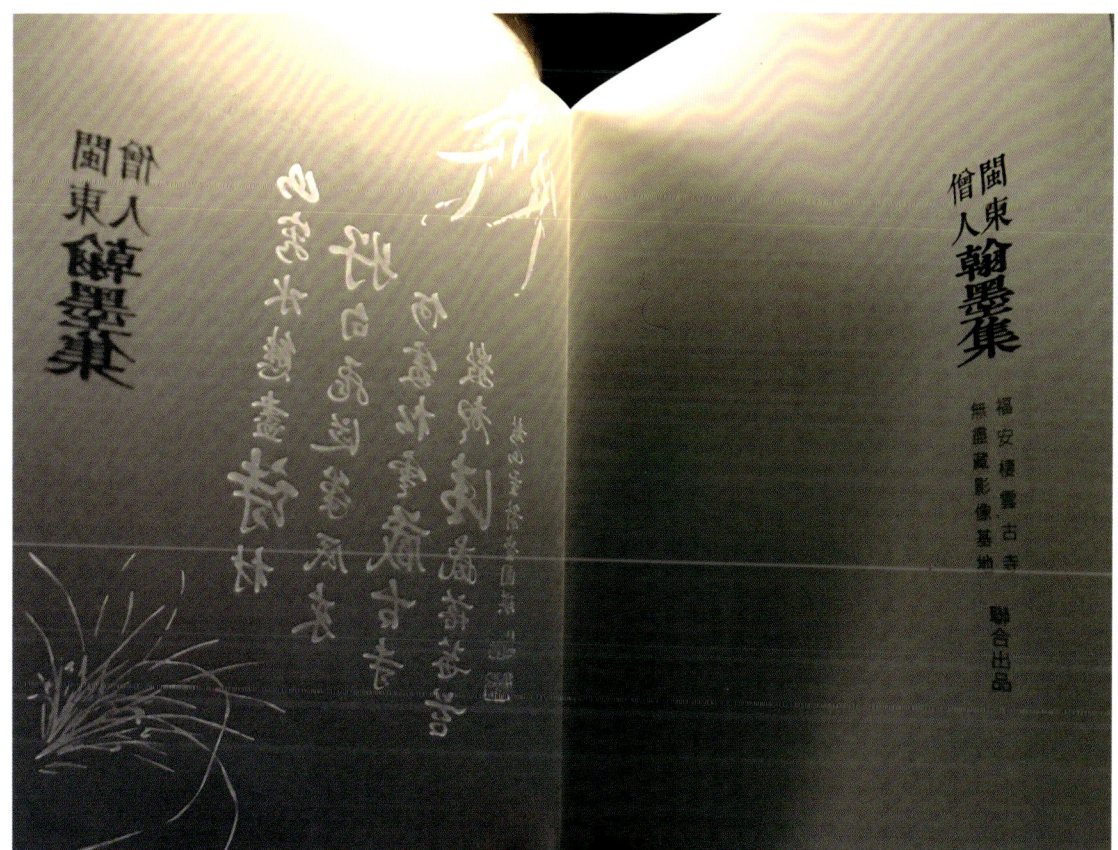

慧照法師

祖籍莆田
畢業於福田廣化寺福建佛學院
福安市佛教協會秘書長，福安市天馬山天堂禪寺方丈。

伯圓長老 一〇〇九．祖籍福

八一年受邀吉隆坡弘法，創建湖濱精舍，並任馬來

Monk Hanmo from
Eastern Fujian

Designer: Hanxian Huang
Design agency: Wisdom Beijing International Cultural Development Co.,LTD.
Country: China

Monk Hanmo from
Eastern Fujian

Designer: Hanxian Huang
Design agency: Wisdom Beijing International Cultural Development Co.,LTD.
Country: China

Suminami Specimen Book

Designer: Carolina Barbosa
Country: USA
Photographer: Carolina Barbosa

The Suminami Specimen Book is a process book to showcase the display typeface Suminami and its process from conceptualization to completion.

Due to the designer's passion for Japanese culture, her main sources of inspiration for this piece were found in Japanese woodblock paintings (ukiyo-e) and in Japanese and Chinese calligraphy. Every letter, along with all ornamentation, was done with bamboo brush and ink before digitalized.

Suminami Specimen Book

Designer: Carolina Barbosa
Country: USA
Photographer: Carolina Barbosa

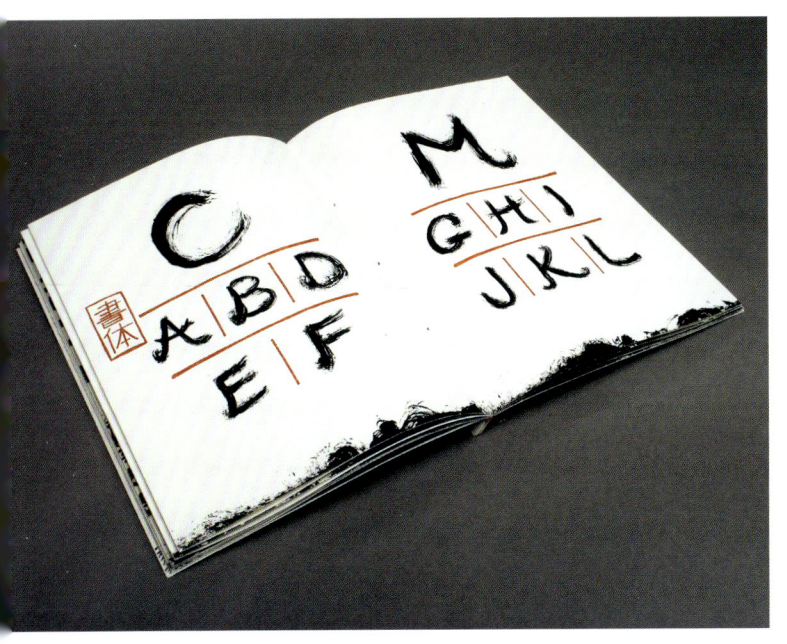

Sketchbook

As an early project, I tried to reproduce a Japanese calligraphy alphabet. I diffused brushwork. I have experience with the practice of calligraphy using only a Sharpie brush, but it was the first time I had the chance to reinterpret it into full line and order of stroke to...

I did another with soft brush pen, but the effect that a reality wanted to specifically seek was this. I quickly jumped into the sketches book. I did an enormous variety of studies when I was trying to aim for the effect of... with a bigger course of breaks.

Some letters have a fine tip to break through lowercase and combined what I felt in the essential...

345

statement

I'm happy to say that I'm very satisfied with my display typeface. This is the first project in which I had the opportunity to input my love for Japanese culture, so it's something I put a lot of thought and ideas into. I've been learning Japanese for about five years now, so this project book is almost a gift to myself for dedicating such time to Japanese culture. I was concerned at first with my typeface looking too much like calligraphy and not having structure, but I managed to find a middle ground between structure and inspiration from free-flowing Japanese calligraphy.

It feels like a system to me, but not that rigid enough that it loses the calligraphic quality to it. I've gained an appreciation for the intrigued yet delicate process of laying strokes in specific orders, of different thicknesses and shapes, together to form one beautifully composed character. This type of calligraphy is a work of art on its own. I can see my display typeface being used to advertise Japanese and Chinese art exhibitions, be in on posters or flyers. Perhaps even for the title of a book on East Asian calligraphy. Ideally I see it on a banner for an exhibition on woodblock paintings, a great part of my inspiration.

This, however, is not the end of my work on this typeface, as I'd still like to create lowercase letters, numbers and punctuation for it in the future.

'The Great Wave of Kanagawa' by Katsushika Hokusai, c. 1830-33

19

rbor wave." The
nd when they'd
a massive
see it at
not be

'A Brief History of Japan - Susanoo no Mikoto' by Tsukioka Yoshitoshi, 1887.

Suminami Specimen Book

Designer: Carolina Barbosa
Country: USA
Photographer: Carolina Barbosa

BOOOOOOK III
CONTENTS
—

Thomas Wirtz

Thomas Wirtz (*1981) lives in Düsseldorf, Germany, and works as a freelance communications designer. He completed his Master's Degree in 2016 at the University of Applied Sciences Düsseldorf under the supervision of Prof. Philipp Teufel and Prof. Gabi Schillig. His focus concentrates on experimental approaches, especially by use of typography and physical phenomena, and the possibilities to apply them functionally to various fields of design.
www.thomaswirtz.net

Masaomi Fujita

Born in 1983 in Shizuoka Prefecture. After graduating from the Faculty of Design of Shizuoka University of Art and Culture, engaged in planning, editing and directing for several years. Reinvented myself as a designer, and worked in an advertising production company as a design and art director for cosmetics, fashion and magazines. Established a design office tegusu in 2012. Now performs a wide variety of works from concept planning to design work in CI and VI development for companies and shops, graphic designs and web designs.

Alfidiya Kuchukbaeva

Alfidiya Kuchukbaeva is a young designer, artist and 3-year student of HSE Art and Design School in Moscow. She was born in 1996 in Tashkent, Uzbekistan. She graduated from the Republic Design college in Tashkent and continues to receive a bachelor's degree in HSE Art and Design School, majoring in Communication Design. She takes possession of packaging and book design, which amazed the possibility of experiments. She tries to experiment with an emphasis on the experience gained over 5 years of study and personal search for a visual language.

Makekaky Mlouha

Books designer from Poland.

Chujing Long

Book designer from China.

Lucas Blat

Lucas Blat was born in São Paulo, Brazil, where he currently lives and works. Master in Graphic Design and Editorial Projects at the Faculty of Fine Arts of the University of Porto (Portugal), he has worked in graphic design offices in São Paulo and Berlin with special focus on cultural scenes. His works were published in Brazilian, European and Asian publications.

Mose （叶昊）

I like to define myself as a wild designer who is thought-free, fancy-free and imagination-free. I hope I am always 21 years old. That is the age of displaying individuality and freedom without restraint.
The first rule of my creation is to follow my inclinations. My creations have no boundary or limit, no concrete meaning, just represent a state of being. Through my creations, my thoughts and skills were fused into my design, and I hope to show this wonderful fusion to all the people. And I also want my design contains various emotions that allows people to indulge in it again and again.

Matto Lau

Matto Lau is a designer from Beijing China, focusing on graphic design, illustration, web design, branding, typography, editorial design. She is pursing an MA degree in Communication University of China (CUC).

Cheryl Chong

I enjoy exploring areas that lies between art and design, believes that design is a combination of aesthetics and framing an experience for the viewer. Good design should be simple yet multi-dimensional, allowing layers of meanings and thoughts to be threaded within. The designer does not merely create a piece of design, but breathes life into his/her work. Only then will people be able to truly feel and connect with the creation.
My interest lies in publication and multi-disciplinary design, experimenting with various mediums and materials.

Alessandro Latela

I'm a visual designer from Italy.
Currently I'm working as a freelance, paying specific attention to each step of the workflow, both for digital and print design.

Chun-Ta Chu

Chun-Ta Chu is an independent contributor.
Born in 1990, Graphic Designer.
Currently studying at National Taiwan Normal University, M.A. Program, Department of design. His works have been featured in publications like Asia-Pacific Design No.10, and awarded by 11 Golden Bee Global Biennale Moscow, and Biennial of Poster Bolivia 2015 and Graphic Design in China 2013, etc.

Chiwai Cheang

Ck, Chiwai Cheang, SomethingMoon Design.
Part-time graphic designer, full-time idiot, sometime writer. Cheang participated in many big yet low profile projects and feels good about it. Find me at somethingmoon.com.

Dora Balla

Dora Balla is a graphic designer and design researcher based in Budapest. She is an associate professor of Graphic Design History and Visual Research with an emphasis in Experiential Typography at Moholy-Nagy University of Art and Design. Her personal and research works focus primarily on editorial design and typography within a broad range of fields and based on visual and historical research.

Estúdio Guayabo

Guayabo is a Brazilian design studio fundamentally based in co-working experience and in skill sharing. Through collaborative processes, we develop comercial and personal projects in interdisciplinary teams, mainly composed of designers, illustrators and graphic artists.

Jiani Lu

Jiani Lu is a multidisciplinary graphic designer and photographer born in China. She currently lives and works out of Toronto, Canada, where she received her Bachelors in Design at York University/Sheridan College. Her work takes on a simplistic, minimalistic and understated tone that can be found transferred across her print, branding and package design work. Jiani was named one of PRINT Magazine's 15 New Visual Artist under 30. Her work has received numerous awards from Adobe, D&AD, AIGA, Graphis, The Dieline and others.

MEDIADESIGN Hochschule Munich

This project was designed by a group of former students from Munich. (MEDIADESIGN HOCHSCHULE Munich).

Kristine H. Kawakubo

Kristine is an independent visualise graphic designer. She has an insatiable passion and a fondness for visual communication, editorial design, publishing, book art, brand & concept visual identity, visual grammar, colour theory, and paper structure. She works on commissioned and self-initiated projects in all stages of printed matter such as editorial design, typography, book cover design, brand & concept development, brand visual identity, photojournalism, corporate communication and art direction from concept to production.
She believes good design comes from unlimited questioning, challenging convention and creating innovative methods to solve visual tasks in unique ways. To emphasis that it is concept-driven design. The form is often learning towards anti-esthetics. The process is often based on a strong idea or a fundamental concept and exploiting to the maximum with no preconceptions. Visual communication is a paradox; that this actually is an esthetic in itself.

One Thousand Times

Started in 2014, One Thousand Times is a Beijing-based studio that provides integrated visual solutions to the community, with a dedication to artistic thinking and innovative design. Here, we work with artists, businesses, and cultural institutions in areas of design and publishing. We takes pride in the way we work. We believe communication is key to satisfactory relationship with the clients and transparency leads to effectiveness and quality.

BOOOOOOK III
CONTENTS
—

BOOOOOOK III

ACKNOWLEDGEMENTS

DESIGNERBOOKS (DB) sincerely thanks all the artists, designers and companies that contributed to this book, meanwhile thank all the staff, translators and printing companies involved in the design and production of this book. Without their efforts and contributions, the book will not be presented to readers in a graceful manner. We will pay attention to all the valuable suggestions from all our friends, and DB will make every effort to do well in every book.

JOIN US

If you want to join DESIGNERBOOKS for future projects and publications, please submit your work and information to edit@designerbooks.com.cn.

DESIGNERBOOKS